NCERT SOLUTIONS

with Chapterwise **Study Notes**

SCIENCE 9th

NCERT SOLUTIONS

with Chapterwise **Study Notes**

SCIENCE 9th

Author

Sushant Batra
Tarnija Midha
Nidhi Sehgal

Including Selected Questions of **DIKSHA**

arihant
SUCCESS AND NOTHING LESS

ARIHANT PRAKASHAN (Series), MEERUT

卐 **Administrative & Production Offices**

Regd. Office

'Ramchhaya' 4577/15, Agarwal Road, Darya Ganj, New Delhi -110002
Tele: 011- 47630600, 43518550

卐 **Head Office**

Kalindi, TP Nagar, Meerut (UP) - 250002
Tel: 0121-7156203, 7156204

卐 **Sales & Support Offices**

Agra, Ahmedabad, Bengaluru, Bareilly, Chennai, Delhi, Guwahati, Hyderabad, Jaipur, Jhansi, Kolkata, Lucknow, Nagpur & Pune.

卐 **PRICE** ₹225.00

卐 PO No. : TXT-59-T065885-07-25

Published by Arihant Publications (India) Ltd.

For further information about the books published by Arihant, log on to www.arihantbooks.com or e-mail at info@arihantbooks.com

Follow us on

Preface

Feeling the immense importance and value of NCERT books, we are presenting this book, having the **NCERT Exercises Solutions**. For the overall benefit of the students we have made this book unique in such a way that it presents not only solutions but also detailed explanations. Through these detailed and through explanations, students can learn the concepts which will enhance their thinking and learning abilities.

We have introduced some Additional Features with the solutions which are given below:

- **Explanatory Solutions** Along with the solutions to questions we have given all the points that tell how to approach to solve a problem. Here we have tried to cover all those loopholes which may lead to confusion. All formulae and hints are discussed in full detail.
- Also included **Thinking Process** and **Mistake Alert** to understanding 'How to solve question' and points of mistakes.
- **Note** We have provided notes also to solutions in which special points are mentioned which are of great value for the students.

Apart from all those who helped in the compilation of this book a special note of thanks to all. With the hope that this book will be of great help to the students, we wish great success to our readers.

Sushant Batra
Tarnija Midha
Nidhi Sehgal

Contents

Matter in Our Surroundings

CHAPTER 01

Important Points

01 Anything that has mass and occupies space is known as **matter.**

02 Early Indian Philosophers classified matter into five basic elements, the *'Panch Tatva'*–Air, Earth, Fire, Sky and Water.

03 Matter is made up of tiny particles.

04 Molecules are extremely small so that they cannot be seen with the naked eyes or even with the help of a microscope.

05 In any matter, molecules are held together by a force of attraction called the **intermolecular force of attraction.**

06 There is some distance between the particles (molecules) of matter, called the **intermolecular space.**

07 The three states of matter, *i.e.*, **solid, liquid and gas** vary among themselves due to the difference in the attractive forces and intermolecular spaces between their molecules. For example, ice is a solid, water is a liquid and steam is a gas.

08 Solids have the maximum attractive forces between their molecules and gases have the least.

09 Gases have the maximum intermolecular space and solids have the least.

10 The particles of matter are continuously moving, *i.e.*, they possess kinetic energy. As the temperature rises, the kinetic energy of the particles increases and they move faster.

11 The smell of perfume reaches our nose quickly due to the process of diffusion.

12 **Diffusion** is the process of movement of molecules from a region of higher concentration to a region of lower concentration. Due to this phenomenon, the particles of two different types of matter can intermix.

13 Solids have a definite shape, distinct boundaries and a fixed volume. They have negligible compressibility. They may break under force but it is difficult to change their shape, so they are rigid.

14 Liquids do not have a fixed shape, but have a fixed volume. They take up the shape of the container in which they are kept. They have a tendency to flow, so they are called **fluid**.

15 Gases neither have fixed shape nor fixed volume. They are highly compressible as compared to solids and liquids.

16 A gas in a container exerts pressure due to the force exerted by the random movement of gas particles per unit area on the walls of the container.

17 A definite temperature at which a solid starts melting to become a liquid is called its **melting point.** The temperature at which vapour pressure of a liquid becomes equal to the atmospheric pressure is called **boiling point** of that liquid. Boiling is a **bulk** phenomenon.

18 The amount of heat energy that is required to change 1kg of a solid into liquid at atmospheric pressure at its melting point is known as **latent heat of fusion.**

19
- When a liquid boils, its temperature (boiling point) remains constant because during this period the heat energy is utilised in breaking the intermolecular forces of attraction between the water molecules. This heat is called **latent heat of vaporisation**.
- Latent heat of vaporisation is the heat energy required to change 1 kg of a liquid to gas at atmospheric pressure at its boiling point.

20 $T\,°C + 273 = T\,K$ where, °C = Celsius and K = Kelvin (K is the SI unit of temperature)

Relation between °C and °F $= \frac{C}{5} = \frac{F-32}{9}$

21 Camphor, ammonium chloride, naphthalene and iodine are some solids that change directly from solid to gas on heating **(sublimation)**.

22 Dry ice is solid carbon dioxide.

23 (a) Solid state $\xrightleftharpoons[\text{Cool}]{\text{Heat}}$ Liquid state $\xrightleftharpoons[\text{Cool}]{\text{Heat}}$ Gaseous state

(b) 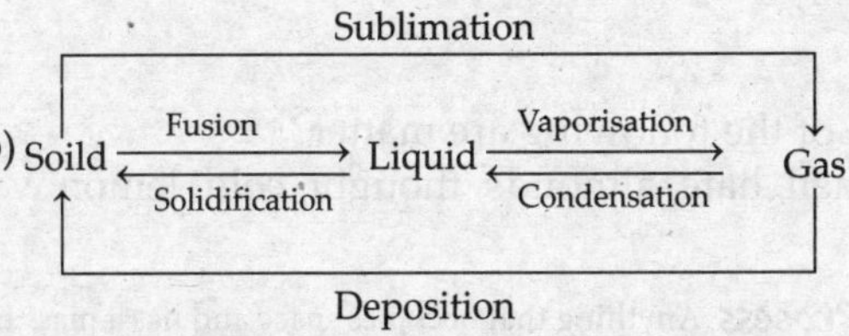

24 Pressure and temperature determine the state of a substance, whether it will be solid liquid or gas. Applying pressure and reducing temperauture can liquefy gases.

25 The phenomenon of change of liquid into vapours at any temperature below its boiling point is called **evaporation.** It is a **surface phenomenon** and occurs due to collision between liquid molecules.

26 Rate of evaporation increases on

(i) increasing surface area. (ii) decreasing humidity.
(iii) increasing temperature. (iv) increasing wind speed.

27 Evaporation causes cooling as the particles of liquid absorb energy from the surroundings, reducing the temperature to regain the energy lost during evaporation.

28 Light coloured cotton clothes are preferred during summers because

(i) cotton absorbs the sweat which evaporates easily (as evaporation causes cooling).

(ii) light colours absorb less heat.

29 Earthern pots like a pitcher (matka) keep water cool because water evaporates through the tiny pores of the pitcher (matka). As high energy water molecules get evaporated, the temperature of the remaining water decreases making it cool.

30 Some measurable quantities and their units are given below:

1. Temperature	Kelvin (K)
2. Length	metre (m)
3. Mass	kg (kilogram)
4. Weight	Newton (N)
5. Volume	Cubic metre (m^3)
6. Density	kilogram per cubic metre (kg/m^3)
7. Pressure	Pascal (Pa)

Intext Questions

On Page 3

Question 1 Which of the following are matter?
Chair, air, love, smell, hate, almonds, thought, cold, lemon water, smell of perfume.

◎ *Thinking Process* Anything that occupies space and has a mass is called matter.

Sol. Chair, air, almonds, lemon water and smell of perfume are matter because they have some mass and occupy space.

Mistake Alert The sense of smell is not a matter but the smell originates from particles of a substance, is a matter.

Question 2 Give reasons for the following observation :
The smell of hot sizzling food reaches you several metres away, but to get the smell from cold food you have to go close.

Sol. The smell of hot sizzling food reaches you from several metres away because at higher temperatures, the aroma particles (volatile molecules) possess greater kinetic energy. This increased energy makes the particles move faster and evaporate more easily into the air. As a result, they diffuse quickly through the surrounding air and spread over a larger distance in a short time. In contrast, cold food has molecules with lower kinetic energy, so fewer aroma particles evaporate and their movement is slower, limiting the spread of the smell.

Question 3 A diver is able to cut through water in a swimming pool. Which property of matter does this observation show?

◎ *Thinking Process* The order of forces of attraction between the particles is **Solid > Liquid > Gas.**

So, the order of the intermolecular space between its particles is :

Solid < Liquid < Gas

Sol. The phenomenon of cutting through the water by a diver shows that matter has space between its particles. The weak forces of attraction between the water molecules due to some intermolecular space between them, is the reason why a diver is able to cut through water in pool.

Question 4 What are the characteristics of the particles of matter?

Sol. Characteristics of the particles of matter are :

1. Particles of matter have space between them.
2. Particles of matter are continuously moving.
3. Particles of matter have a force of attraction between them.
4. Particles of matter are very small in size.

On Page 6

Question 1 The mass per unit volume of a substance is called density.
(Density = mass/volume). Arrange the following in order of increasing density – air, exhaust from chimneys, honey, water, chalk, cotton and iron.

◎ *Thinking Process* Among solid, liquid and gas, the order of density is gas < liquid < solid.

Sol. The order of increasing density is based on the arrangement of particles in each substance. Air and exhaust gases have the least density due to widely spaced particles. Cotton, being fibrous and containing air pockets, is less dense than water. Liquids like water and honey have higher densities due to closely packed molecules, while solids like chalk and iron have the highest densities due to their tightly packed particle structures.

Thus, the correct order of increasing density is

Air < Exhaust from chimneys < Cotton < Water < Honey < Chalk < Iron.

Question 2

(a) Tabulate the differences in the characteristics of states of matter.

(b) Comment upon the following:
rigidity, compressibility, fluidity, filling a gas container, shape, kinetic energy and density.

Sol. (a) Difference in the characteristic and state of matter.

S.No.	Solids	Liquids	Gases
1.	Generally solids have a definite shape (exceptions are sponge, rubber band etc).	Liquids do not have a definite shape. They take the shape of the container.	Gases do not have a definite shape.
2.	Solids have a definite volume.	Liquids have a definite volume too.	Gases do not have a definite volume. (Their volume also varies with the container in which they are stored.)
3.	Solids have high densities hence they are hard too.	Generally, liquids have low densities.	Gases also have low densities.
4.	Solids are rigid.	Liquids are not rigid.	Gases are not rigid.
5.	Solids are generally incompressible (except sponge, rubber etc.)	Liquids are almost incompressible.	Gases are highly compressible.
6.	Solids do not tend to flow.	Liquids tend to flow.	Gases also tend to flow.

S.No.	Solids	Liquids	Gases
7.	Powdered solids can be heaped.	Liquids cannot be heaped.	Gases cannot be heaped.
8.	In solids, molecules are packed in a closed arrangement.	In liquids, molecules are loosely packed as compared to solids.	In gases, molecules are very far from each other.
9.	There is a strong attraction force between the molecules of a solid.	There is less force of attraction between the liquid molecules as compared to that of solid molecules.	Attraction force between the gaseous molecules is the least, *i.e.*, negligible.
10.	There is negligible (least) intermolecular space between the molecules of a solid.	Intermolecular space between the molecules of a liquid is less than that in solid molecules.	There is large intermolecular space between gas molecules.

(b) (i) **Rigidity** The property due to which an object retains its shape and size is known as rigidity. Solids are rigid whereas, liquids and gases are not.

(ii) **Compressibility** Compressibility is the property due to which a substance can be compressed, i.e., its volume can be decreased. Gases are compressible whereas, solids and liquids are not.

(iii) **Fluidity** The property due to which a substance tends to flow is called fluidity. Gases and liquids are fluids, whereas solids are not.

(iv) **Filling a gas container** A gas can be filled in a gas container by compressing it under high pressure.

(v) **Shape** The property of having a definite geometry is called shape of a particular substance. Solids have a definite shape whereas, gases and liquids do not.

(vi) **Kinetic energy** The energy possessed by an object or by the molecules of an object due to its state of motion is called kinetic energy. **Molecules of gases possess highest kinetic energy.** Increasing the temperature also increases the kinetic energy of a substance (or its molecules), due to increased collision of molecules.

(vii) **Density** The mass per unit volume of a substance is called density.

$$\text{Density} = \frac{\text{Mass}}{\text{Volume}} = \frac{m}{V}$$

Unit of density is kg m^{-3} or g cm^{-3}.

Question 3 Give reasons

(a) A gas fills completely the vessel in which it is kept.

(b) A gas exerts pressure on the walls of the container.

(c) A wooden table should be called a solid.

(d) We can easily move our hand in air but to do the same through a solid block of wood we need a karate expert.

Sol. (a) There is negligible force of attraction between the molecules of gases. Therefore, they occupy the maximum space available to them. Hence, a gas fills completely the vessel in which, it is kept. High kinetic energy possessed by their molecules also helps for the same.

(b) In the gaseous state, the particles move randomly at high speed. Due to this random movement, the particles hit each other and also the walls of the container. The pressure exerted by the gas is due to this force exerted by these particles per unit area on the walls of the container.

(c) There is a strong force of attraction between the molecules of wood and the intermolecular space between them is the least. So, a wooden table has a definite shape and volume, and thus it should be called a solid.

(d) Air molecules are very far away from each other due to negligible force of attraction working between them. So, our hand gets sufficient space to move in air. But a solid block of wood has closely packed molecules which are bound by strong forces of attraction, so we cannot move our hand through it.

Question 4 Liquids generally have lower density as compared to solids. But you must have observed that ice floats on water. Find out why?

Sol. Generally, liquids have lower density than that of solids. Water is also expected to have a lower density than that of ice. But it is the opposite case. The reason is that ice has a cage-like structure, *i.e.*, the vacant spaces are left when water (H_2O) molecules are linked in ice. The number of these spaces are comparatively less in water. So, ice being more porous than water, is lighter than water and floats over the surface of water.

Mistake Alert One can make a mistake in considering that the density of ice is greater than that of water.

On Page 9

Question 1 Convert the following temperature to celsius scale

(a) 300 K (b) 573 K

Sol. For converting the temperature scale from kelvin to celsius, we have to subtract 273 from the given value $T\text{ K} - 273 = t°\text{C}$

(a) 300 K − 273 = 27°C (b) 573 K − 273 = 300°C

Question 2 What is the physical state of water at

(a) 250°C (b) 100°C ?

Sol. As the boiling point of water is 100°C so,

(a) at 250°C, the state of water will be steam or water vapour, *i.e.*, gaseous state.

(b) at 100°C, there is a transition of liquid state into the gaseous state. So, at this temperature, water can exist in both liquid and gaseous state.

Question 3 For any substance, why does the temperature remain constant during the change of state?

Thinking Process Latent heat is the hidden heat which is used up in overcoming the forces of attraction between the particles, while changing the states of matter.

Sol. The temperature remains constant during the change of state of a substance. This can be understood with the help of an example : when a solid is heated to its melting point, the temperature first rises and becomes constant when reaches its melting point. Now, on further heating, the heat energy provided to the substance helps to break the force of attraction between the solid molecules. This heat is called latent heat. Because this energy is used to change the state only, the temperature remains constant until the change is complete.

Question 4 Suggest a method to liquefy atmospheric gases.

Sol. Applying high pressure and cooling a gas at low temperature helps in the liquefaction of atmospheric gases. The reason is that under such conditions of temperature and pressure, the molecules of gases come closer, their kinetic energy becomes less and the gas is liquefied.

On Page 10

Question 1 Why does a desert cooler cool better on a hot dry day?

Sol. The rate of evaporation increases with an increase in temperature and decrease in humidity. A desert cooler functions on the basis of evaporation, which causes cooling. As evaporation increases when the day is hot and dry, so the desert cooler also cools to a better extent.

Question 2 How does the water kept in an earthen pot (matka) become cool during summer?

Sol. The surface of the earthen pot (matka) has tiny pores. Molecules of water inside the matka remain in motion i.e. have kinetic energy, so they collide with each other. Particles near the surface (pores) of the matka gains high energy and therefore they get evaporated and overall temperature of water becomes low. The water stored in the earthen pot evaporates faster through these pores due to the increased exposed surface area. As the process of evaporation causes cooling, the stored water inside the earthen pot becomes cool.

Question 3 Why does our palm feel cold when we put some acetone or petrol or perfume on it?

Thinking Process Evaporation causes cooling.

Sol. Acetone, petrol, perfume, etc., being volatile in nature evaporate very fast when exposed to larger surfaces. During this process, they absorb the required latent heat of vaporisation from the palm (if kept on palm). So, the process causes cooling and the palm feels cold.

Question 4 Why are we able to sip hot tea or milk faster from a saucer rather than a cup?

Sol. The rate of evaporation increases with increase in surface area and evaporation also causes cooling. Since, in a saucer, the exposed surface area of tea or milk is greater as compared to the cup. Therefore, the evaporation process is faster in saucer and it is easier to sip colder tea or milk.

Question 5 What type of clothes should we wear in summer?

Sol. We should wear light coloured cotton clothes in summer because

1. Cotton is a good absorber of water and sweat. It provides more surface area for the sweat to evaporate, which gives a cooling effect in summer.
2. Light colours absorb less heat.

So, wearing light coloured cotton clothes helps us feeling cool and comfortable.

Exercises

Question 1 Convert the following temperatures to the celsius scale.

(a) 293 K (b) 470 K

Sol. In order to convert temperature from kelvin to celsius scale, we have to subtract 273 from the given value because K − 273 = °C

(a) 293 K − 273 = 20 °C (b) 470 K − 273 = 197 °C

Question 2 Convert the following temperatures to the kelvin scale.

(a) 25°C (b) 373°C

Sol. To convert temperature from celsius to kelvin scale, add 273 to the given values because °C + 273 = K

(a) 25 °C + 273 = 298 K (b) 373 °C + 273 = 646 K

Question 3 Give reason for the following observations.

(a) Naphthalene balls disappear with time without leaving any solid.

(b) We can get the smell of perfume sitting several metres away.

◎ ***Thinking Process***

(a) Sublimation is a process in which a solid changes into gas directly, without converting into liquid.

(b) The movement or inter mixing of particles from areas of high concentration to areas of low concentration is known as diffusion.

Sol. (a) Naphthalene is a substance which directly changes from solid to gas on heating by the process of sublimation. So, the naphthalene balls disappear with time as they sublime into gaseous state due to heat of surroundings.

(b) Air have gaseous particles which are far away from each other due to very less forces of attraction between them. So, particles of perfume diffuse or intermix into the air easily. Thus, the smell (aroma) of perfume reaches a person sitting several metres away due to this fast diffusion of the gaseous perfume particles through the air.

Question 4 Arrange the following substances in increasing order of forces of attraction between the particles-water, sugar, oxygen.

Sol. The intermolecular forces of attraction are strongest in solids and weakest (or negligible) in case of gases. Sugar is a solid, water is in liquid state and oxygen is a gas so, the order of forces of attraction is

oxygen < water < sugar

Question 5 What is the physical state of water at

(a) 25°C (b) 0°C (c) 100°C ?

Sol. 0° is the temperature at which water (liquid) starts to convert into its solid form (ice) and 100°C is the temperature at which water (liquid) starts to change into water vapour. Between 0° to 100°C, it remains in the liquid state. Thus,

(a) Liquid state

(b) Solid and liquid state (Transition state)

(c) Liquid and gaseous state (Transition state)

Mistake Alert At transition state or at melting and boiling points, two states of matter co-exists.

Question 6 Give two reasons to justify

(a) water at room temperature is a liquid.

(b) an iron almirah is a solid at room temperature.

Sol. (a) Water is a liquid at room temperature because

(i) It has a tendency to flow.

(ii) It does not have a fixed shape and takes the shape of the container in which it is filled, but its volume remains the same.

(iii) It has weak intermolecular forces of attraction between the particles.

(b) An iron almirah is a solid at room temperature because

(i) Its shape and volume are definite.

(ii) It is hard and rigid.

(iii) Its density is high.

(iv) It possess strong forces of attraction between its particles.

(v) It is incompressible.

Question 7 Why is ice at 273 K more effective in cooling than water at the same temperature?

Sol. When ice melts, it also absorbs the energy equal to the latent heat of fusion from the surroundings so it causes cooling more effectively than the water at same temperature (because water does not absorb energy from the surroundings).

Question 8 What produces more severe burns, boiling water or steam?

◎ *Thinking Process* Latent heat of vaporisation is the heat energy required to change 1kg of a liquid to a gas at atmospheric temperature at its boiling point.

Sol. Steam causes more severe burns than boiling water. The reason is that it releases the extra amount of heat (latent heat of vaporisation) which it has already taken during vaporisation (when the steam was formed from water).

Question 9 Name *A, B, C, D, E* and *F* in the following diagram showing change in its state.

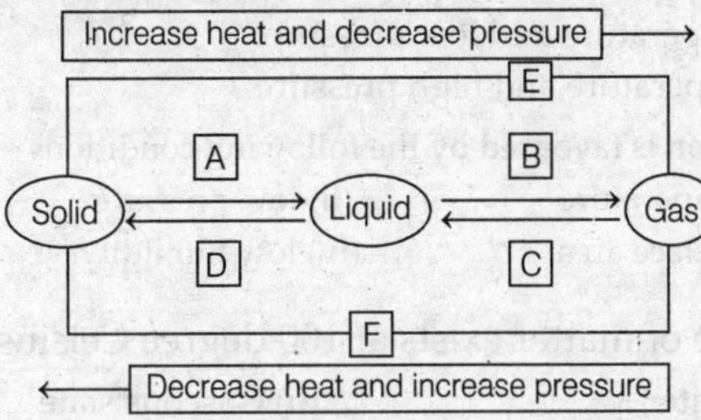

Sol. *A* = Melting or fusion, here the solid changes into liquid.
B = Evaporation or vaporisation, here the liquid changes into gas.
C = Condensation or liquefaction, here the gas changes into liquid.
D = Freezing or solidification, here the liquid changes into solid.
E = Sublimation, here solid directly changes into gas without coming in liquid state.
F = Deposition here gas changes into solid without coming to liquid state.

DIKSHA APP Questions

☐ Multiple Choice Questions

Q.1 Which of the following phenomenon leads to the cooling of water in earthen pot?

(a) Evaporation (b) Fusion

(c) Diffusion (d) Sublimation

Sol. (a) Evaporation leads to the cooling of water in the earthen pot. Molecules of water inside the earthen pot remains in motion and collide with each other. The molecules present near the surface of the pot gets evaporated and overall temperature of water inside it becomes low.

Q.2 State the condition which favours evaporation of water?

(a) Low temperature and low pressure.

(b) High temperature and high pressure.

(c) High temperature and low pressure.

(d) Low temperature and high pressure.

Sol. (c) Evaporation is favoured by the following conditions

(i) high temperature (ii) low pressure

(iii) large surface area (iv) low humidity

Q.3 Which state of matter exists at 100 degree Celsius?

(a) Liquid state (b) Gaseous state

(c) Both liquid and gaseous state (d) None of these

Sol. (a) At 100°C, matter exists as in both liquid and gaseous state, because at 100°C, matter starts to boil.

Q.4 As the pressure of air decreases the boiling point of a liquid

(a) increase (b) decrease

(c) remains fixed (d) none of these

Sol. (b) As the pressure of air decreases, boiling point of liquid also decrease *i.e.* liquid will boil earlier.

Q.5 The smell of perfume spread out by the process known as

(a) Evaporation (b) Diffusion

(c) Condensation (d) Fusion

Sol. (b) The smell of perfume is spread out via phenomenon of diffusion, as in diffusion, movement of perfume particles takes place from high concentration to low concentration.

Q.6 The melting point of ice in kelvin is

◎ *Thinking Process* Melting point is the minimum temperature at which a solid melts to become a liquid at atmospheric pressure.

(a) 0 K (b) 100 K
(c) 273.15 K (d) 298 K

Sol. (c) Melting point of ice is 0°C. In kelvin it will be 0 + 273.15 = 273.15 K.

Q.7 Fluidity is a property unique to fluids. Which one of the following statements is correct in accordance with the above statement?

(a) Only gases behave like fluids.
(b) Gases and solids behave like fluids.
(c) Gases and liquids behave like fluids.
(d) Only liquids are fluids.

Sol. (c) Gases and liquids both behave like fluids because they have a tendency to flow.

Q.8 Which among the following factors will increase the rate of evaporation of water?

(a) Increase in temperature of water.
(b) Decrease in temperature of water.
(c) Less exposed surface area of water.
(d) Adding common salt to water.

Sol. (a) Rate of evaporation of water increases with increase in temperature, increase in surface area, decrease in humidity and increase in wind speed.

Q.9 A solid is one

(a) which has definite mass but has not definite shape.
(b) it is highly compressible.
(c) particles of solid are held by weak forces of attraction.
(d) which has definite volume and definite shape.

Sol. (d) A solid is one which has a definite shape and volume. The particles of solid are tightly held together by strong forces of attraction, so the solids are not compressible.

Q.10

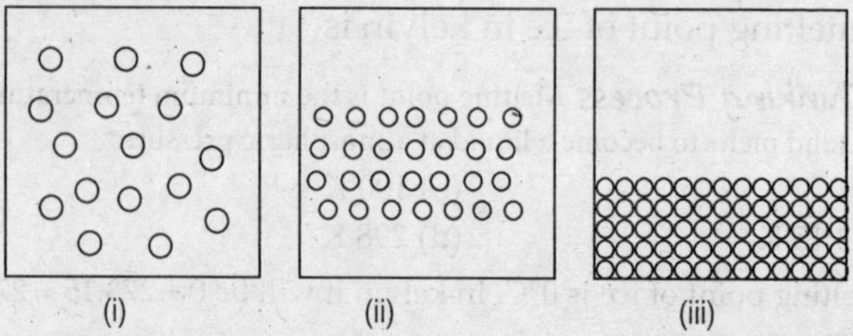

Given above are the figures showing particles of a matter in its three states at the same temperature and pressure and contained in separate containers of the same volume.

The circles indicate the particles in the three states of a matter. Which figure shows minimum attraction between the particles of the matter?

(a) Figure (i)
(b) The figures do not indicate any thing about the interparticle attraction
(c) Figure (iii)
(d) Figure (ii)

Sol. (a) The attraction between the particles of the matter is related to inter-particle distance. As the distance between the particles is maximum in Figure (i), the attraction between them is minimum.

☐ Very Short Answer Type

Q.1 Convert –50°C into kelvin scale.

Sol. $K = °C + 273 = -50°C + 273 = 223\text{ K}$

Q.2 Why is the density of solids higher than gases?

Sol. The density of solids is higher than gases because the particles in solids are closely packed together, with strong forces of attraction between them. While in gases, the particles are spread out and have weaker forces of attraction, resulting in lower density.

Q.3 When we put salt in water, it dissolves. Where do the salt particles disappear?

◎ ***Thinking Process*** The particles of liquid, like water are not very close to each other as they are bound by weak forces of attraction.
So, they have some interparticle space present between them.

Sol. The salt particles disappear as they try to occupy the vacant spaces between the particles of water.

Q.4 Name the temperature at which solid and liquid states of matter co-exist.

Sol. The temperature at which solid and liquid states of matter coexist is called the melting point. It is the minimum temperature at which a solid melts to become a liquid at the atmospheric pressure.

Q.5 Name the physical state of matter which is most compressible.

Sol. The physical state of matter that is most compressible is gas. In gases, particles are far away from each other and can be compressed easily when pressure is applied.

☐ Short Answer Type

Q.1 Why diffusion becomes faster on heating?

Sol. Diffusion becomes faster on heating because heating increases the kinetic energy of the particles. As the temperature increases, the particles move more quickly and collide with each other more frequently. This faster movement allows particles to spread out and intermix more easily, therefore, speeding up the process of diffusion.

Q.2 How does evaporation causes a cooling effect?

Sol. Evaporation causes a cooling effect because when a liquid evaporates, the faster-moving molecules (which have higher kinetic energy) escape into the air. This leaves behind the slower-moving, lower kinetic energy molecules, causing the temperature of the remaining liquid to drop. As a result, the surface from which the liquid is evaporating feels cooler.

Q.3 Why do solids do not possess fluidity?

Sol. The particles of solid are tightly held together by strong forces of attraction, which prevents them from moving freely. Hence, they do not flow or show the property of fluidity.

Q.4 Why wet clothes dry very quickly in hot summer as compared to rainy days? Explain.

Sol. Wet clothes dry quickly in hot summer because the rate of evaporation increases with higher temperature. In summer, the heat provides more energy to the water molecules, allowing them to escape into the air faster. On rainy days, the humidity in the air is high, which slows down evaporation as the air is already saturated with water vapour, making it harder for the water in the clothes to evaporate.

Q.5 Explain why ice starts melting as the temperature of the container containing ice increases?

Sol. Ice starts melting as the temperature of the container increases because the heat energy is absorbed by the ice, which raises its temperature. As the temperature of the ice reaches its melting point, the ice gains enough energy to overcome the forces holding the solid particles together. This causes the ice to change from a solid to a liquid state.

□ Long Answer Type

Q.1 Fill in the blanks

(a) Evaporation of a liquid at room temperature leads to a .... effect.

(b) At room temperature the forces of attraction between the particles of solid substances are .... than those which exist in the gaseous state.

(c) The arrangement of particles is less ordered in the ...... state. However, there is no order in the .... state.

(d) .... is the change of solid state directly to vapour state without going through the .... state.

(e) The phenomenon of change of a liquid into the gaseous state at any temperature below its boiling point is called ....

Sol. (a) cooling (b) stronger

(c) liquid, gaseous (d) sublimation, liquid

(e) evaporation

Q.2 Rahul wants to wear his favourite shirt to a party, but the problem is that it is still wet after a wash. What steps would you suggest to dry it faster.

Sol. To help Rahul dry his wet shirt faster, there are several steps he can follow.

(i) **Increase the temperature** Rahul can hang the shirt under the sun or near a heat source like a heater. Increase in temperature speeds up the evaporation process by providing energy to the water molecules, helping them escape into the air faster.

(ii) **Increase wind speed** He can hang the shirt in an airy area or near a fan. The more is the wind speed around the shirt, the faster the water will evaporate.

(iii) **Increase the surface area** Rahul can spread out the shirt flat for drying as it increases the exposed surface area for evaporation. The larger the exposed area, the more water can evaporate at once, making the drying process faster.

Is Matter Around us Pure?

CHAPTER 02

Important Points

01 A **pure substance** is made up of single type of particle (atoms or/ and molecules). Whereas, a **mixture** is made up of two or more pure substances.

02 Elements and compounds are considered to be pure as they have characteristic melting point and boiling point.

03 A pure substance always exhibits the same characteristic properties, irrespective of the source from which they are obtained.

04 A mixture may be homogeneous or heterogeneous in nature. **Homogeneous mixtures** have uniform composition throughout, whereas, **heterogeneous mixtures** have non-uniform compositions and physically distinct parts.

05
- A solution is a homogeneous mixture of two or more substances.
- The particles of solution are smaller than 1nm in diameter, so they do not scatter a beam of light passing through the solution.
- The solution is stable and its solute particles cannot be separated from the mixture by the process of filtration.

06 **Alloys** are mixtures of two or more metals or a metal and a non-metal. They are often considered solutions of solid in solid and can be homogeneous (*e.g.* brass, Cu in gold) or heterogeneous (*e.g.* steel). Alloys cannot be separated into their components by physical methods.

07 Solution is made up of two components: **solute** (present in lesser quantity) and **solvent** (present in larger quantities).

08 Air is a homogeneous mixture of **gases.**

09
- A solution in which no more solute can be dissolved at a given temperature is called a **saturated solution**.

- A solution in which the amount of solute contained is less than the saturation level is called an **unsaturated solution**.

10 The amount (mass or volume) of solute present in a given amount (mass or volume) of the solution is called **concentration of a solution.**

11 Mass by mass percentage of a solution $= \frac{\text{Mass of solute}}{\text{Mass of solution}} \times 100$

12 Mass by volume percentage of a solution $= \frac{\text{Mass of solute}}{\text{Volume of solution}} \times 100$

13 Volume by volume percentage of a solution

$$= \frac{\text{Volume of solute}}{\text{Volume of solution}} \times 100$$

14 Particles of a **suspension** are visible through naked eye while those of a **true solution** are not. It is a heterogeneous mixture in which the solute particles (solid) do not dissolve in the bulk of the medium (liquid) and remain suspended.

15
- The particles of suspension scatter the beam of light passed through it and make its path visible. A suspension is unstable and its particles can be separated from the mixture by the process of filtration.
- Suspension is a heterogeneous mixture in which the solute particles do not dissolve but remain suspended throughout the bulk of the medium.

16
- A **colloid** is a heterogeneous mixture in which the size of the particles is too small. It is quite stable and particles of colloids cannot be separated from the mixture by the process of filtration.
- **Centrifugation** is a special technique used to separate the colloidal particles.

17 When a beam of light is passed through a colloidal solution, its particles scatter light because of this scattering the path of light becomes visible **(Tyndall effect).**

18 Colloidal solutions are composed of two components : **dispersed phase** (solute-like) and **dispersion medium** (solvent-like).

19 Classification of colloids on the basis of the state of the dispersed phase and the dispersing medium is given below in the tabulated form.

Dispersed Phase	Dispersing Medium	Type	Example
Liquid	Gas	Aerosol	Fog, clouds, mist
Solid	Gas	Aerosol	Smoke, automobile exhaust
Gas	Liquid	Foam	Shaving cream
Liquid	Liquid	Emulsion	Milk, face cream
Solid	Liquid	Sol	Milk of magnesia, mud
Gas	Solid	Foam	Foam, rubber, sponge, pumice
Liquid	Solid	Gel	Jelly, cheese, butter
Solid	Solid	Solid Sol	Coloured gemstone, milky glass

20 Physical changes involves the changes in physical properties such as size, shape and physical state. In contrast, chemical changes involve a change in the chemical composition of a substance resulting in the formation of a new substance.

21 Elements are the building blocks of matter that cannot be broken down into simpler substances by chemical reactions.

22 Elements can be divided into **metals, non-metals and metalloids**.

(a) Metals have a lustre (shine). They conduct heat and electricity. They are ductile, malleable and sonorous.

(b) Non-metals display a variety of colours. They are not lustrous, sonorous or malleable. They are poor conductors of heat and electricity.

(c) Metalloids have intermediate properties between those of metals and non-metals.

23 A compound is a substance composed of two or more elements, chemically combined with one another in a fixed proportion.

24 A compound does not exhibit the properties of its constituent 2elements while a mixture does so.

25 A mixture can be separated into its constituents by simple physical methods while a compound cannot be divided into its constituents by these methods.

Intext Questions

On Page 15

Question 1 What is meant by a substance?

Sol. A substance is a type of matter which is made up of a single type of particle.

For example : Hydrogen, water etc., are pure substances.

Note All elements and compounds are considered to be pure.

Question 2 List the points of differences between homogeneous and heterogeneous mixtures.

Sol.

S.No.	Homogeneous mixture	Heterogeneous mixture
1.	It has a uniform composition throughout.	It has a non-uniform composition.
2.	There are no visible boundaries of separation in a homogeneous mixture.	There are clear and visible boundaries of separation between the constituents.
3.	Its constituents cannot be easily separated.	Its constituents can be separated by simple methods.
4.	Its constituent particles cannot be seen easily.	Its constituent particles can be seen easily.
5.	**Examples :** Alloys, solution of salt in water, etc.	**Examples :** Mixture of sand and common salt, mixture of sand and water, etc.

On Page 18

Question 1 Differentiate between homogeneous and heterogeneous mixtures with examples.

Sol. Same as the previous question.

Question 2 How are sol, solution and suspension different from each other?

Sol.

S.No.	Solution	Sol (colloidal solution)	Suspension
1.	Solution or true solution is homogeneous.	Sol or colloidal solution is heterogeneous (may appear homogeneous).	Suspension is also heterogeneous.
2.	The particle size of solute is less than 1 nm.	The particle size ranges from 1 to 100 nm.	The particle size is greater than 100 nm.
3.	It does not show Tyndall effect.	It shows Tyndall effect.	It also shows Tyndall effect.
4.	The particles pass through the filter paper *i.e.,* solute particles cannot be filtered by the filtration method.	The particles pass through the filter paper so the constituents cannot be separated by the filtration method.	The particles are quite large, so they do not pass through the filter paper and can be easily separated by the filtration method.
5.	True solution is transparent.	It may be transparent or translucent.	It may be translucent or opaque.
6.	The particles do not settle at all.	The particles settle on centrifugation or some other specific conditions *e.g.,* curdling of milk.	The particles settle down when the suspension is left undisturbed.
7.	**Examples :** Sea water, alloys, solution of lemon juice in water, soda water, etc.	**Examples :** Milk of magnesia, cough syrup, mist, fog, clouds, smoke, mud, blood, etc.	**Examples :** Mixture of sand in water, mixture of chalk in water, etc.

Question 3 To make a saturated solution, 36 g of sodium chloride is dissolved in 100 g of water at 293 K. Find its concentration at this temperature.

◎ ***Thinking Process*** Mass by mass percentage of solution

$$= \frac{\text{Mass of solute}}{\text{Mass of solution}} \times 100$$

Sol. Mass of sodium chloride (solute) = 36 g

Mass of water (solvent) = 100 g

We know that, mass of solution = mass of solute + mass of solvent

$$= 36\text{ g} + 100\text{ g} = 136\text{ g}$$

Concentration (mass percentage) of the solution

$$= \frac{\text{Mass of solute}}{\text{Mass of solution}} \times 100 = \frac{36\text{ g}}{136\text{ g}} \times 100$$

$$= 26.47\%$$

On Page 19

Question 1 Classify the following as chemical or physical changes :

- Cutting of trees,
- Melting of butter in a pan,
- Rusting of almirah,
- Boiling of water to form steam,
- Passing of electric current, through water and the water breaking down into hydrogen and oxygen gases,
- Dissolving common salt in water,
- Making a fruit salad with raw fruits, and
- Burning of paper and wood,

◎ *Thinking Process* Physical changes involve change in physical state of a substance and no new substance is formed.
Chemical changes involve change in chemical composition of a substance and a new substance is formed during this change.

Sol.

Physical Changes	Chemical Changes
• Cutting of trees.	• Rusting of almirah.
• Melting of a butter in a pan.	• Passing of electric current through water and the water breaking down into hydrogen and oxygen gases.
• Boiling of water to form steam.	• Burning of paper and wood.
• Dissolving common salt in water.	
• Making a fruit salad with raw fruits.	

Question 2 Try segregating the things around you as pure substances or mixtures.

Sol. Pure substance : Water, salt, sugar, etc.
Mixture : Air, soil, steel, etc.

Exercises

Question 1 Which separation techniques will you apply for the separation of the following?

(a) Sodium chloride from its solution in water.

(b) Ammonium chloride from a mixture containing sodium chloride and ammonium chloride.

(c) Small pieces of metal in the engine oil of a car.

(d) Different pigments from an extract of flower petals.

(e) Butter from curd.

(f) Oil from water.

(g) Tea leaves from tea.

(h) Iron pins from sand.

(i) Wheat grains from husk.

(j) Fine mud particles suspended in water.

Sol. (a) **Evaporation** Water will evaporate on heating the mixture leaving behind sodium chloride (salt).

(b) **Sublimation** On heating the mixture,ammonium chloride will sublime into the vapour phase. On collecting and cooling these vapours, solid ammonium chloride is recovered. Sodium chloride remains as the residue in the container.

(c) **Filtration** Small metal pieces can be filtered by using a suitable filter.

(d) **Chromatography** Pigments (different colours) of flower petal extract are separated by chromatography.

(e) **Centrifugation** Butter from curd can be separated by the process of centrifugation. When curd is churned by hand or using a centrifugal machine, the less denser particles (butter) separate from the liquid (curd).

(f) **Decantation by using separating funnel** Oil and water form separate layers (as they are immiscible) which are separated by using separating funnel.

(g) **Filtration** Tea leaves are separated with the help of a tea-strainer through the process of filtration.

(h) **Magnetic separation** Iron pins are separated from sand by the process of magnetic separation (Iron is magnetic and can be attracted by a magnet).

(i) **Winnowing** Husk from wheat grains is separated by the process of winnowing.

(j) **Coagulation and decantation** Alum is added to the muddy water which makes the soil particles heavier so they settle down. The clear water is then separated by decantation process.

Question 2 Write the steps you would use for making tea. Use the words solution, solvent, solute, dissolve, soluble, insoluble, filtrate and residue.

Sol. **Preparation method of tea**

(i) Take some water (solvent) in a pan and heat it.

(ii) Add some sugar (solute) and boil to dissolve the sugar completely. The obtained homogeneous mixture is called solution.

(iii) Add tea leaves (or tea) in the solution and boil the mixture.

(iv) Now add milk and boil again.

(v) Filter the mixture through a tea strainer and collect the filtrate or soluble substances, *i.e.*, tea in a cup. The insoluble tea leaves are left behind as residue in the strainer.

Question 3 Pragya tested the solubility of three different substances at different temperatures and collected the data as given below (results are given in the following table, as grams of substance dissolved in 100 grams of water to form a saturated solution).

Substance dissolved	Temperature in K				
	283	293	313	333	353
	Solubility				
Potassium nitrate	21	32	62	106	167
Sodium chloride	36	36	36	37	37
Potassium chloride	35	35	40	46	54
Ammonium chloride	24	37	41	55	66

(a) What mass of potassium nitrate would be needed to produce a saturated solution of potassium nitrate in 50 grams of water at 313 K?

(b) Pragya makes a saturated solution of potassium chloride in water at 353 K and leaves the solution to cool at room temperature. What would she observe as the solution cools? Explain.

(c) Find the solubility of each salt at 293 K. Which salt has the highest solubility at this temperature?

(d) What is the effect of change of temperature on the solubility of a salt?

◎ ***Thinking Process*** Solubility of a solid is that amount in gram which can be dissolved in 100 g of water (solvent) to make saturated solution at a particular temperature.

Sol. (a) Since, Mass of potassium nitrate required to produce its saturated solution in 100 g of water at 313 K = 62 g

$\therefore$ Mass of potassium nitrate required to produce its saturated solution in 50 g of water at 313 K = $\frac{62}{100} \times 50$ g = 31 g

(b) On cooling, Crystals of potassium chloride are formed. This happens as solubility of a solid decreases with a decrease in temperature.

(c) **Solubility of each salt at 293 K**

Potassium nitrate = 32 g per 100 g water

Sodium chloride = 36 g per 100 g water

Potassium chloride = 35 g per 100 g water

Ammonium chloride = 37 g per 100 g water

Ammonium chloride has the maximum solubility (37 g per 100 g of water) at 293 K.

(d) Solubility of a (solid) salt decreases with decrease in temperature while it increases with rise in temperature.

Question 4 Explain the following giving examples.

(a) Saturated solution

(b) Pure substance

(c) Colloid

(d) Suspension

Sol. (a) **Saturated Solution** A solution in which no more amount of solute can be dissolved at a particular temperature is called saturated solution *e.g.*, when sugar is dissolved repeatedly in a given amount of water, a condition is reached at which further dissolution of sugar is not possible in that amount of water at room temperature. This is a saturated solution.

(b) **Pure Substance** A substance made up of single type of particle (atoms and/or molecules) is called pure substance. All elements and compounds are said to be pure, *e.g.* water, sugar, etc.

(c) **Colloid** A Colloid is a heterogeneous mixture in which the solute particle size is too small to be seen with the naked eye, but is big enough to scatter light. The solute particles are called the dispersed phase and the medium in which they are spread is called the dispersion medium. Milk, clouds, etc., are the example of colloid.

(d) **Suspension** A suspension is a heterogeneous mixture in which the solute particles do not dissolve but remain suspended throughout the bulk of the medium. Particles of a suspension are visible to the naked eye. *e.g.*, mixture of sand, water and muddy water, etc.

Question 5 Classify each of the following as a homogeneous or heterogeneous mixture.

Soda water, wood, air, soil, vinegar, filtered tea

◎ *Thinking Process* Homogeneous mixtures have same composition (uniform) throughout but the composition of heterogeneous mixture is not uniform.

Sol. **Homogeneous mixtures** Air, soda water, vinegar, filtered tea.
Heterogeneous mixtures Wood, soil,

Question 6 How would you confirm that a colourless liquid given to you is pure water?

Sol. Boiling point is a characteristic feature of a pure substance. Boiling point of pure water is 100°C. If the given colourless liquid boils sharply at 100°C then it is pure water, otherwise it is impure.

Question 7 Which of the following materials fall in the category of a "pure substance"?

(a) Ice (b) Milk (c) Iron (d) Hydrochloric acid
(e) Calcium oxide (f) Mercury (g) Brick (h) Wood (i) Air

Sol. Ice, iron, hydrochloric acid, calcium oxide, mercury are pure substance as they have a definite composition.

Note Milk is a colloid, so it is a heterogeneous mixture. Air is a mixture of various gases while wood and brick are made up of many substances, so they are also mixtures.

Question 8 Identify the solutions among the following mixtures.

(a) Soil (b) Sea water
(c) Air (d) Coal
(e) Soda water

◎ *Thinking Process* A solution is a homogeneous mixture of two or more substances.

Sol. Sea water, air and soda water, are considered as solution because they are the homogeneous mixtures of two or more substances.

Note
- Coal is a heterogeneous mixture of carbon, hydrogen, sulphur and other impurities.
- Soil is a heterogeneous mixture of sand, clay, air, microorganisms, etc.

Question 9 Which of the following will show "Tyndall effect"?

(a) Salt solution (b) Milk

(c) Copper sulphate solution (d) Starch solution

Thinking Process Tyndall effect is the phenomenon in which the particles scatter the beam of light passing through their solution.

Sol. Milk and starch solution will show "Tyndall effect" as both of these are colloids. On the other hand, salt solution and copper sulphate ($CuSO_4$) solutions are true solution so they do not show Tyndall effect.

Mistake Alert Only colloids and suspensions show Tyndall effect and not true solution.

Question 10 Classify the following into elements, compounds and mixtures.

(a) Sodium (b) Soil (c) Sugar solution

(d) Silver (e) Calcium carbonate (f) Tin

(g) Silicon (h) Coal (i) Air

(j) Soap (k) Methane (l) Carbon dioxide

(m) Blood

Sol. Elements consists of only one type of atoms, compounds have atoms or elements of more than one kind but in definite proportion whereas mixtures have two or more substance in any proportion (*i.e.*, composition of mixture is not definite). Thus, the correct classification is;

Elements Sodium, silver, tin and silicon.

Compounds Calcium carbonate, methane and carbon dioxide.

Mixtures Soil, sugar solution, coal, air, soap and blood.

Question 11 Which of the following are chemical changes?

(a) Growth of a plant. (b) Rusting of iron.

(c) Mixing of iron filings and sand. (d) Cooking of food.

(e) Digestion of food. (f) Freezing of water.

(g) Burning of a candle.

Sol. Growth of a plant, rusting of iron, cooking of food, digestion of food and burning of a candle are chemical changes, because here the chemical composition of substance changes and a new substance is formed during the change.

Mistake Alert Burning of a candle involves both physical and chemical changes.

- Melting of wax is a physical change.
- The wax near the wick of a candle burns with oxygen to give carbon dioxide, soot, heat, light, etc., as new substances. Thus, it is also a chemical change.

DIKSHA APP Questions

☐ Multiple Choice Questions

Q.1 Tincture of iodine has antiseptic properties. This solution dissolving is made by

(a) iodine in potassium iodide.
(b) iodine in vaseline.
(c) iodine in water.
(d) iodine in alcohol.

Sol. (d) Tincture of iodine is an antiseptic solution of iodine dissolved in alcohol.

Q.2 When a beam of light is passed through a colloidal solution, it gets

(a) reflected
(b) absorbed
(c) scattered
(d) refracted

Sol. (c) Due to Tyndal effect, scattering of light takes place when a beam of light passes through a colloidal solution.

Q.3 In a sugar solution

(a) sugar is solute, water is solvent.
(b) sugar is solvent, water is solute.
(c) Both are solutes.
(d) Both are solvents.

Sol. (a) Sugar solution is a homogeneous solution in which solute is sugar and solvent is water.

Q.4 Mixture can be

(a) homogeneous
(b) heterogeneous
(c) Both (a) and (b)
(d) pure substance

Sol. (c) A mixture can be homogeneous or heterogeneous.

Q.5 Identify any two statements that are true for pure substances among the following

(i) Pure substances contain only one kind of particle.
(ii) Pure substances may be compounds or mixtures.
(iii) Pure substances have the same composition throughout.
(iv) Pure substances can be exemplified by all elements other than nickel.

(a) (i) and (ii)
(b) (i) and (iii)
(c) (iii) and (iv)
(d) (ii) and (iii)

Sol. (b) Pure substances are those which contain only one kind of particle and they have the same composition throughout.

Q.6 A mixture of two or more metals or a metal and non-metal is known as

(a) pure compound (b) heterogeneous mixture
(c) alloy (d) pure solid

Sol. (c) Alloys are mixtures of two or more metals or a metal and a non-metal. They cannot be separated into their components by physical methods. But still, an alloy is considered as a mixture because it shows the properties of its constituents and can have variable composition. *e.g.*, brass, bronze, etc.

Q.7 If naphthalene balls are kept in warm clothes, their amount goes on decreasing due to the phenomenon of

(a) precipitation (b) evaporation
(c) sublimation (d) condensation

Sol. (c) When naphthalene balls are kept in warm clothes, their amount decreases due to the phenomenon of sublimation. Sublimation is the process in which a solid changes directly into a gas without passing through the liquid phase. At room temperature, naphthalene balls are solid, but they sublime and transition from solid to vapour, when exposed to warm air or clothes. As a result, it gradually decreases in size as they turn into gas.

Q.8 The amount of solute present per unit mass of the solution/solvent is known as

(a) composition of solute (b) concentration of a solvent
(c) concentration of a solute (d) concentration of a solution

Sol. (d) The amount of solute 'present per unit mass of the solution or solvent is known as the **concentration of a solution**.

Q.9 Which of the following statement(s) is/are correct regarding the mixture of milk in water in a proportion of 1:2?

(1) It is a true solution. (2) It shows Tyndall effect.
(3) It is a suspension. (4) It is colloidal solution.

(a) 2 & 4 only (b) 2 & 3 only (c) 1 & 2 only (d) 1 & 3 only

Sol. (a) Milk in water forms a **colloidal mixture**, so it shows **Tyndall effect** due to its bigger particle size. It is not a true solution because it does not dissolve completely and it is also not a suspension as its particles do not settle over time.

Q.10 A solution is made by dissolving 9.0 grams of common salt in water so as to get 150 grams of solution. The mass by mass percentage of the solution is

(a) 6 (b) 9 (c) 4 (d) 12

Sol. (a) To find the mass percentage of the solution, we use the formula

$$\text{Mass percentage} = \left(\frac{\text{Mass of solute}}{\text{Mass of solution}}\right) \times 100$$

Here,

- Mass of solute = 9.0 g (Common salt)
- Mass of solution = 150 g

On substituting the values into the formula, we get

$$\text{Mass percentage} = \left(\frac{9.0}{150}\right) \times 100$$

$$= 6\%$$

So, the mass by mass percentage of the solution is 6%.

Q.11 Which of the following are chemical changes?

(i) Condensation of vapours to liquid
(ii) Conversion of water to steam
(iii) Cutting of iron rod
(iv) Burning of candle wax.
(v) Combustion of LPG in the burner

(a) (iii) and (iv)
(b) (i), (ii) & (v)
(c) (iv) & (v)
(d) (i), (ii) & (iii)

Sol. (c) In (i), (ii) & (iii), only physical state of the substance is changing and no new substance is formed. Therefore, these are examples of a physical change. On the other hand, the changes (iv) and (v) involve the formation of new substances and in these changes the chemical composition of the substances are changing. Therefore, these two represent chemical changes.

Note Burning of candle wax involves both physical and chemical changes.

- **Physical change** Melting of wax.
- **Chemical Change** combustion of wax vapour.

Q.12 Which one of the following sets of general properties is exhibited by non-metals?

(a) Good conductor, non-lustrous, malleable.
(b) Poor conductor, brittle, non sonorous.
(c) Poor conductor, lustrous, non-ductile.
(d) Malleable, ductile, good conductor.

Sol. (b) Non-metals are poor conductors of heat and electricity. They are brittle (they break easily when struck, unlike metals which are malleable). They are non-sonorous, meaning they do not produce a ringing sound when struck, unlike metals that tend to be sonorous.

☐ Very Short Answer Type

Q.1 Name two metalloids.

Sol. Silicon and Germanium are two metalloids. They have have intermediate properties between those of metals and non- metals.

Q.2 Define a solute and a solvent.

Sol. The component of the solution that dissolves the other component in it (usually the component present in larger amount) is called the **solvent**. The component of the solution that is dissolved in the solvent (usually present in lesser quantity) is called the **solute**.

Q.3 Give an example of a solid and a gaseous solution.

Sol. **Alloys** are an example of solid solution, whereas air is an example of gaseous solution.

Q.4 Give one example of each homogeneous and heterogeneous mixtures.

Sol. One example of homogeneous mixture is sugar solution. A solution of sand in water is an example of heterogeneous solution.

☐ Short Answer Type

Q.1 Calculate the concentration by mass percentage in a solution that contains 30g of salt in 100g of water.

Sol. To calculate the mass percentage of a solution, we use the formula

$$\text{Mass percentage} = \left(\frac{\text{Mass of solute}}{\text{Mass of solution}}\right) \times 100$$

Where,

- Mass of solute = 30 g (salt)
- Mass of solvent = 100 g (water)
- Mass of solution = Mass of solute + Mass of solvent = 30 g + 100 g = 130 g

On substituting the value into the formula, we get

$$\text{Mass percentage} = \left(\frac{30}{130}\right) \times 100 = 23.08\ \%$$

Thus, the mass percentage of the salt in the solution is approximately 23.08 %.

Mistake Alert One can make a mistake in considering the mass of a solvent for writing the mass percentage of a solution.

Q.2 What is Tyndall effect? Why does solution of sodium chloride not show Tyndall effect whereas the mixture of water and milk shows it.

Sol. The Tyndall effect is the scattering of light by colloidal particles or larger particles suspended in a medium. When a beam of light passes through a colloidal solution or suspension, the particles scatter the light, making the path of the light visible.

A solution of sodium chloride in water is a true solution and not a colloid. In a true solution, the solute (sodium chloride) dissolves completely in water, and the size of the particles is too small to scatter light. In a mixture of water and milk, the milk forms a colloidal solution, and therefore shows Tyndall effect.

Q.3 Write two points with example to distinguish element and compound.

Sol.

Element	Compound
It is made up of only one kind of atom.	It is made up of two or more than two types of atoms.
It is a pure substance.	It is also a pure substance but it is made up of two or more different elements chemically combined in a fixed ratio.
Examples gold, copper, sodium, etc.	Examples water, carbon dioxide, sodium chloride, etc.

Q.4 What is meant by the terms dispersed phase and dispersion medium?

Sol. The solute-like component or the dispersed particles in a colloid form the dispersed phase, and the component in which the dispersed phase is suspended is known as the dispersion medium.

☐ Long Answer Type

Q.1 Classify each of the following, as a physical or a chemical change.

(a) Drying of a shirt in the sun.
(b) Rising of hot air over a radiator.
(c) Burning of kerosene in a lantern.
(d) Change in the colour of black tea on adding lemon juice to it.
(e) Churning of milk cream to get butter.

Sol. (a) Drying a shirt in the sun is a physical change. The water in the shirt evaporates due to heat, but no new substance is formed.

In other words, the process involves a change in state (from liquid water to water vapour) but does not alter the chemical composition of the water or the shirt.

(b) Rising of hot air over the radiator is a physical change as water in a radiator converts to vapour on heating and hot air becomes lighter and rises up.

(c) Burning of kerosene in a lantern is a chemical change because kerosene burns in the presence of oxygen to give carbon dioxide, heat and light, as new substances.

(d) Change in the colour of black tea on adding lemon juice to it is a chemical change. The acid in lemon juice chemically reacts with the compounds in the tea, such as flavonoids, causing a colour change.

(e) The churning of milk cream to make butter is a physical change. The process separates the fat (butter) from the liquid (milk cream) through mechanical action, but no new substances are chemically formed.

Q.2 Write four differences between mixtures & compounds.

Sol.

Mixtures	Compounds
Mixtures are impure substances.	Compounds are pure substances.
It is formed when two or more substances are physically combined without a fixed ratio.	It is made up of two or more different elements chemically combined in a fixed ratio.
The properties of a mixture are similar to those of the individual substances.	The properties of a compound are different from the properties of the individual elements.
Mixtures can be separated by physical methods (*e.g.* filtration evaporation).	Compounds can only be separated by chemical methods (e.g., filtration).
Examples air, sugar solution etc.	Examples : Water, carbon dioxide, etc.

Atoms and Molecules

CHAPTER 03

Important Points

01 Previously the atom (Parmanu) was thought to be indivisible or the smallest known particle. Maharishi Kanad, Democritus, Dalton and Leucippus supported this idea.

02 According to the **'Law of conservation of mass'**, matter can neither be created nor destroyed during a chemical reaction.

03 **'Law of constant (or definite) proportions'** states, 'In a chemical substance, the elements are always present in definite proportions by mass'.

04 **Dalton's Atomic Theory**

- According to Dalton's atomic theory all matter, whether an element, a compound or a mixture is made up of microscopic particles called **atoms** (indivisible).
- He also proposed that atoms of the same element are identical in mass and chemical properties. While atoms of different elements have different masses and properties.
- Atoms combine in simple whole number ratio to form compounds.

05 Atoms are very reactive and most of them cannot exist independently. Molecules are groups of two or more atoms that are chemically bonded to each other. These molecules or ions aggreyate in large numbers to form matter that we can see feel or touch.

06 Atomic radius is measured in nanometres. ($1 \text{ nm} = 10^{-9}$ m)

07 Symbols of elements are just like abbreviations, based on their Latin names.

e.g., Gold	Latin Name	Symbol
	Aurum	Au

08 IUPAC, *i.e.,* International Union of Pure and Applied Chemistry governs all the rules and regulations related to chemistry.

09 **Atomicity** is the number of atoms present per molecule of an element or compound. *e.g.*, atomicity of He is 1,N_2 is 2, P_4 is 4 and SO_2 is 3.

10 Anion is the negatively charged ion and cation is the positively charged ion. A cluster of atoms which can act as an ion are known as **polyatomic ions.** They carry fixed charge on them.

11 Valency of an element is the combining capacity of the element with other elements.

12 The chemical formula of a compound is the symbolic representation of its composition.

13 While writing the formula of a compound, atoms (or groups) are written with their own valencies. Then the valencies are exchanged with each other.

e.g.,

Symbol	C	Cl
Valency	4	1

Formula : CCl_4

14 A mole is a group of **6.022 × 10^{23}** particles (atoms, molecules or ions).

15 6.022 × 10^{23} is also known as **'Avogadro's number'**.

16 Mass of one mole atom of an element is equal to its **atomic mass.** One atomic mass unit is a mass unit equal to exactly one twelfth $\left(\frac{1}{12}\text{th}\right)$ the mass of one atom of carbon-12.

17 **Molecular mass** of a substance is a sum of the atomic masses of all the atoms in a molecule of the substance. It is expressed in **atomic mass units** (u).

18 **Formula unit mass** of a substance is a sum of the atomic masses of all atoms in a unit of a formula compound. It is expressed in **atomic mass units** (u).

19 Mass of one mole of a substance (element or compund is equal to the molar mass (formula mass) of the element or compound.

Intext Questions

On Page 27

Question 1 In a reaction, 5.3 g of sodium carbonate reacted with 6 g of acetic acid. The products were 2.2 g of carbon dioxide, 0.9 g water and 8.2 g of sodium acetate. Show that these observations are in agreement with the law of conservation of mass.

Sodium carbonate + Acetic acid $\longrightarrow$ Sodium acetate + Carbon dioxide + Water

Sol. $$\underset{5.3\text{ g}}{Na_2CO_3} + \underset{6\text{ g}}{2CH_3COOH} \longrightarrow \underset{8.2\text{ g}}{2CH_3COONa} + \underset{2.2\text{ g}}{CO_2} + \underset{0.9\text{ g}}{H_2O}$$

'Law of conservation of mass' states that mass is neither created nor destroyed during a chemical reaction.

It means that the mass remains the same before and after the reaction. So, we add the mass of the reactants on LHS and add the mass of all products on RHS.

$$\text{LHS} = 5.3\text{ g} + 6\text{ g} = 11.3\text{ g}$$
$$\text{RHS} = 8.2\text{ g} + 2.2\text{ g} + 0.9\text{ g} = 11.3\text{ g}$$
$$\therefore \quad \text{LHS} = \text{RHS}$$

So, the observations are in agreement with the law of conservation of mass.

Question 2 Hydrogen and oxygen combine in the ratio of 1 : 8 by mass to form water. What mass of oxygen gas would be required to react completely with 3 g of hydrogen gas?

Sol. 'Law of constant proportions' states that composition of a compound is always fixed. Applying this,

$\because$ 1 g of hydrogen gas combines with oxygen = 8 g

$\therefore$ 3 g of hydrogen gas will combine with oxygen = $8 \times 3 = 24$ g

Quick Solution

As we know ratio of H and O in H_2O molecule is 1 : 8.

i.e. 1 g H_2 reacts with 8g O.

so 3 g H_2 will react with $= \dfrac{8 \times 3}{1} = 24$ g

Question 3 Which postulate of Dalton's atomic theory is the result of the law of conservation of mass?

Sol. Following postulate of Dalton's atomic theory is the result of the law of conservation of mass. 'Atoms are indivisible particles, which cannot be created or destroyed in a chemical reaction.'

Question 4 Which postulate of Dalton's atomic theory can explain the law of definite proportions?

Sol. Following postulate of Dalton's atomic theory can explain the 'law of definite proportions'. 'The relative number and kinds of atoms are constant in a given compound.'

On Page 30

Question 1 Define the atomic mass unit.

Sol. One atomic mass unit (amu) is a mass unit equal to exactly one-twelfth ($1/12^{th}$) the mass of one atom of carbon-12. The relative atomic masses of all the elements have been found with respect to an atom of carbon-12.

Question 2 Why is it not possible to see an atom with naked eyes?

Sol. As an atom is extremely small in size, it is not possible to see it with naked eyes. Generally, radius of an atom is of the order of nanometres. For example, atomic radius of hydrogen atom is 10^{-10} m (or 10^{-1} nm). According to Indian saga kannad, size of one atom is $\frac{1}{60}$th of a dust particle.

On Page 34

Question 1 Write down the formulae of

(i) sodium oxide (ii) aluminium chloride

(iii) sodium sulphide (iv) magnesium hydroxide

◎ ***Thinking Process*** While writing the formula of a compound, the valencies of the atoms/groups are written along with their formulae and then exchanged.

Sol. (i) **Sodium oxide**

Symbol Na S

Charge 1+ 2–

Formula = $\mathbf{Na_2O}$

(ii) **Aluminium chloride**

Symbol Al Cl

Charge 3+ 1–

Formula = $\mathbf{AlCl_3}$

(iii) **Sodium sulphide**

Symbol Na S

Charge 1+ 2–

Formula = $\mathbf{Na_2S}$

(iv) **Magnesium hydroxide**

Symbol Mg OH

Charge 2+ 1–

Formula = $\mathbf{Mg(OH)_2}$

Question 2 Write down the names of compounds represented by the following formulae.

(i) $Al_2(SO_4)_3$ (ii) $CaCl_2$ (iii) K_2SO_4 (iv) KNO_3 (v) $CaCO_3$

Sol. (i) Aluminium sulphate, (ii) Calcium chloride, (iii) Potassium sulphate, (iv) Potassium nitrate, (v) Calcium carbonate.

Question 3 What is meant by the term chemical formula?

Sol. Chemical formula of a compound (or element) is the symbolic representation of its composition. It gives information about the number and kind of atoms present per molecule of the compound.

Question 4 How many atoms are present in a
(i) H_2S molecule and (ii) PO_4^{3-} ion?

Sol. (i) 2 atom of hydrogen + 1 atom of sulphur
= three (3) atoms (in a H_2S molecule).

(ii) 1 atom of phosphorus + 4 atoms of oxygen
= five (5) atoms (in a PO_4^{3-} ion).

On Page 35

Question 1 Calculate the molecular masses of
$H_2, O_2, Cl_2, CO_2, CH_4, C_2H_6, C_2H_4, NH_3, CH_3OH$.

◎ *Thinking Process* Molecular mass of a substance is the sum of the atomic masses of all the atoms in a molecule of that substance.

Sol. (i) Molecular mass of H_2 (hydrogen) = Atomic mass of hydrogen × 2
= 1u × 2 = 2 u

(ii) Molecular mass of O_2 (oxygen) = Atomic mass of oxygen × 2
= 16 u × 2 = 32 u

(iii) Molecular mass of Cl_2 (chlorine) = Atomic mass of chlorine × 2
= 35.5 u × 2 = 71 u

(iv) Molecular mass of CO_2 (carbon dioxide)
= (Atomic mass of carbon × 1) + (Atomic mass of oxygen × 2)
= 12u + (16u × 2) = (12 + 32)u = 44 u

(v) Molecular mass of CH_4 (methane)
= (Atomic mass of carbon × 1) + (Atomic mass of hydrogen × 4)
= 12u + (1u × 4) = (12 + 4)u = 16 u

(vi) Molecular mass of C_2H_6 (ethane)
= (Atomic mass of carbon × 2) + (Atomic mass of hydrogen × 6)
= (12u × 2) + (1u × 6) = (24 + 6)u = 30 u

(vii) Molecular mass of C_2H_4 (ethene)
= (Atomic mass of carbon × 2) + (Atomic mass of hydrogen × 4)
= (12u × 2) + (1u × 4) = (24 + 4)u = 28 u

(viii) Molecular mass of NH_3 (ammonia)

= (Atomic mass of nitrogen × 1) + (Atomic mass of hydrogen × 3)

= (14u × 1) + (1u × 3) = (14 + 3)u = 17 u

(ix) Molecular mass of CH_3OH (methanol or methyl alcohol)

= (Atomic mass of carbon × 1) + (Atomic mass of hydrogen × 3) + (Atomic mass of oxygen × 1) + (Atomic mass of hydrogen × 1)

= 12u + 3u + 16u + 1u = 32 u

Mistake Alert Carefully calculate the molecular mass of the compounds by adding the atomic masses of the atoms present in the molecule.

Question 2 Calculate the formula unit masses of ZnO, Na_2O, K_2CO_3. Given atomic masses of Zn = 65 u, Na = 23 u, K = 39 u, C = 12 u and O = 16 u.

Thinking Process Formula unit mass of a substance is a sum of the atomic masses of all atoms in a unit of a formula compound.

Sol. (i) Formula unit mass of ZnO (zinc oxide) = 65u + 16u = 81u

(ii) Formula unit mass of Na_2O (sodium oxide) = (23u × 2) + (16u × 1)

= 46u + 16u = 62 u

(iii) Formula unit mass of K_2CO_3 (potassium carbonate)

= (39u × 2) + (12u × 1) + (16u × 3)

= 78u + 12u + 48 = 138 u

Exercises

Question 1 A 0.24 g sample of compound of oxygen and boron was found by analysis to contain 0.096 g of boron and 0.144 g of oxygen. Calculate the percentage composition of the compound by weight.

Sol. Mass of the compound = 0.24 g

Mass of boron = 0.096 g

Mass of oxygen = 0.144 g

$$\text{Percentage of boron} = \frac{\text{Mass of boron}}{\text{Mass of the compound}} \times 100 = \frac{0.096 \text{ g}}{0.240 \text{ g}} \times 100 = 40\%$$

$$\text{Percentage of oxygen} = \frac{\text{Mass of oxygen}}{\text{Mass of the compound}} \times 100 = \frac{0.144 \text{ g}}{0.240 \text{ g}} \times 100 = 60\%$$

Quick Solution

Percentage of oxygen = 100 − percentage of boron

= 100 − 40 = 60%

Question 2 When 3.0 g of carbon is burnt in 8.00 g oxygen, 11.00 g of carbon dioxide is produced. What mass of carbon dioxide will be formed when 3.00 g of carbon is burnt in 50.00 g of oxygen? Which law of chemical combination will govern your answer?

Sol. First we find the mass proportion of carbon and oxygen in carbon dioxide.

In CO_2, $C : O = 12 : 32$ or $3 : 8$

In other words, we can say that

$\because$ 12.00 g carbon reacts with oxygen = 32.00 g

$\therefore$ 3.00 g carbon will react with oxygen $= \frac{32}{12} \times 3 = 8$ g

$$\begin{array}{ccccc} C & + & O_2 & \longrightarrow & CO_2 \\ 12\text{ g} & & 32\text{ g} & & 12 + 16 \times 2 = 44\text{ g} \\ 3\text{ g} & & 8\text{ g} & & 3 + 8 = 11\text{ g} \end{array}$$

Therefore, 3.00 g of carbon will always react with 8.00 g of oxygen to form CO_2 (11.00 g), even if a large amount (50.00 g) of oxygen is present. This answer will be governed by 'the law of constant proportions'.

Question 3 What are polyatomic ions? Give examples.

Sol. The group of atoms which carry a fixed charge (either positive or negative) on them and behave as ions are called polyatomic ions.

For example

(i) Carbonate ion (CO_3^{2-}) (ii) Sulphate ion (SO_4^{2-})

(iii) Ammonium ion (NH_4^+) (iv) Phosphate ion (PO_4^{3-})

Question 4 Write the chemical formulae of the following.

(i) Magnesium chloride (ii) Calcium oxide

(iii) Copper nitrate (iv) Aluminium chloride

(v) Calcium carbonate

Sol. (i) **Symbol** Mg Cl

Charge 2+ 1–

Formula = $MgCl_2$ (Magnesium chloride)

(ii) **Symbol** Ca O

Charge 2+ 2–

Formula = Ca_2O_2 or CaO (Calcium oxide)

(iii) **Symbol** Cu NO_3

Charge 2+ 1–

Formula = $Cu(NO_3)_2$ (Copper nitrate)

(iv) **Symbol** Al Cl

Charge 3+ 1–

Formula = $AlCl_3$ (Aluminium chloride)

(v) **Symbol** Ca CO_3

Charge 2+ 2–

Formula = $CaCO_3$ (Calcium carbonate)

Question 5 Give the names of the elements present in the following compounds.

(a) Quick lime (b) Hydrogen bromide
(c) Baking powder (d) Potassium sulphate

Note First write the chemical name and chemical formula of the compound. Then, with the help of formula, name the elements.

Sol. (a) **Quick lime** – Calcium oxide – CaO.
Elements – Calcium and oxygen.

(b) **Hydrogen bromide** – HBr
Elements – Hydrogen and bromine.

(c) **Baking powder** – Sodium hydrogen carbonate — $NaHCO_3$
Elements – Sodium, hydrogen, carbon and oxygen.

(d) **Potassium sulphate** – K_2SO_4
Elements – Potassium, sulphur and oxygen.

Question 6 Calculate the molar mass of the following substances.

(a) Ethyne, C_2H_2
(b) Sulphur molecule, S_8
(c) Phosphorus molecule, P_4 (Atomic mass of phosphorus = 31)
(d) Hydrochloric acid, HCl
(e) Nitric acid, HNO_3

Sol. (a) Molar mass of C_2H_2

$$= (2 \times \text{Atomic mass of C}) + (2 \times \text{Atomic mass of H})$$
$$= (2 \times 12\text{u}) + (2 \times 1\text{u}) = 26 \text{ u}$$

(b) Molar mass of S_8 = (8 × Atomic mass of S) = 8 × 32 u = 256 u

(c) Molar mass of P_4 = 4 × Atomic mass of P = 4 × 31u = 124 u

(d) Molar mass of HCl = Atomic mass of hydrogen + Atomic mass of Cl

$$= 1\text{u} + 35.5\text{u} = 36.5 \text{ u}$$

(e) Molar mass of HNO_3 = Atomic mass of H + Atomic mass of N

$$+ (3 \times \text{Atomic mass of O})$$
$$= 1\text{u} + 14\text{u} + (3 \times 16\text{u}) = 15\text{u} + 48\text{u} = 63 \text{ u}$$

DIKSHA APP Questions

Multiple Choice Questions

Q.1 The chemical symbol for sodium is

(a) So (b) Sd (c) NA (d) Na

Sol. (d) Symbol of sodium is Na.

Q.2 The chemical symbol for nitrogen gas is

(a) Ni (b) N_2 (c) N^+ (d) N

Sol. (b) Symbol of nitrogen atom is N while, symbol of nitrogen gas is N_2.

Q.3 Which of the following contains maximum number of molecules?

(a) 1g CO_2 (b) 1g N_2 (c) 1g H_2 (d) 1g CH_4

Sol. (c) As we know that, Number of molecules

$$= \frac{\text{mass}}{\text{molar mass}} \times N_A (6.022 \times 10^{23})$$

Therefore, the number of molecules for the given options can be calculated as,

For option (a), No. of mulecules $= \frac{1}{44} \times N_A$

For option (b), No. of mulecules $= \frac{1}{28} \times N_A$

For option (c), No. of mulecules $= \frac{1}{2} \times N_A$

For option (d), No. of mulecules $= \frac{1}{16} \times N_A$

Hence, option (c), 1g H_2, contains the maximum numbers of molecules.

Quick Solution

From the above solution, we can observe that if the masses of given compounds in the options are same, then the compound having least molar mass will contain maximum number of molecules.

Q.4 Which of the following statements is false about an atom?

(a) Atoms are not able to exist independently.

(b) Atoms are the basic units from which molecules and ions are formed.

(c) Atoms are always neutral in nature.

(d) Atoms aggregate in large numbers to form the matter that we can see, feel or touch.

Sol. (a) Only statement (a) is incorrect. The correct form of this statement is as follows :

Atoms are able to exist independently, *e.g.*, He, Ne, Cl, F, Na, K

Q.5 Which of the following correctly represents 360 g of water.

(a) 2 moles of H_2O. (b) 202 moles of water.
(c) 6.022×10^{23} molecules of water. (d) 1.2044×10^{25} molecules of water.

Thinking Process Number of moles $= \dfrac{\text{mass of a substance}}{\text{Molar mass}} = \dfrac{N}{N_A}$

Sol. (d) As we know that, No. of moles $= \dfrac{\text{Mass of a substance}}{\text{Molar mass}}$

Therefore, for the given options, mass can be calculated as,

For option (a), $2 = \dfrac{m}{18} = 36$ g.

For option (b), $202 = \dfrac{m}{18}$, $m = 3636$ g

For option (c), No. of molecules $= \dfrac{\text{mass}}{\text{molar mass}} \times N_A$

$$\therefore \quad 6.022 \times 10^{23} = \frac{\text{mass}}{18} \times 6.022 \times 10^{23}$$

$$m = 18 \text{ g}$$

Similarly, For option (d), $1.2044 \times 10^{25} = \dfrac{m}{18} \times 6.022 \times 10^{23}$

$$m = 360 \text{ g}$$

Thus, option (d) is correct.

Q.6 Number of moles of water in 180g will be

(a) 5 (b) 10 (c) 15 (d) 18

Sol. (b) No. of moles $= \dfrac{\text{Mass of a substance}}{\text{Molar mass}}$

Where, molar mass of water = 18 g mol^{-1}

Mass of water = 180 g

$\therefore$ No. of moles $= \dfrac{180\text{g}}{18 \text{ g mol}^{-1}} = 10$ moles

Q.7 Molecular mass of ozone is

(a) 16 u (b) 32 u (c) 48 u (d) 64 u

Sol. (c) Ozone (O_3) has molecular mass of ($3 \times$ mass of oxygen) *i.e.*, $3 \times (16\text{u}) = 48$ u

Q.8 The correct formula of aluminium sulphate is

(a) $AlSO_4$ (b) $Al_2(SO_4)_2$ (c) Al_2SO_4 (d) $Al_2(SO_4)_3$

Sol. (d) Symbol Al SO_4

Charge 3+ 2−

Formula : $Al_2(SO_4)_3$

Q.9 Which of the following molecule has an atomicity of four?

(a) H_2O (b) NH_3 (c) CH_4 (d) CO_2

Sol. (b) The number of atoms constituting a molecule is known as atomicity. NH_3 has 4 atoms, so its atomicity is four.

Q.10 Calcium carbonate decomposes to calcium oxide and carbon dioxide. The valency of calcium ion in calcium oxide and oxygen in carbon dioxide are :

(a) 2 and 2 (b) 1 and 2 (c) 2 and 1 d) 1 and 1

Sol. (a) The reaction for decomposition of calcium carbonate ($CaCO_3$) is

$$CaCO_3(s) \longrightarrow (CaO(s)) + CO_2(g)$$

Now, calcium oxide is formed as

Symbol Ca O

Valency 2^+ 2^-

∴ Calcium has valency of 2 in calcium oxide.

Similarly, Carbon dioxide (CO_2) is formed as

Symbol C O

Valency 4 2

Formula : $C_2O_4 = CO_2$

Thus, valency of oxygen in carbon dioxide is 2.

□ Very Short Answer Type

Q.1 The chemical formula of oxide of an element "X" is X_2O_5. Write the chemical formula of its chloride.

Sol. The charge on the oxide is −2, So, the compound X_2O_5 is formed when X has a charge of +5, *i.e.*,

Symbol X O

Charge 5+ 2−

So, the formula of its chloride is

Symbol X Cl

Charge 5+ 1–

Formula : XCl_5

Q.2 What is an atom?

Sol. An atom is the indivisible smallest particle of an element capable of independent existence.

Q.3 State the law of constant proportion.

Sol. The law of constant proportion states that "In a chemical substance the elements are always present in definite proportions by mass."

Q.4 Using the concept of valency, derive the formulae of the following compounds.

(i) Aluminium oxide

(ii) Calcium phosphate

Sol. (i) Aluminium oxide

Symbol Al O

Valency 3 2

Formula : Al_2O_3

(ii) Calcium phosphate

Symbol Ca PO_4

Valency 2 3

Formula : $Ca_3(PO_4)_2$

☐ Short Answer Type

Q.1 You are provided with a fine white coloured powder which is either sugar or salt. How would you identify it without tasting?

Sol. (a) On heating the powder, if it chars then it is a sugar, otherwise it is a salt.

(b) When we dissolve the powder in water and check for its electricity conduction, if it conducts electricity then it is a salt, otherwise it is a sugar

Q.2 Does the solubility of a substance change with temperature? Explain with the help of an example.

Sol. Yes, solubility of a substance is a temperature dependent property. The solubility generally increases with an increase in temperature. For example, more sugar can be dissolved in hot water than in cold water.

Q.3 What is an ion? What are cations and anions?

Sol. An ion is a charged particle. The negatively charged ion is called as an 'anion' and the positively charged ion is known as a 'cation'.

☐ Long Answer Type

Q.1 State the chemical symbols for the following elements : Sodium, Potassium, Iron, Copper, Mercury, Silver.

Sol. Sodium : Na, Potassium : K, Iron : Fe, Copper : Cu, Mercury : Hg, Silver : Ag.

Q.2 Write the formulae of the following compounds. Also name the elements present in them.

(a) Water (b) Ammonia (c) Methane (d) Sulphur dioxide
(e) Ethanol

Sol.

Compound	Formula	Elements Present
(a) Water	H_2O	Hydrogen (H) and oxygen (O)
(b) Ammonia	NH_3	Nitrogen (N) and Hydrogen (H)
(c) Methane	CH_4	Carbon (C) and Hydrogen (H)
(d) Sulphur dioxide	SO_2	Sulphur (S) and Oxygen (O)
(e) Ethanol	C_2H_5OH	Carbon (C), Hydrogen (H) and Oxygen (O)

Q.3 What is the atomicity of the following?

(a) Oxygen (b) Ozone (c) Neon (d) Sulphur
(e) Phosphorus

◎ ***Thinking Process*** The number of atoms constituting a molecule is known as atomicity.

Sol. The atomicity of the following are:

(a) Oxygen (O_2) = 2
(b) Ozone (O_3) = 3
(c) Neon (Ne) = 1
(d) Sulphur (S_8) = 8
(e) Phosphorus (P_4) = 4

Structure of the Atom

CHAPTER 04

Important Points

01 **J.J. Thomson** is credited for the discovery of an electron while Eugen Goldstein worked on canal rays and contributed to the understanding of the proton.

02 Dalton's idea of atoms being indivisible failed after the discovery of electrons and protons, leading to the study of their arrangement in atoms.

03 **J.J. Thomson** proposed a Christmas pudding model for an atom in which 'electrons were embedded in the sphere of a positive charge.'

04 **Alpha particles** (^4_2He) are nuclei of helium having + 2 charge and a mass of 4 units.

05 Gold foil is exclusively used for α-particle scattering experiment as gold is having extraordinary **malleability** *i.e.*, very thin foil (1000 atom thick) can be made from it.

06 **Ernest Rutherford** discovered the nucleus of an atom through α-particle scattering experiment (Gold Foil Experiment). It has described the presence of nucleus in an atom.

07 Rutherford's model of an atom did not describe the stability of the atom as it predicted that electrons would spiral into the nucleus due to energy loss.

08 **Neils Bohr** proposed that electrons revolve around the nucleus in definite paths (orbits/shells/energy levels) having definite energy (K, L, M, N, ...).

09 The maximum number of electrons in a shell is given by **$2n^2$ rule.** where n is shell number energy level.

10 The combining capacity of an element is known as its **valency.**

11 Presence of complete octet (8 electrons in the outermost shell) provides an atom a stable configuration.

[Helium is an exception, as it has a stable configuration with 2 electrons in its K shell known as duplet.]

12 **Atomic number (Z)** = Number of protons (p)

Mass number (A) = Number of protons (p) + Number of neutrons (n)

13 Atoms having same number of protons (same atomic number) but different number of neutrons are called **isotopes** of an element. *e.g.,* ${}^1_1H$, ${}^2_1H$, ${}^3_1H$

14 **Isobars** are the atoms with same mass number but different atomic number. *e.g.,* ${}^3_2He$, ${}^3_1H$

15 **Atomic mass** of an element is taken as the average mass of all the naturally occurring atoms of that element. During the calculation, the percentage of isotopes is also considered.

16 **James Chadwick** discovered neutrons, the neutral particle in the atom.

17 The isotope of hydrogen, ${}^1_1H$ (or protium) does not have a neutron.

18 Electronic configuration of some elements are given below.

S.No.	Element	Symbol	Atomic number	Configuration				Valency
				K	*L*	*M*	*N*	
1.	Hydrogen	H	1	1				1
2.	Helium	He	2	2				0
3.	Lithium	Li	3	2	1			1
4.	Beryllium	Be	4	2	2			2
5.	Boron	B	5	2	3			3
6.	Carbon	C	6	2	4			4
7.	Nitrogen	N	7	2	5			3
8.	Oxygen	O	8	2	6			2
9.	Fluorine	F	9	2	7			1
10.	Neon	Ne	10	2	8			0
11.	Sodium	Na	11	2	8	1		1
12.	Magnesium	Mg	12	2	8	2		2
13.	Aluminium	Al	13	2	8	3		3
14.	Silicon	Si	14	2	8	4		4
15.	Phosphorus	P	15	2	8	5		3
16.	Sulphur	S	16	2	8	6		2
17.	Chlorine	Cl	17	2	8	7		1
18.	Argon	Ar	18	2	8	8		0
19.	Potassium	K	19	2	8	8	1	1
20.	Calcium	Ca	20	2	8	8	2	2

19 Average atomic mass $= \left[(\text{Atomic mass of isotope I})\left(\frac{\%\text{ of isotope I}}{100}\right)\right.$

$$\left. + \text{atomic mass of isotope II}\left(\frac{\%\text{ of isotope II}}{100}\right)\right]$$

Intext Questions

On Page 39

Question 1 What are canal rays?

Sol. Canal rays or anode rays are the positively charged rays which are originated from anode and seen moving from the anode towards cathode in a specially designed discharge tube (with a porous cathode), when a high voltage is applied across the electrodes.

Question 2 If an atom contains one electron and one proton, will it carry any charge or not?

◎ *Thinking Process* An electron carries a negative charge of –1 and a proton carries a positive charge of +1.

Sol. The charge (– 1) on an electron and that on a proton (+1) balance and neutralise each other. Thus, the atom will not carry any charge.

On Page 41

Question 1 On the basis of Thomson's model of an atom, explain how the atom is neutral as a whole?

Sol. According to Thomson's model an atom consists of both negatively and positively charged particles. As the magnitude of positive and negative charges are equal, the atom is electrically neutral.

Question 2 On the basis of Rutherford's model of an atom, which subatomic particle is present in the nucleus of an atom?

Sol. Nucleus is positively charged according to Rutherford's model of an atom, *i.e.*, proton is present inside the nucleus of an atom.

Question 3 Draw a sketch of Bohr's model of an atom with three shells.

Sol.

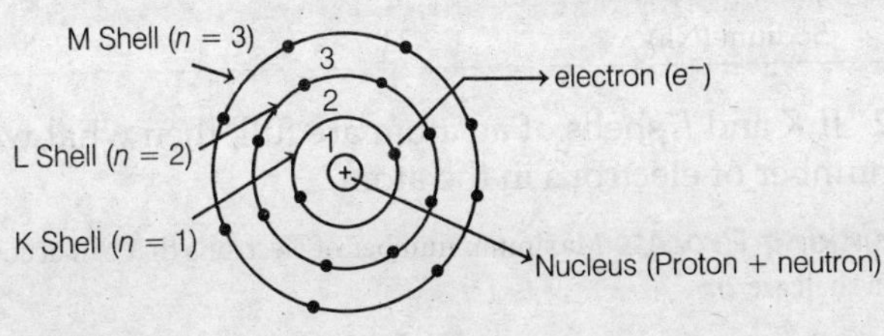

Mistake Alert Nucleus contains both protons and neutrons.

Question 4 What do you think would be the observation if the α-particle scattering experiment is carried out using a foil of a metal other than gold?

Sol. Rutherford used gold for α-particle scattering experiment because gold is the **most malleable** metal. A very thin foil of 10^{-7} m thickness (or 1000 atoms thick) can be made with gold. Malleability of silver is next to gold (10^{-6} m thick foil can be made). More thick foils can be made by other metals like platinum. As the thickness of the foil increases, the possibility of correctness of the experiment decreases. So, use of gold in this case is preferred.

Question 5 Name the three sub-atomic particles of an atom.

Sol. The three sub-atomic particles in an atom are **protons, electrons** and **neutrons.**

Question 6 Helium atom has an atomic mass of 4 u and two protons in its nucleus. How many neutrons does it have?

◎ ***Thinking Process*** Atomic mass (A) = no. of neutrons (n) + no. of protons (p)

Sol. Atomic mass of helium = 4 u, Number of protons = 2

Let the number of neutrons = x

$\because$ Number of protons + Number of neutrons = Atomic mass

$\therefore$ $x + 2 = 4, x = 4 - 2 = 2$

Thus, the number of neutrons = 2

On Page 42

Question 1 Write the distribution of electrons in carbon and sodium atoms.

Sol.

S.No.	Element	Atomic number	Electronic configuration K, L, M
1.	Carbon (C)	6	2, 4
2.	Sodium (Na)	11	2, 8, 1

Question 2 If K and L shells of an atom are full, then what would be the total number of electrons in the atom?

◎ ***Thinking Process*** Maximum number of electrons that can accommodate in a shall are $2n^2$.

Sol. Maximum number of electrons in K-shell = $2 \times (1)^2 = 2$

Maximum number of electrons in L-shell = $2 \times (2)^2 = 2 \times 4 = 8$

Total number of electrons in the atom = 2 + 8 = 10 electrons

On Page 44

Question 1 How will you find the valency of chlorine, sulphur and magnesium?

◎ *Thinking Process*

- Valency is the combining capacity of an elements.
- Valency of a metal = number of valence electrons
  (*i.e.*, number of electrons present in the outermost shell.)
- Valency of a non-metal = 8 – number of valence electrons.

Sol. Magnesium is a metal while chlorine and sulphur are non-metals.

(i) ${}_{12}Mg$ = 2, 8, 2 Valency of magnesium = 2
(ii) ${}_{16}S$ = 2, 8, 6 Valency of sulphur = 8 – 6 = 2
(iii) ${}_{17}Cl$ = 2, 8, 7 Valency of chlorine = 8 – 7 = 1

Mistake Alert One can make a mistake in confusing metals and non-metals, while calculating their valency.

Question 2 If number of electrons in an atom is 8 and number of protons is also 8, then

(i) what is the atomic number of the atom? and
(ii) what is the charge on the atom?

◎ *Thinking Process*

- Atomic number (Z) = no. of protons (p) = no. of electrons (e^-)
- mass number (A) = no. of neutron (n) + no. of protons (p)

Sol. (i) Atomic number (Z) = number of protons (p) = 8.

(ii) The charge on the atom is zero because number of electrons and number of protons is equal.

Question 3 Find the mass number of oxygen and sulphur atom.

Sol. Mass number = no. of protons + no. of neutrons

(i) In oxygen, protons = 8, neutrons = 8
$\therefore$ Mass number of oxygen = 8 + 8 = 16
(ii) In sulphur, protons = 16, neutrons = 16
$\therefore$ Mass number of sulphur = 16 + 16 = 32

On Page 45

Question 1 For the symbol H, D and T tabulate three sub-atomic particles found in each of them.

Sol.

Symbol	Protons	Neutrons	Electrons
^1_1H	1	0	1
^2_1D	1	1	1
^3_1T	1	2	1

Question 2 Write the electronic configuration of any one pair of isotopes and isobars.

Thinking Process

- Isotopes have the same atomic number but different mass numbers.
- Isobars are atoms of different elements with different atomic numbers, but same mass number.

Sol. **Isotopes** *e.g.,* $^{35}_{17}Cl$ and $^{37}_{17}Cl$.

Electronic configuration of both the isotopes of chlorine is same as their atomic number is same, *i.e.,*

$$_{17}Cl = \begin{matrix} K & L & M \\ 2 & 8 & 7 \end{matrix}$$

Now, **Isobars** *e.g.,* $^{40}_{20}Ca$ and $^{40}_{18}Ar$.

Electronic configuration of both the elements are :

$$\begin{matrix} & K & L & M & N \\ _{20}Ca = & 2 & 8 & 8 & 2 \\ _{18}Ar = & 2 & 8 & 8 & \end{matrix}$$

Exercises

Question 1 Compare the properties of electrons, protons and neutrons.

Sol.

Property	Electron	Proton	Neutron
Absolute charge	$(-) 1.6 \times 10^{-19}$ C	$(+) 1.6 \times 10^{-19}$ C	Nil (zero)
Relative charge	-1	$+1$	Nil (zero)
Absolute mass	9.1×10^{-31} kg	1.67×10^{-27} kg	1.67×10^{-27} kg
Relative mass	1/1840	1	1
Discovered by	J.J Thomson	E. Goldstein	J. Chadwick

Question 2 What are the limitations of J.J Thomson's model of the atom?

Sol. Limitations of Thomson's model of atom

1. Thomson's model could not explain the experimental results of other scientists such as Rutherford, as there is no nucleus in the atomic model proposed by Thomson.
2. It does not have any experimental evidence in its support.

Question 3 What are the limitations of Rutherford's model of the atom?

Sol. Limitations of Rutherford's model of an atom

1. It could not explain the stability of the atom.

   Reason When a charged particle revolves in a circular orbit, it radiates energy continuously due to accelerated motion. This makes the atom highly unstable. But we know that the atom is stable.
2. Rutherford's model could not explain the distribution of electrons in the extra nuclear portion of the atom.

Question 4 Describe Bohr's model of the atom.

Sol. Bohr's model of atom

1. Electrons revolve in well defined paths, known as orbits or shells around the nucleus.
2. These orbits are also called **energy levels.**
3. These are named as *K, L, M, N* ..... or 1, 2, 3, 4 ..... and so on.
4. The order of energy increases from *K* onwards. It means $K < L < M < N$....
5. While revolving in an orbit, the electron neither loses or gains energy. As the energy of an orbit is stationary, these are also known as **stationary states.**

Question 5 Compare all the proposed models of an atom given in this chapter.

S.No.	Thomson's model	Rutherford's model	Bohr's model
1.	Nucleus is not present.	Nucleus is present.	Nucleus is present.
2.	Positive charge present in the form of a sphere.	Positive charge (protons) present inside the nucleus.	Positive charge (protons) present inside the nucleus.
3.	Electrons embedded in the positive sphere (uniform distribution).	Electrons revolve around the nucleus.	Electrons revolve around the nucleus in well defined orbits with definite energy.

Question 6 Summarise the rules for writing of distribution of electrons in various shells for the first eighteen elements.

Sol. **Rules for writing the electronic configuration**

1. The maximum number of electrons in a shell is given by $2n^2$ rule, where n is the shell number (1, 2, 3 ...). Thus, K shell can accomodate maximum of 2 electrons, while L, M and N shell can have a maximum number of 8, 18, 32 electrons respectively.
2. The outermost or valence shell of an atom can accomodate only 8 electrons (or less) but not more than 8 electrons.
3. Electrons are not accomodated in a given shell untill the inner shells are filled, *i.e.*, the shells are filled in a stepwise manner.

Question 7 Define valency by taking examples of silicon and oxygen.

Sol. **Valency** The combining capacity of the atom of an element with the atom (s) of other element (s) in order to complete its octet is called the valency of that element.

Examples

(i) The electronic configurationof $_{14}Si = 2, 8, 4$. Its outermost shell has 4 electrons. Thus, its valency is 4.

(ii) The electronic configuration of 8° is 2,6. Its outermost shell has 6 electrons. Since, it can easily gain 2 e^- to complete its octet. Thus, its valency is 2.

Question 8 Explain with examples

(i) Atomic number, (ii) Mass number, (iii) Isotopes and,

(iv) Isobars.

Give any two uses of isotopes.

Sol. (i) **Atomic number (Z)** The number of protons present in the nucleus of the atom of an element is called its atomic number.

$$\text{Atomic number}\,(Z) = \text{Number of protons}\,(p)$$

For example : Sodium (Na) atom has 11 protons. Thus, its atomic number is 11. It is represented as $_{11}Na$.

(ii) **Mass number (A)** (or atomic mass) The total number of protons and neutrons (nucleons) present in an atom is called its mass number.

Mass number = no. of protons + no. of neutrons

For example : Sodium atom has 11 protons and 12 neutrons. Its mass number is 23. It is represented as ^{23}Na.

(iii) **Isotopes :** Atoms of an element that have same atomic number but different mass number are called isotopes of that element.
For example : Hydrogen has 3 isotopes ^1_1H, ^2_1H and ^3_1H.

(iv) **Isobars :** Atoms of different elements that have same mass number but different atomic number are called isobars.
For example : $^{40}_{18}Ar$ and $^{40}_{20}Ca$ are isobars.

Uses of Isotopes

1. Radioactive isotope of iodine (^{131}I) is used in the treatment of goitre.
2. Radioactive uranium (^{235}U) is used as a fuel in the nuclear reactors.
3. Radioactive isotope of cobalt (^{60}Co) releases γ-radiations so it is used in the treatment of cancer.

Question 9 Na^+ has completely filled K and L shells. Explain.

Sol. Sodium (Na) atom has the following electronic configuration, K, L, M = 2, 8, 1

When an atom loses one electron, it acquires a positive charge. Thus, Na atom will have lose one electron from its M shell to get converted into Na^+ ion.

Na^+(ion) = 2, 8

As the maximum capacity of K shell is 2 electrons and that of L shell is 8 electrons, therefore, Na^+ has completely filled K and L shells.

Question 10 If bromine atom is available in the form of, say, two isotopes $^{79}_{35}Br$ (49.7%) and $^{81}_{35}Br$ (50.3%), calculate the average atomic mass of bromine atom.

Sol. Average atomic mass of an element

$$= \left[\left(\text{Atomic mass of I isotope} \times \frac{\text{\% of I isotope}}{100}\right) + \left(\text{Atomic mass of II isotope} \times \frac{\text{\% of II isotope}}{100}\right)\right]$$

$$\text{Average atomic mass of bromine} = \left[\left(79\text{u} \times \frac{49.7}{100}\right) + \left(81\text{u} \times \frac{50.3}{100}\right)\right]$$

$$= 39.263\text{u} + 40.743\text{u} = 80.006\text{u}$$

Question 11 The average atomic mass of a sample of an element X is 16.2 u. What are the percentages of isotopes $^{16}_{8}X$ and $^{18}_{8}X$ in the sample?

Sol. Let the percentage of $^{16}_{8}X = x$

Then, the percentage of $^{18}_{8}X = (100 - x)$ ...(i)

Average atomic mass of X = 16.2 u

According to the given data,

$$16 \times \frac{x}{100} + 18 \times \frac{(100 - x)}{100} = 16.2 \quad \text{...(ii)}$$

$$\frac{16x}{100} + \frac{1800 - 18x}{100} = 16.2$$

$$16x + 1800 - 18x = 1620$$

$$-2x = -1800 + 1620$$

$$x = \frac{180}{2} = 90\%$$

Placing the value of x in Eq. (i)

$$\% \text{ of } {}^{18}_{8}X = 100 - 90 = 10\%$$

Isotope ${}^{16}_{8}X = 90\%$; Isotope ${}^{18}_{8}X = 10\%$

Question 12 If $Z = 3$, what would be the valency of the element? Also, name the element.

Sol. Electronic configuration of element $Z = \begin{matrix} K, & L \\ 2, & 1 \end{matrix}$

Valency of an element = Number of valence electrons = 1

Name of the element with atomic number $(Z) = 3$ is Lithium

Question 13 Composition of the nuclei of two atomic species X and Y are given as under.

	X	Y;
Protons =	6	6;
Neutrons =	6	8

Give the mass numbers of X and Y. What is the relation between the two species?

Sol. Mass number = Number of protons + Number of neutrons

Mass number of $X = 6 + 6 = 12$

Mass number of $Y = 6 + 8 = 14$

To find the relation between X and Y,

Atomic number of X = Number of protons = 6

Atomic number of Y = Number of protons = 6

As the atomic numbers of both elements X and Y are same (6) but their mass numbers are different, thus, X and Y are isotopes of the same element (carbon), *i.e.*, X and Y are ${}^{12}_{6}C$ and ${}^{14}_{6}C$ respectively.

Question 14 For the following statements, write T for (True) and F for (False).

(a) J.J. Thomson proposed that the nucleus of an atom contains only nucleons.

(b) A neutron is formed by an electron and a proton combining together. Therefore, it is neutral.

(c) The mass of an electron is about $\frac{1}{2000}$ times that of proton.

(d) An isotope of iodine is used for making tincture iodine, which is used as a medicine.

Sol. (a) False (F). Because in J.J. Thomson model nucleus was not present.

(b) False (F). A neutron is a fundamental particle and is not formed by the combination of a proton and a neutron.

(c) True (T). Mass of an electron is $\frac{1}{1840}$ times *i.e.*, about $\frac{1}{2000}$ times that of the proton.

(d) False (F). Tincture is made by dissolving iodine in alcohol, not from the isotope of iodine.

Question 15 Rutherford's alpha-particle scattering experiment was responsible for the discovery of

(a) atomic nucleus
(b) electron
(c) proton
(d) neutron

Sol. (a) On the basis of his experiment, Rutherford predicted that the centre part of the atom is solid, positively charged and is responsible for the mass of the atom. He called this portion atomic nucleus.

Question 16 Isotopes of an element have

(a) the same physical properties.
(b) different chemical properties.
(c) different number of neutrons.
(d) different atomic numbers.

Sol. (c) Isotopes of an element have similar chemical properties, same atomic number (same number of protons) but different mass number. (different number of neutrons).

Question 17 Number of valence electrons in Cl^- ion are

(a) 16 (b) 8
(c) 17 (d) 18

Sol. (b) Valence electrons are the electrons present in the outermost shell of an atom.

$_{17}Cl$ (atom) = 2, 8, $\underline{7}$; Valence electrons = 7

Cl^- (ion) = 2, 8, $\underline{8}$; Valence electrons = 8

Question 18 Which one of the following is a correct electronic configuration of sodium?

(a) 2, 8 (b) 8, 2, 1
(c) 2, 1, 8 (d) 2, 8, 1

Sol. (d) Atomic number of Na is 11.

Electronic configuration $_{11}Na$ = 2, 8, 1

Question 19 Complete the following table.

Atomic number	Mass number	Number of neutrons	Number of protons	Number of electrons	Name of the atomic species
9	—	10	—	—	—
16	32	—	—	—	Sulphur
—	24	—	12	—	—
—	2	—	1	—	—
—	1	0	1	0	—

Sol.

Atomic number	Mass number	Number of neutrons	Number of protons	Number of electrons	Name of the atomic species
9	**19**	10	**9**	**9**	**Fluorine**
16	32	**16**	**16**	**16**	Sulphur
12	24	**12**	12	**12**	**Magnesium**
1	2	**1**	1	**1**	**Deuterium**
1	1	0	1	0	**Hydrogen ion**

Explanation

(i) **Fluorine** ($^{19}_{9}F$) Atomic number = 9 ; Number of neutrons = 10
Mass number = atomic no. + number of neutrons = 9 + 10 = 19
Number of protons = Atomic number = Number of electrons = 9
Thus, the element is fluorine ($^{19}_{9}F$).

(ii) **Sulphur** ($^{32}_{16}S$) Atomic number = 16
Number of protons = Number of electrons = 16
Number of neutrons = Mass number – Atomic number
= 32 – 16 = 16

(iii) **Magnesium** ($^{24}_{12}Mg$) Number of protons = 12
Atomic number = Number of protons = 12
Number of electrons = Number of protons = 12
Number of neutrons = Mass number – Atomic number = 24 – 12 = 12

(iv) **Deuterium** ($^{2}_{1}D$) Number of protons = Number of electrons = 1
∴ Atomic number = 1; Mass number = 2
Number of neutrons = 2 – 1 = 1

(v) **Hydrogen ion** ($_1H^+$) Mass number = 1
Number of protons = 1 ; Number of neutrons = 0
Number of electrons = 1 – 1 = 0
Atomic number = Number of protons = 1
Because, number of electrons is zero, so the species is hydrogen ion (H^+), not hydrogen atom.

DIKSHA APP Questions

☐ Multiple Choice Questions

Q.1 In an atom, valence electrons are present in

(a) 1st shell (b) 2nd shell (c) outermost shell (d) last but one shell

Sol. (c) Valence electrons are those electrons which are present in the outermost shell (valence shell).

Q.2 The first model of an atom was given by

(a) N. Bohr (b) E. Goldstein (c) Rutherford (d) J.J. Thomson

Sol. (d) First model of an atom was given by J.J. Thomson.

Q.3 The ion of an element has 3 positive charges. Mass number of the atom is 27 and the number of neutrons is 14. What is the number of electrons in the ion?

(a) 13 (b) 10 (c) 14 (d) 16

Sol. (b) Let x is an ion, *i.e.*, x^{3+}

Mass number $(A) = 27$ $n = 14$ $e^- = ?$

$A =$ no. of protons (p) + no. of neutrons (n)

$p = A - n = 27 - 14 = 13$

As, Atomic number (Z) = no. of protons (p)

So, $Z = 13$ *i.e.* element is Al.

As it contains +3 charge, therefore, it contains $13 - 3 = 10$ electrons

Q.4 (i) Electrons have negative charge.

(ii) The mass and positive charge of the atom is concentrated in the nucleus.

(iii) Neutrons exists in the nucleus.

(iv) Most of the space in atom is empty

Which of the above statements are correct?

(a) (i) and (iii) (b) (ii) and (iv) (c) (i) and (iv) (d) All of these

Sol. (d) All the statements given above are correct.

Q.5 Rutherford's alpha particles scattering experiment resulted into discovery of

(a) electron (b) proton
(c) nucleus in the atom (d) atomic mass

Sol. (c) Rutherford's α-particle experiment resulted in the discovery of nucleus in atom.

Q.6 The cathode ray experiment was done for the first time by

(a) J.J Thomson (b) John Dalton
(c) Goldstein (d) Rutherford

Sol. (a) The cathode ray experiment was done for the first time by J.J Thomson.

Q.7 The magnitude of charge on an electron is

(a) 1.6×10^{-6}C (b) 1.6×10^{-20}C (c) 1.6×10^{-19}C (d) 1.6×10^{-16}C

Sol. (c) The charge on an electron is 1.6×10^{-19}C

Q.8 As per the theory of Neils Bohr, the maximum number of electrons that can be accommodated in third shell $(n=3)$ is

(a) 2 (b) 8 (c) 18 (d) 10

Sol. (c) The maximum electrons that can be accommodated in a shell is given by $2n^2$

For $n=3$, $2n^2 = 2(3)^2 = 2\times9 = 18$

So, maximum 18 electrons can be accommodated in a shell.

Q.9 The nucleus of an atom contains.

(a) protons (b) electrons
(c) protons and neutrons (d) neutrons

Sol. (c) The nucleus of an atom contains both protons and neutrons.

Q.10 What is the number of valence electrons of Al ?

(a) 5 (b) 2 (c) 3 (d) 4

Sol. (c) The number of valence electrons of Al is 3 as its electronic configuration is 2, 8, 3.

Q.11 An element X has two orbits and 7 valence electrons. Identify X.

(a) Chlorine (b) Fluorine
(c) Nitrogen (d) Neon

Sol. (b) An element X has electronic configuration 2, 7 and it has 9 electrons so, it is fluorine (F).

Q.12 The number of electrons in an element with atomic number X and atomic mass Y will be

(a) $(X-Y)$ (b) $(Y-X)$ (c) $(X+Y)$ (d) X

Sol. (d) $\because$ Atomic number (X) = no. of protons = no. of electrons

Similarly, Atomic mass (X) = no. of neutrons + no. of protons

So, number of electrons is X.

Q.13 Which of the following describes an isotope with a mass number of 99 that contains 56 neutrons in its nucleus?

(a) $^{99}_{56}Ba$ (b) $^{43}_{56}Ba$ (c) $^{99}_{43}Tc$ (d) $^{56}_{43}Tc$

Sol. (c) As we know that, Atomic number (Z) = no. of protons (p) = no. of electrons (e^-)

Mass number (A) = no. of neutrons (n) + no. of protons (p)

Given, $n = 56$

$A = 99$

So; $p = A - n = 99 - 56$

$p = 43 \Rightarrow Z = 43$

$\therefore$ Element is $^{99}_{43}Tc$

Mistake Alert The representation of the elements symbol is : $^{A}_{Z}X$ and not $^{Z}_{A}X$.

☐ Very Short Answer Type

Q.1 Why do some elements lose and some gain electrons?

Sol. Some elements lose and some gain electrons to attain a stable state or nearest noble gas configuration.

Q.2 What is an octet of electrons?

Sol. Octet of electrons means having 8 electrons in the valence shell.

Q.3 What is the charge of the rays used by Rutherford in his experiment?

Sol. Rutherford used positively charged alpha particles for his experiment.

Q.4 Name the scientist who discovered the neutron?

Sol. James Chadwick discovered the neutron.

☐ Short Answer Type

Q.1 An atom contains five protons and six neutrons. What is its atomic number and mass number.

Sol. An atom has atomic number (Z) as Z = no. of protons (p) = no. of electrons (e^-) and mass number (A) of an atom is :

$$A = \text{no. of neutrons } (n) + \text{no. of protons } (p)$$

According to the question,

$$p = 5$$

$$n = 6$$

$\therefore Z = p = e = 5$ and $A = n + p$

$A = 5 + 6 = 11$

So, atomic number of an element is 5 and its mass number is 11.

Q.2 Isotopes have similar chemical properties but different physical properties. Justify

Sol. Physical properties are determined by the intermolecular forces of attraction in the bulk. It is affected by the mass number. Chemical properties are determined by the outer shell electrons or valency. It is affected by the atomic number.

Since, isotopes have same atomic number but different mass numbers therefore, they have similar chemical properties but different physical properties.

Q.3 The atomic composition of element A is the number of neutrons $= x$, Atomic mass $= 12$, number of electrons $= 6$ and of B is number of neutrons $= y$, atomic mass $= 28$, number of electrons $=$ number of electrons in $A + 8$. Find the ratio of x and y.

Sol. For an element A,

No. of neutrons $(n) = x$

Atomic mass $(A) = n + p = 12$

No. of electrons $(e^-) = 6 \Rightarrow e^- = p = 6$

So, $A = x + 6 = 12$

$\Rightarrow x = 6$

For an element B,

No. of neutrons $(n) = y$

Atomic mass $(A) = n + p = 28$

No. of electrons $e^- = 6 + 8 = 14$

$e^- = p = 14$

So, $A = y + 14 = 28$

$\Rightarrow y = 14$

Thus, ratio of x and $y = 6 : 14 = 3 : 7$

☐ Long Answer Type

Q.1 In what way is the Rutherford's atomic model different from that of Thomson's atomic model?

Sol. Rutherford proposed a model in which electrons revolve around the nucleus in well-defined orbits. There is a positively charged centre in an atom called the nucleus. He also proposed that the size of the nucleus is very small as compared to the size of the atom and nearly all the mass of an atom is centred in the nucleus.

Whereas, Thomson proposed the model of an atom to be similar to a Christmas pudding. The electrons are studded like currents in a positively charged sphere like Christmas pudding and the mass of the atom was supposed to be uniformly distributed.

Q.2 Why do Helium, Neon and Argon have a zero valency?

Sol. Helium has two electrons in its only energy shell, while Argon and Neon have 8 electrons in their valence shells. As these have maximum number of electrons in their valence shells, they do not have any tendency to combine with other elements. Hence, they have a valency equal to zero.

Q.3 Show diagramatically the electron distributions in a sodium atom and a sodium ion and also give their atomic number.

Sol. Since, the atomic number of sodium atom is 11, it has 11 electrons arranged as 2, 8, 1. A positively charged sodium ion (Na^+) is formed by the removal of one electron from a sodium atom. So, a sodium ion has 11-1 = 10 electrons in it.

Thus, electronic distribution of sodium ion will be 2, 8. The atomic number of an element is equal to the number of protons in its atom. Since, sodium atom and sodium ion both contains the same number of protons, therefore, the atomic number of both is 11.

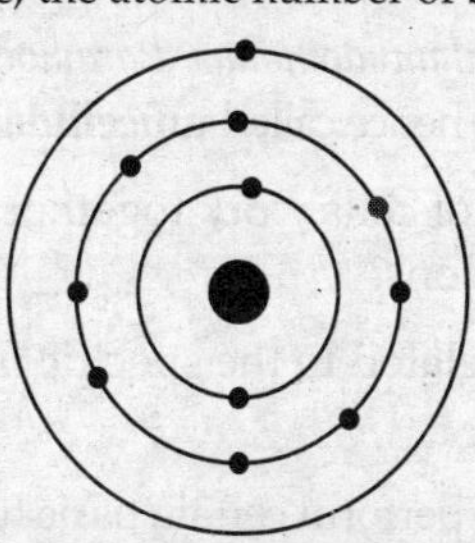
Sodium (Na)

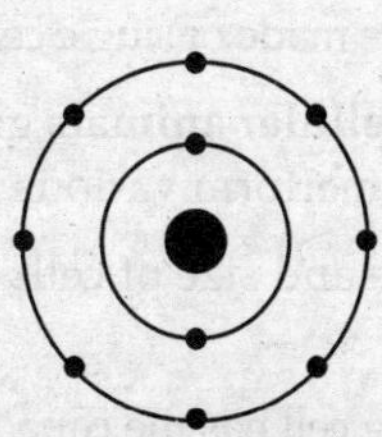
Sodium ion (Na^+)

The Fundamental Unit of Life

CHAPTER 05

Important Points

01 **Robert Hooke** (1665) observed honey comb-like structures or boxes from a thin slice of cork through his self-designed microscope. He called these boxes as **cells**.

02 **Antonie van Leeuwenhoek** (1674) discovered free living cells in pond water for the first time, with the help of improved microscope.

03 **Robert Brown** (1831) discovered the nucleus in the cell.

04 **Jan Evangelista Purkinje** (1839) coined the term 'protoplasm' for the fluid substance of the cell.

05 **Matthias Schleiden** (1838) and **Theodor Schwann** (1839) proposed the cell theory. According to this theory
(i) All plants and animals are composed of cells.
(ii) The cell is the basic unit of life.

06 **Rudolf Virchow** (1855) further expanded this theory, suggesting that all cells arise from pre-existing cells.

07 Small organisms like *Amoeba, Chlamydomonas, Paramocium* and bacteria are made of single cell and hence called **unicellular organisms.**

08 In **multicellular animals** group of cells work together in a single body and perform various functions.

09 The shape and size of cells are related to the specific function they perform.

10 Each living cell has the capacity to perform certain basic functions that are characteristic of all living forms besides some special functions.

11 Each type of cell shows the property of division of labour.

12 Each cell contains specific components within it known as cell organelles, each performing a special function.

13 Cells can be classified as

(i) **Prokaryotic cells** These are simple cells and do not have nuclear membrane as well as the membrane bound organelles.

(ii) **Eukaryotic cells** These are complex cells and possess a nuclear membrane as well as membrane bound organelles.

14 The **plasma membrane** or cell membrane, is the outermost covering of cell that separates the contents of the cell from its external environment.

15 The plasma membrane is extremely thin, elastic and selectively permeable. It is made up of lipids and proteins.

16 It provide definite shape to the cell as well as control movement of substances in and out, maintaining cellular balance.

17 **Diffusion** is the spontaneous movement of substances such as CO_2 or O_2 from the area of higher conc to area of lower conc.

18 **Osmosis** is the diffusion of water through a selectively permeable membrane.

Different solutions have different effect on the cell, as described below.

(i) **Hypotonic Solution** a cell will gain water.

(ii) **Hypertonic Solution** a cell will lose water, which can lead to a process known as plasmolysis.

(iii) **Isotonic Solution** A cell will neither gain nor lose water.

19 **Endocytosis** is the process of ingestion of food and other material by cells through the plasma membrane.

20 The cell wall is present in plant cells only. It is non-living and mainly contains cellulose, gives rigidity to the plant cell and also offers mechanical support, safe guarding the cell's internal structure.

21 **Nucleus** is the largest cell organelle which controls all the cell activities. It has a double-layered porous covering called **nuclear membrane**.

22 The nucleus contains rod-shaped structures called **chromosomes**. They are composed of DNA and protein.

23 Chromosomes contain information for inheritance of characters from parents to next generation in the form of DNA.

24 **DNA** (Deoxyribonucleic acid) contain the information necessary for constructing and organising cells. The functional segments of DNA are called **genes.**

25 In a cell, which is not dividing, this DNA is present as chromatin material, which is a thread-like entangled mass. Whenever, the cell is about to divide, the chromatin material gets organised into chromosomes.

26 The functions of nucleus are

(i) It controls all the functions of cell directly or indirectly.

(ii) It controls cell division.

27 The Cytoplasm is a viscous, homogeneous, colloidal fluid that contains various molecules of water, amino acids, carbohydrates, protein and lipids, etc.

28 It provide turgidity to the cell, facilitate intercellular transport as well as serves as the site of many metabolic reactions.

29 Cell organelles are mostly visible only with an electron microscope. These are membrane-bound structures except ribosomes. The important cell organelles are endoplasmic reticulum, golgi apparatus, lysosomes, mitochondria, plastids and vacuoles.

30 The **Endoplasmic Reticulum (ER)** is a large network of membrane-bound tubes and sheets.

31 The endoplasmic reticulum is of two types :

(i) Rough Endoplasmic Reticulum (RER)

(ii) Smooth Endoplasmic Reticulum (SER)

32 The endoplasmic reticulum synthesizes proteins (RER) and lipids (SER), transport material, support biochemical reactions and detoxifies, substances in liver cells.

33 **Ribosomes** are the smallest cell organelles and lack a membrane. They are found freely in the cytoplasm or attached to the rough endoplasmic reticulum (RER). Ribosomes are the main site of protein synthesis in a cell.

34 The Golgi apparatus also known as Golgi bodies or Golgi complex, was first described by **Camillo Golgi**. It consists of membrane-bound vesicles, arranged approximately parallel to each other in stocks called cisterns.

35 The Golgi apparatus modifies, packages and stores materials synthesized in the ER, such as proteins and lipids. It is involved in the fomation of lysosomes and synthesis of complex sugars.

36 Lysosomes are small sized hydrolytic enzyme (digestive enzymes) containing vesicles, which are bounded by a single membrane. These are also known as **'suicidal bags'** or **'digestive bags'.**

37 Lysosomes digest foreign materials and worn-out organelles. It can also trigger cell death by releasing digestive enzymes when the cell is damaged.

38 **Mitochondria** are double membraned bean-shaped structures. Their outer membrane is porous and the inner membrane is deeply folded.

39 Mitochondria are known as strange organelle because they contains their own DNA and ribosomes.

40 They help in cellular respiration and release of energy in the form of ATP molecules.

41 Mitochondria are popularly known as 'power house of the cell'.

42 **Plastids** are present only in plant cells. The internal organisation of plastids consists of numerous membrane layers embedded in a material called the stroma. Like the mitochondria, plastids also have their own DNA and ribosomes.

43 The plastids are of two types *i.e.,* leucoplast and chromoplast. The chromoplast containing the pigment chlorophyll are known as chloroplast.

44 Plastids are responsible for photosynthesis (chloroplast), storage of starch, oils and protein (leucoplast) as well as the pigmentation of flowers and fruits (chromoplasts).

45 Vacuoles are storage sacs for solids or liquid contents. They are small sized in animal cells while plant cells have very large vacuoles.

46 Vacuole maintain turgidity and rigidity in plant cells. It also store essential substances (like food and water) as well as assist in expelling excess water and waste in unicellular organisms.

47 **Cell division** is the process by which new cells are formed for growth, replacing dead cells and forming gametes for reproduction.

Two type of cells division are

(i) **Mitosis** → involved in growth and repair.

(ii) **Meiosis** → occurs in reproductive cells.

Intext Questions

On Page 51

Question 1 Who discovered cells and how?

Sol. Robert Hooke discovered cells in 1665 with the help of his self-designed microscope. He examined a thin slice of cork and observed that it has the structure of a honey comb, consisting of many tiny compartments. He called these compartments "cells" because they reminded him of the small rooms, or cells, in a monastery.

Question 2 Why is the cell called the structural and functional unit of life?

Sol. The cell is called the structural and functional unit of life because it is the smallest unit that has a defined structure and organisation as well as carry out all the processes necessary for life. Living cells contain specific components called cell organelles, each of which performs a particular function necessary for the cell's survival. These functions include making new materials, releasing waste, transporting substance, and generating energy. The coordinated activities of the cell organelles ensure that the cell can maintain homeostasis, grow, reproduce, and respond to its environment. Thus, the cell, with its organelles, is the basic building block of all living organisms, performing all essential life functions.

On Page 53

Question 1 How do substances like CO_2 and water move in and out of the cell? Discuss.

Sol. Substances like CO_2 and water move in and out of the cell through different mechanisms:

Diffusion CO_2, a cellular waste product, move out of the cell from a region of higher concentration, inside the cell, to a region of lower concentration outside the cell until equilibrium is reached.

Osmosis Water moves in and out of the cell by osmosis, which is the diffusion of water across a selectively permeable membrane from a region of lower to a region of higer solute concentration. This helps in maintaining the cell's internal environment.

Question 2 Why is the plasma membrane called a selectively permeable membrane?

Sol. The plasma membrane is called selectively permeable because it regulates the movement of substances in and out of the cell. It allows certain molecules to pass through while restricting others, based on factors like size, charge and solubility.This selective control helps maintains the cell's internal environment and ensure proper functioning.

On Page 55

Question 1 Fill in the gaps in the following table illustrating differences between prokaryotic and eukaryotic cells.

S.No.	Prokaryotic Cell	Eukaryotic Cell
1.	Size : generally small (1 - 10 μm) $1 \mu m = 10^{-6}$ m	Size : generally large (5 - 100 μm).
2.	Nuclear region : .... and known us	Nuclear region : well defined and surrounded by a nuclear membrane
3.	Chromosome : single	More than one chromosome
4.	Membrane bound cell organelles absent	....

Sol.

S.No.	Prokaryotic Cell	Eukaryotic Cell
1.	Size : generally small (1 - 10 μm) $1 \mu m = 10^{-6}$ m	Size : generally large (5 - 100 μm).
2.	Nuclear region : undefined nuclear region, containing only nucleic acids (genetic material) and known as nucleoid	Nuclear region : well defined and surrounded by a nuclear membrane.
3.	Chromosome : single	More than one chromosome
4.	Membrane-bound cell organelles absent	Membrane bound cell organelles present

On Page 57

Question 1 Can you name the two organelles we have studied that contain their own genetic material?

Sol. Mitochondria and plastids are two organelles with their own DNA and ribosomes. These organelles are also capable of producing their own proteins.

Question 2 If the organisation of a cell is destroyed due to some physical or chemical influence, what will happen?

Sol. Living cells are capable of performing certain basic functions due to the presence of certain cell organelles. If this organisation of cell is destroyed, then cell will not be able to perform its basic functions like metabolism, protein synthesis and cell division and will eventually die.

Question 3 Why are lysosomes known as suicide bags?

Sol. The lysosomes contain powerful digestive enzymes which are capable of breaking down organic matter. In case of any disturbance in cellular metabolism, such as when a cell gets damaged, then lysosomes burst and release these enzymes, which digest their own cell. Hence, the lysosomes are known as 'suicide bags' of cells.

Question 4 Where are protein synthesised inside the cell?

Sol. Protein is synthesised inside the cell on ribosomes which can be found free-floating in the cytoplasm or attached to the surface of endoplasmic reticulum.

Exercises

Question 1 Make a comparison and write down ways in which plant cells are different from animal cells.

Sol. Comparison of plant cell and animal cell is as follows

S.No.	Plant Cell	Animal Cell
1.	Cell wall is present, outside the plasma membrane.	Cell wall is absent.
2.	Generally regular in shape.	Generally irregular in shape.
3.	Larger in size than animal cells.	Smaller in size than animal cells.
4.	Plastids are present.	Plastids are absent.
5.	A permanent and large vacuole is present.	Vacuoles are many, small and temporary.

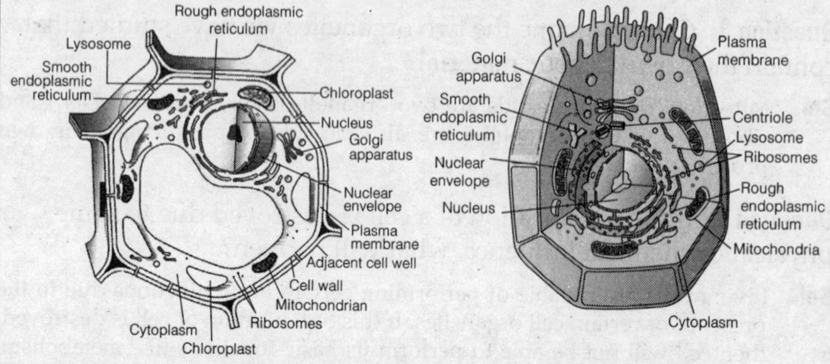

Question 2 How is a prokaryotic cell different from a eukaryotic cell?

Sol. The differences between prokaryotic and eukaryotic cells are as follows

S.No.	Feature	Prokaryotic Cell	Eukaryotic Cell
1.	Size	Generally small (1-10 μm)	Generally large (5-100 μm)
2.	Nucleus	No true nucleus; nuclear region (nucleoid) is not membrane-bound	True nucleus, enclosed by a nuclear membrane
3.	Cell organelles	Membrane-bound organelles are absent	Membrane-bound organelles (*e.g.*, mitochondira, ER, Golgi apparatus) are present
4.	Cell division	Binary fission	Mitosis (and meiosis for reproductive cells)
5.	Cell wall	Usually present and chemically complex (*e.g.*, peptidoglycan in bacteria)	When present, chemically simple (*e.g.*, cellulose in plants, chitin in fungi)
6.	Endoplasmic Reticulum	Absent	Present
7.	Golgi Apparatus	Absent	Present
8.	Mitochondria	Absent	Present
9.	Chloroplasts	Absent; photosynthesis occurs in infolded plasma membrane structures (in photosynthetic prokaryotes).	Present in plant cells and algae

Question 3 What would happen if the plasma membrane ruptures or breaks down?

Sol. If the plasma membrane ruptures or breaks down, the following consequences will occur

(i) All useful substances would move out of the cell due to the loss of selectively permeability.

(ii) The cell would lose its normal shape and integrity.

(iii) There would be no difference between cell contents and its external environment. The cell's internal environment would become unstable, disrupting cellular processes, potentially leading to cell death.

Question 4 What would happen to the life of a cell if there was no Golgi apparatus?

Sol. The effect of absence of Golgi apparatus on life of a cell are as follows

(i) The packaging and transportation of different types of proteins to various targets inside and outside the cell, would be disrupted.

(ii) Lysosomes formation would be affected, leading to the accumulation of worn-out and dead cell organelles within the cell, which may cause cell death.

Question 5 Which organeile is known as the power house of the cell? Why?

Sol. Mitochondria are known as power house of the cell because they contain oxidative enzymes that oxidise the food and convert it into energy currency of the cell *i.e.,* ATP (Adenosine Triphosphate). This energy is used by body for making new chemical compounds and for doing other works.

Question 6 Where do the lipids and proteins constituting the cell membrane get synthesised?

Sol. The synthesis of lipids occur in Smooth Endoplasmic Reticulum (SER). The proteins are synthesised in the ribosomes which are attached to the Rough Endoplasmic Reticulum (RER).

Question 7 How does an *Amoeba* obtain its food?

Sol. *Amoeba* acquires its food through endocytosis, a process of ingestion of food through the plasma membrane. This occurs due to flexible nature of plasma membrane which enable the *Amoeba* to engulf food and other materials from its surroundings.

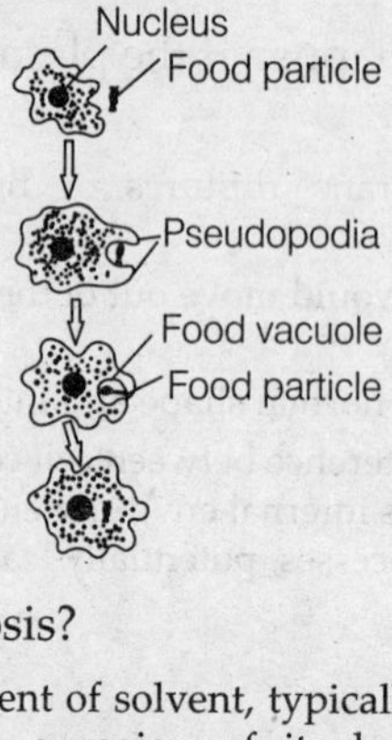

Question 8 What is osmosis?

Sol. Osmosis is the movement of solvent, typically water, from a region of its high concentration to a region of its low concentration through a semipermeable membrane. During osmosis, the water molecules (solvent) move freely across the plasma membrane in both the directions.

Question 9 Carry out the following osmosis experiments

Take four peeled potato halves and scoops each one out to make potato cups. One of these potato cups should be made from a boiled potato. Put each potato cup in a trough containing water. Now

(a) Keep cup *A* empty

(b) Put one tea spoon sugar in cup *B*.

(c) Put one tea spoon salt in cup *C*.

(d) Put one tea spoon sugar in the boiled potato cup *D*.

Keep these for two hours. Then observe the four potato cups and answer the following:

(i) Explain why water gathers in the hollowed portion of *B* and *C*?

(ii) Why is potato *A* necessary for this experiment?

(iii) Explain why water does not gather in the hollowed out portion of *A* and *D*?

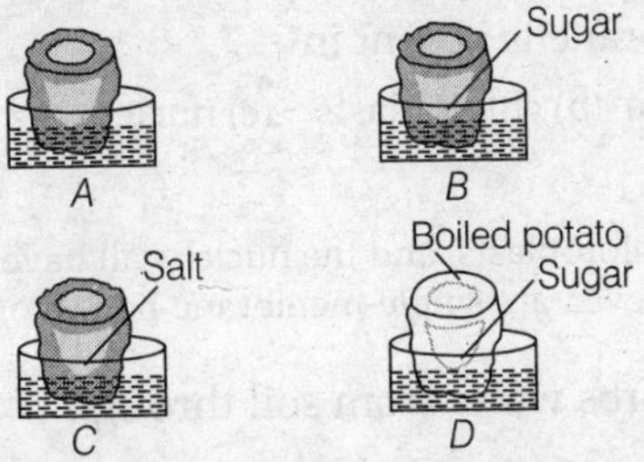

Sol. (i) Water gathers in the hollowed portion of B and C due to osmosis. Since, the concentration of solute (sugar in cup B and salt in cup C) is higher inside the cup as compared to the water, which is outside the cup. Hence, water from its higher concentration (outside the cup) will move towards the lower concentration (inside the cup). This process of osmosis (moving in of solvent) is called **endosmosis**.

(ii) Potato A acts as a control for the experiment. This is required for comparing the results to demonstrate the effect of adding solute (sugar or salt) on osmosis.

(iii) Water does not gather in the hollowed out portions of A and D because of the following reasons:

- The hollowed portion of potato *A* is empty. So, because of absence of concentration difference, no osmosis can occur.
- The hollowed portion of potato *D* contains sugar in it but it is in boiled state. So, osmosis cannot occur as its semipermeable membrane is destroyed by boiling.

Question 10 Which type of cell division is required for growth and repair of body and which type is involved in formation of gametes?

Sol.
- Mitosis cell division is required for growth and repair of body.
- Meiosis is required for the formation of gametes.

DIKSHA APP Questions

☐ Multiple Choice Questions

Q.1 If a cell is placed in a hypotonic solution, water will move .... of the cell, causing it to ....

(a) into, swell

(b) out of, shrink

(c) in and out of the cell, stay the same

(d) None of the above

Sol. (a) In a hypotonic solution. the concentration of solutes outside the cell is lower than inside the cell. This causes water to move into the cell by osmosis, causing the cell to swell and potentially burst if too much water enters.

Q.2 Double membrane is absent in

(a) mitochondria (b) chloroplasts (c) nucleus (d) lysosomes

Sol. (d) Lysosome

Mitochondria, chloroplasts, and the nucleus all have double membranes. Lysosomes, however, are single-membrane-bound organelles.

Q.3 Root hair absorbs water from soil through

(a) osmosis (b) active transport (c) diffusion (d) endocytosis

Sol. (a) Osmosis

Root hair cells absorb water from the soil through osmosis, which is the movement of water across a semi-permeable membrane from an area of lower solute concentration to an area of higher solute concentration.

Q.4 Which of the cell organelles consists of chloroplast?

(a) Plastids (b) Mitochondria (c) Vacuoles (d) Cell wall

Sol. (a) Plastids

Chloroplast is a type of plastid, found in the cells of plants and algae. Mitochondria, vacuoles, and cell walls do not contain chloroplasts.

Q.5 The cells were discovered for the first time by?

(a) Robert Hooke (b) Anton Von Leeuwenhoek

(c) Robert Brown (d) Rudolf Virchow

Sol. (a) Robert Hooke discovered cells in 1665 through his self-designed microscope.

Q.6 Who Proposed cell theory?

(a) Robert Hooke (b) Anton Von Leeuwenhoek
(c) Robert Brown (d) Schleiden and Schwann

Sol. (d) Schleiden and Schwann proposed the cell theory. According to this theory,

(a) All plants and animals are made up of cells.

(b) A cell is the basic unit of life.

Q.7 The prokaryotic cells lack .... :

(a) chlorophyll (b) DNA
(c) nuclear membrane (d) all of these

Sol. (c) The prokaryotic cells lack nuclear membrane and membrane bound organelles.

Q.8 Cellulose forms which of the part of a plant cell?

(a) Chloroplast (b) Cell wall (c) Cell membrane (d) None of these

Sol. (b) The plant cell wall is made up of cellulose.

Q.9 Which one of the following best describes the function of the cell membrane?

(a) It keeps the cell in shape
(b) It controls substance entering the cell
(c) It controls the substance entering and leaving the cell
(d) It supports the cell structure

Sol. (c) The cell membrane is known as selectively permeable membrane as it allows entry and exit of some of the substances while blocking others.

Q.10 Chromosomes are composed of

(a) DNA and protein (b) DNA and RNA
(c) RNA and protein (d) DNA only

Sol. (a) Chromosomes are composed of DNA and protein.

Q.11 Which of the following is the site of protein synthesis?

(a) Golgi apparatus (b) Mitochondria
(c) Lysosomes (d) Ribosome

Sol. (d) Ribosomes are the site of protein synthesis.

Q.12 Which organelle is involved in the formation of lysosomes?

(a) Plastid (b) Ribosome
(c) Golgi apparatus (d) All of these

Sol. (c) Golgi apparatus is involved in the formation of lysosomes. It processes and packages digestive enzymes, which are then transported to form lysosomes within the cell.

Q.13 Which one is absent in a plant cell?

(a) Chloroplast (b) Centriole
(c) Cell membrane (d) Vacuole

Sol. (b) Centrioles are present in animal cells only. They are involved in spindle fibre formation during cell division.

Q.14 Identify the incorrect combination:

(a) Nucleus-	control centre of the cell
(b) Mitochondria-	powerhouse of the cell
(c) Chloroplast-	kitchen of the cell
(d) Lysosomes-	site of protein synthesis

Sol. (d) Lysosomes- site of protein synthesis
Ribosomes are the site of protein synthesis.

☐ Very Short Answer Type

Q.1 Define plasmolysis.

Sol. Plasmolysis refers to the shrinkage of contents of cell due to loss of water, upon being placed in a hypertonic solution.

Q.2 Where are genes located?

Sol. Genes are situated on chromosomes within the nucleus of a cell.

Q.3 Damini's mother wanted to make mango pickle. She asked Damini to cut the tender mango into four pieces, smear them with common salt, and keep them for some time. Damini observed that after some time, the mango pieces had started to lose water and shrunk in size. Name the phenomenon observed by Damini.

Sol. Exosmosis

Q.4 Give an example of a unicellular organism.

Sol. Examples include *Amoeba,* Bacteria, and *Paramoecium.*

Q.5 Plasma membrane is made up of which two components?

Sol. The plasma membrane is composed of lipids and proteins.

☐ Short Answer Type

Q.1 What is lacking in a virus which makes it dependent on a living cell to multiply? Give reason.

Sol. Viruses lack cellular machinery, such as enzymes and organelles necessary for metabolism and reproduction. This makes them dependent on the host cell's machinery to replicate and produce new viral particles.

Q.2 Lysosomes are a kind of waste disposal system of a cell, Justify the statement.

Sol. Lysosomes contain powerful digestive enzymes that can break down waste materials and cellular debris. When a cell gets damaged, lysosomes may burst, releasing these enzymes and digesting the cell itself, hence they are known as suicide bags.

Q.3 Draw a neat and well-labeled diagram of a prokaryotic cell.

Sol.

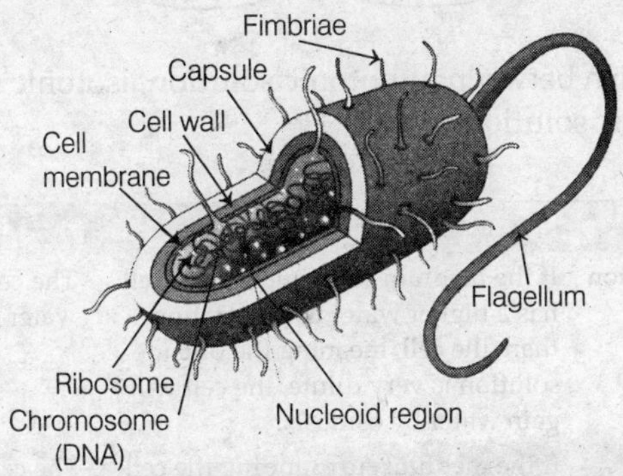

Q.4 What is the significance of pores present on the nuclear membrane.

Sol. The pores on the nuclear membrane facilitate the transport of water-soluble molecules across the nuclear envelope. RNA and ribosomes move out of the nucleus, while carbohydrates, lipids, and proteins move into the nucleus.

Q.5 Describe the microscopic structure of the cell.

Sol. The first cells to be observed were cork cells, which appeared as box-like compartments forming a honeycomb structure. Inside cells, various organelles are embedded in the cytoplasm, all enclosed by the plasma membrane.

Q.6 Create a Venn diagram to compare the structure of plant and animal cells.

Sol.

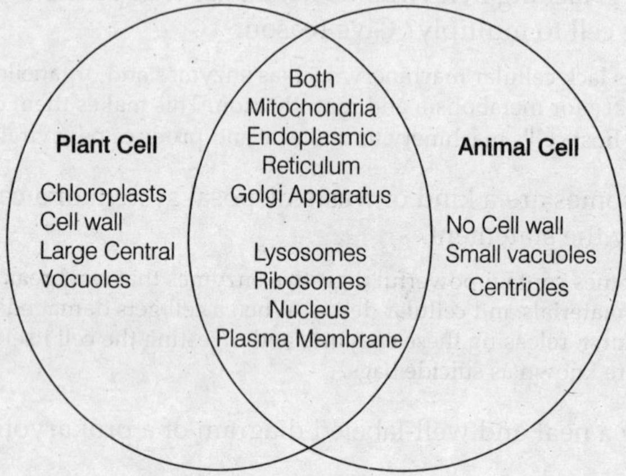

Q.7 Distinguish between hypotonic solution, isotonic solution, and hypertonic solution.

Sol.

Solution Type	Definition	Effect on Cell
Hypotonic Solution	If the medium surrounding the cell has a higher water concentration than the cell, meaning the outside solution is very dilute, the cell will gain water by osmosis.	The cell will swell as water enters the cell.
Isotonic Solution	If the medium surrounding the cell has the same water concentration as the cell, there will be no net movement of water across the cell membrane.	The cell will remain the same size.
Hypertonic Solution	If the medium surrounding the cell has a lower water concentration than the cell, meaning the outside solution is more concentrated, the cell will lose water by osmosis.	The cell will shrink as water leaves the cell.

Q.8 Differentiate between osmosis and diffusion.

Sol.

	Osmosis	Diffusion
1.	Only water or other solvents moves from a region of their high concentration to a region of lower concentration.	Any type of substance moves from an area of its highe concentration to a region of low concentration
2.	Osmosis occurs only in a liquid medium.	Diffusion can occur in both, liquid and gaseous medium.
3.	Osmosis require's a semipermeable membrane.	Diffusion does not require a semipermeable membrane.
4.	The concentration of the solvent does not becomes equal on both sides of the membrane.	The concentration of the diffusing substance equalizes to fill the available space.
5.	Osmosis mainly depends on the number of solute particles dissolved in the solvent.	Diffusion mainly depends on the presence of other particles.

Q.9 What is membrane biogenesis? How is plasma membrane formed during this process?

Sol. The process of formation of plasma membrane formation is called membrane biogenesis.

The proteins and lipids are first synthesised in the rough endoplasmic reticulum and smooth endoplasmic reticulum, respectively. These are then transported to the Golgi complex for their modification. After modification, these are transported to the cell surface through vesicles which bud off from Golgi complex to fuse with cell membrane and form a part of the membrane.

Tissues

CHAPTER 06

Important Points

01 **Tissue** is a group of cells that are similar in structure and work together to perform a specific function. All the cells with in a tissue have a common origin. Blood, muscles, phloem and xylem are examples of some tissues.

02 Plant organs like root, stem, leaves, flowers and fruits are made up of different kinds of tissues to perform specific functions.

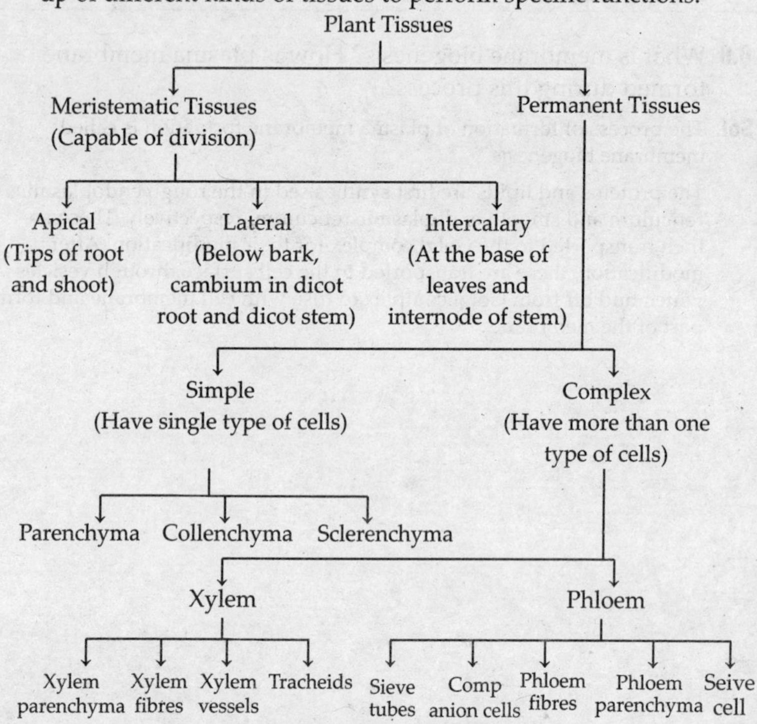

▲ Classification of plant tissues

03 **Differences between Plant and Animal Tissues**

S.No.	Plant Tissue	Animal Tissue
1.	There is an abundance of dead and supportive tissue as compared to living tissue.	Living tissues are more compared to dead tissues.
2.	Some tissues divide throughout life. Growth is limited to certain regions.	Growth in animals do not occurs throughout life.
3.	They are differentiated into meristematic and permanent tissues.	Such differentiation is not present.
4.	They need less energy for maintenance.	They need more energy for maintenance.

04 **Meristematic tissue** occurs only in certain specific regions of a plant. Based on their location, meristematic tissues can be classified into three types

(i) Apical (ii) Lateral (iii) Intercalary

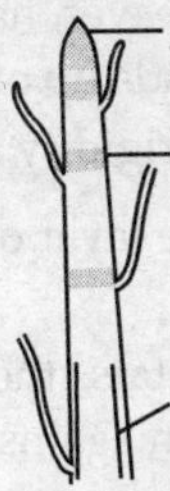

▲ Location of meristematic tissue in plant body

05 **Permanent tissues** are formed when meristematic tissues take up a specific role and lose the ability to divide. This process of taking up a permanent shape, size and a function is called differentiation.

06 **Simple permanent tissues** are made up of structurally and functionally similar cells. On the basis of nature of cells, these are further divided as parenchyma, collenchyma and sclerenchyma.

07 **Parenchyma** is present in stem, roots, leaves, flowers and fruits.

(i) They form the basic packing tissue of the plant body.
(ii) The cells are living and have large intercellular spaces between them.
(iii) Its main function is to store and assimilate food.
(iv) If chloroplast is present in parenchyma, it is called **chlorenchyma** and they carry out photosynthesis.
(v) In aquatic plants, large cavities are present in parenchyma to give buoyancy to the plants to help them float. This type of parenchyma is called **aerenchyma.**

08 **Collenchyma** is a kind of living tissue like parenchyma. It is present below the epidermis of green dicotyledonous stem and leaf stalk (petiole).

(i) It provides flexibility to the plant by allowing it to bend without breaking. It also provides mechanical support to the plant.

(ii) The cells of this tissue are living, elongated, and irregularly thickened at the corners. These cells have very little intercellular space between them.

09 **Sclerenchyma** is a type of dead tissue, that makes the plant hard and stiff.

(i) The cells of tissues are long, narrow as the walls are thickened due to lignin. The cells are closely packed without any intercellular spaces.

(ii) The cells of sclerenchyma are of two types–sclereids and fibres.

(iii) It occurs in stems, roots, veins of leaves, hard covering of seeds and nuts. The husk of coconut is made up of sclerenchyma tissue.

(iv) Sclerenchyma gives strength and rigidity to the plant body.

10 **Epidermis** is the outermost, protective layer of cells. It is usually made up of single layer of cells.

(i) In plants living in very dry habitats, the epidermis may be thicker to provide better protection against water loss.

(ii) Epidermal cells on the aerial parts of the plant often secrete a waxy, water resistant layer on their outer surface. This protect against loss of water, mechanical injury and invasion by parasites fungi.

(iii) Most epidermal cells are relatively flat often their outer and side walls are thicker than the inner wall.

(iv) In the epidermis of leaves, small pores called stomata are present. Stomata are enclosed by kidney-shaped cells called guard cells. These help in exchange of gases and transpiration.

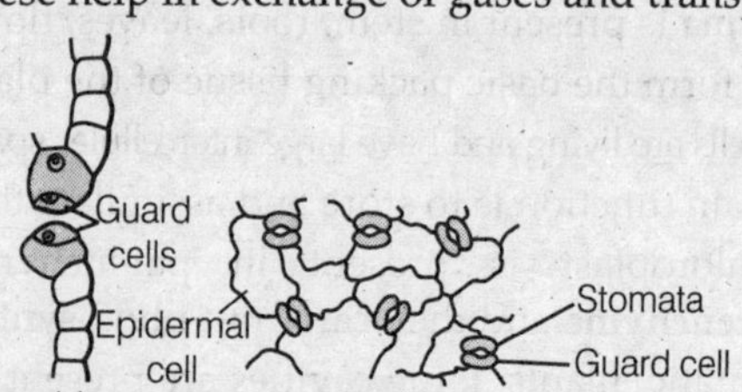

▲ Guard cells and epidermal cells (a) Lateral view (b) Surface view

(v) Epidermal cells of roots, whose function is water absorption, commonly bear long hair like parts that greatly increase the total absorptive surface area.

(vi) In some desert plants, epidermis has a thick waxy coating of **cutin** on its outer surface.

(vii) As plants grow older, epidermis undergo several changes. The secondary meristem in the cortex forms the several layer **thick cork** or the bark of the tree. Cork cells have a chemical called **suberin** in their walls that makes them impervious to gases and water.

11 Complex permanent tissues are made up of more than one type of cells. For example, **xylem** and **phloem**. They are both conducting tissues and constitute a vascular bundle.

12 **Xylem** helps in conduction of water and minerals from roots to all parts of the shoot. It consists of tracheids, vessels, xylem parenchyma and xylem fibres.

(i) Tracheids and vessels are tubular structures, which allows them to transport water and minerals vertically through the plant.

(ii) Parenchyma stores food and helps in the sideways conduction of water with in the plant.

(iii) Xylem fibers mainly provide mechanical support to the plant.

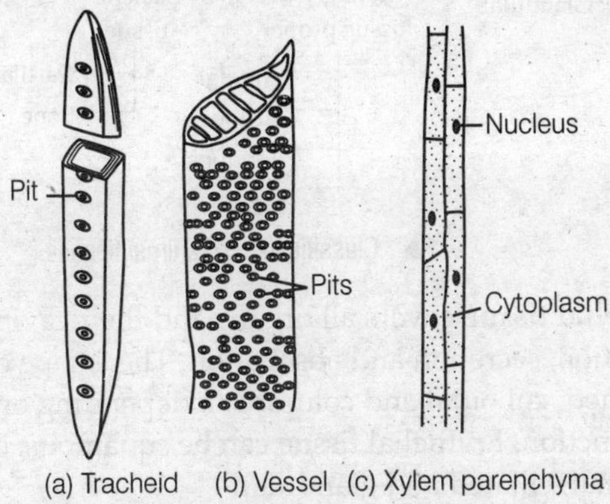

(a) Tracheid (b) Vessel (c) Xylem parenchyma

▲ Elements of xylem tissue

13 **Phloem** It transports food from leaves to other parts of the plant. It is made up of sieve cells, sieve tube, companion cells, phloem fibres and the phloem parenchyma.

(i) Sieve tubes are tubular cells with perforated end walls, allowing the transport of nutrients.

(ii) Phloem cells are living cells, except for phloem fibres.

(iii) Phloem parenchyma helps in storage of food.

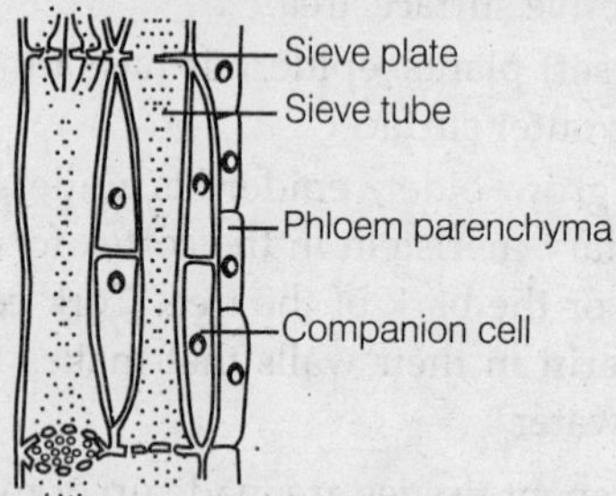

▲ Section of a phloem tissue

14 **Animal tissues** can be classified as following, based on their functions :

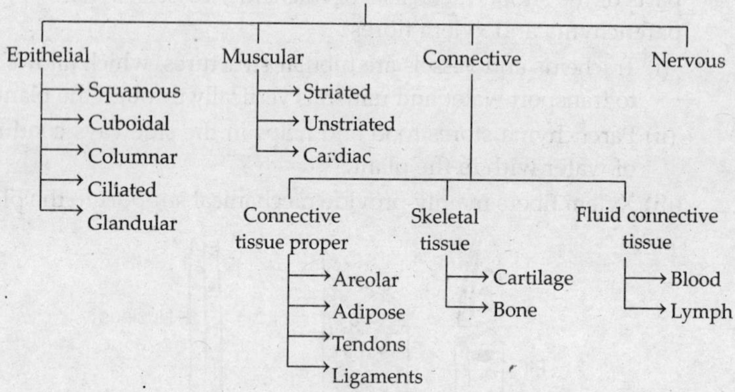

▲ Classification of animal tissues

15 **Epithelial tissue** covers all organs and their cavities, aiding in protection, secretion and absorption. The shape of the cells vary (flattened, cuboidal and columnar), depending on their location and function. Epithelial tissue can be squamous, cuboidal, columnar, ciliated and glandular.

16 **Squamous epithelium** is present on the skin, lining of alveoli of lungs, oesophagus, etc. The cells are flat and thin. These play important role in protection, osmosis and diffusion.

17 **Cuboidal epithelium** is present in glands, ducts and germinal layers of ovary. The cells are cube shaped. The function of cuboidal epithelium is secretion and absorption.

18 **Columnar epithelium** forms the lining of stomach and intestine. The cells are pillar like resting on a thin membrane. This tissue helps in absorption and secretion.

19 **Ciliated epithelium** lines the respiratory tract. The cells are columnar with fine hair-like **cilia.** Cilia cleans the respiratory tract by pushing the mucus forward.

20 **Glandular epithelium** is present in glands. This tissue is mainly involved in secretion.

21 **Connective tissue** connects various body tissues or organs. It connects bones to bones, muscles to bones and also binds tissues

22 The various types of connective tissues are areolar tissue, cartilage, bone, tendon, ligament and blood.

23 **Areolar tissue** is present between the skin and muscles, in the bone marrow etc. The functions of areolar tissue involves

(a) repair of body tissues. (b) support internal organs.

24 **Adipose tissue** is found below the skin and between the internal organs. The cells of this tissue is filled with fat globules.

25 **Tendons** connect muscles to bones. They are fibrous tissue with great strength but limited flexibility.

26 **Ligaments** is a elastic tissue having considerable strenght. It connect one bone to the other bone.

27 **Cartilage** smoothens bone surface at joints. It is present in the wind pipe, nose and ear pinna.

28 **Bone** forms the skeleton framework of the body. Bones cells are embedded in a hard matrix of calcium and phosphorus. Its functions are:

(i) Provide support and shape to the body.
(ii) Protect internal organs.

29 **Blood** flows through the heart and blood vessels, *i.e.*, arteries and veins. It contains plasma and blood corpuscles. The blood corpuscles are of following three types.

(i) Erythrocytes (Red blood cells – RBCs)
(ii) Leucocytes (White blood cells – WBCs)
(iii) Thrombocytes (Platelets)

The functions of blood are transport of food, oxygen, carbon dioxide, waste and hormones.

30 **Muscular tissue** is responsible for movement in the body. Muscles contain contractile proteins, which contract and relax to cause movement. The muscle tissue can be of three types :

(i) **Striated** or **skeletal muscles** are attached to the bones and produce body movement such as walking, running and lifting. These are long, cylindrical, multinucleated cells with alternating dark and light bands (striations). This assists in voluntary movement of the body.

(ii) **Non-striated** or **smooth muscles** are located in walls of internal organs including the lining of blood vessels, respiratory tract, digestive organs, etc. They are spindle-shaped, uninucleated structure without striations. Their function is related to the involuntary movement and peristaltic movements.

(iii) **Cardiac muscles** are located in heart. The cells of heart muscles are cylindrical, branched and uninucleate. These show rhythmic contraction and relaxation throught life.

31 **Nervous tissue** is specialised for communication and control in the body. It is present in brain, spinal cord and nerves.

32 The structural and functional unit of nervous tissue is neuron. The neuron consists of cell body, dendrite and axon. The neuron controls all the body activities, conducts impulses and stimulates other tissues for activity.

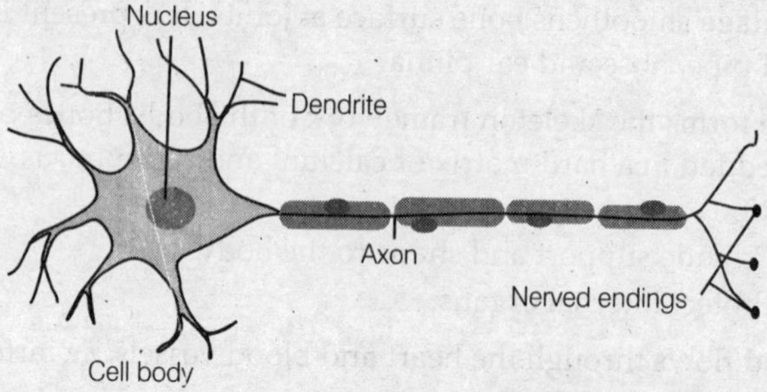

▲ A neuron unit of nervous tissue

33 The functional combination of nerve and muscle tissue is fundamental to most animals. This combination enables animals to move rapidly in response to stimuli.

Intext Questions

On Page 61

Question 1 What is a tissue?

Sol. A group of cells that are similar in structure and/or work together to achieve a particular function is called tissue.

Question 2 What is the utility of tissues in multicellular organisms?

Sol. In multicellular organisms, the body system is based on the division of labour. This means the cells performing a specific function are grouped together to form a particular tissue. The different tissues are organised in a way that provide highest efficiency in functioning of the body. This organisation allows multicellular organisms to perform complex activities and maintain homeostasis effectively.

On Page 65

Question 1 Name types of simple tissues.

Sol. The three main types of simple tissues are

(i) Parenchyma (ii) Collenchyma

(iii) Sclerenchyma

Question 2 Where is apical meristem found?

Sol. Apical meristem is found at the growing tips of stems and roots of plants. It helps in increasing the length of the stem and the root.

Question 3 Which tissue makes up the husk of coconut?

Sol. The husk of coconut is made up of sclerenchymatous tissue. This tissue provides the coconut husk with its tough, fibrous and durable nature, making it resistant to physical damage.

Question 4 What are the constituents of phloem?

Sol. The constituents of phloem tissue are:

(i) Sieve tubes (tubular living cells with perforated end walls)

(ii) Companion cell (living cells)

(iii) Phloem parenchyma (living cells)

(iv) Phloem fibres (non-living and sclerenchyma cells)

These componets work together to transport nutrients, primarily sugars produced during photo synthesis, from the leaves to other parts of the plants.

On Page 69

Question 1 Name the tissue responsible for movement in our body.

Sol. Muscular tissue is responsible for movement in our body. It consists of elongated cells (muscle fibres). These fibres contract and relax to enable voluntary and involuntary movements.

Question 2 What does a neuron look like?

Sol. A neuron consists of a cell body with a nucleus and cytoplasm, from which long, thin hair-like projections arise. Each neuron has a single long part, called the axon and many short, branched parts called dendrites. Many nerve fibres bound together by connective tissue to make up a nerve, facilitating the transmission of nerve implulses throughout the body.

Question 3 Give three features of cardiac muscles.

Sol. Features of cardiac muscles are as follows

(i) These are involuntary and show rhythmic contraction and relaxation throughout life, ensuring the continuous pumping of blood.

(ii) The cells are cylindrical, branched and uninucleate.

(iii) These muscles do not get fatigued under normal conditions, enabling the heart to function efficiently without tiring.

Question 4 What are the functions of areolar tissue?

Sol. Functions of areolar tissue are as follows.

(i) It fills the space inside the organs, thus acts as a packing tissue between the organs, providing structural support and cushioning.

(ii) It supports many delicate organs in the body, by holding them in place

(iii) It plays role in repair of tissues, aiding in wound leading and regeneration.

Exercises

Question 1 Define the term 'tissue'.

Sol. A group of cells that are similar in structure and work together to achieve a particular function is called tissue. Tissues are essential for the organization and specialisation of cells in multicellular organisms.

Question 2 How many types of elements together make up the xylem tissue? Name them.

Sol. The following four types of elements make up xylem tissue:

(i) Xylem tracheids (dead). (ii) Xylem vessels (dead).

(iii) Xylem parenchyma (living). (iv) Xylem fibres (dead).

Question 3 How are simple tissues different from complex tissues in plants?

Sol.

S.No.	Simple Tissue	Complex Tissues
1.	Made up of only one type of cells.	Made up of more than one type of cells.
2.	Mainly responsible for storage and mechanical support. **Examples** Parenchyma, collenchyma and sclerenchyma.	Mainly responsible for the transport of water, minerals, sugars and other metabolites. **Examples** Xylem and phloem.

Question 4 Differentiate between parenchyma, collenchyma and sclerenchyma on the basis of their cell wall.

Sol. Differences between parenchyma, collenchyma and sclerenchyma

S.No.	Parenchyma	Collenchyma	Sclerenchyma
1.	These are living cells with thin walls.	These are living cells having irregular thickening at the corners.	These are dead cells with thick cell walls.
2.	Cells are uniformly thin	Cells are elongated.	Cells are long and narrow.

Question 5 What are the functions of the stomata?

Sol. Functions of stomata are as follows

(i) They are essential for gaseous exchange with the atmosphere, allowing carbon dioxide to enter the leaf for photosynthesis and oxygen to exit as by product.

(ii) They help in transpiration in the form of water vapour through leaves, which aids in cooling the plant.

Question 6 Diagrammatically show the difference between the three types of muscle fibres.

Sol.

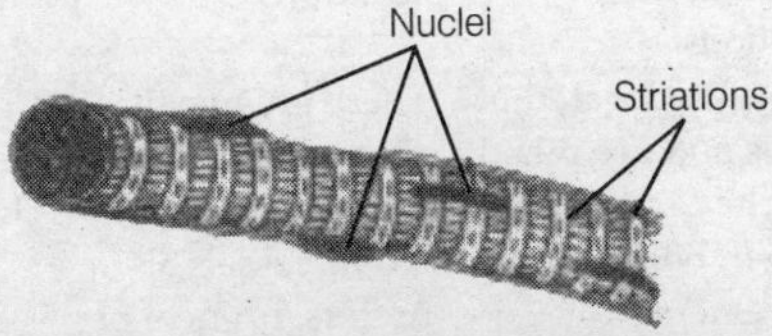

▲ Striated muscle

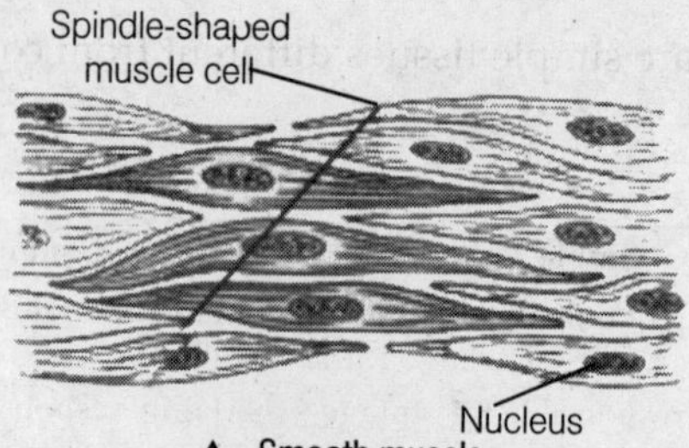

▲ Smooth muscle

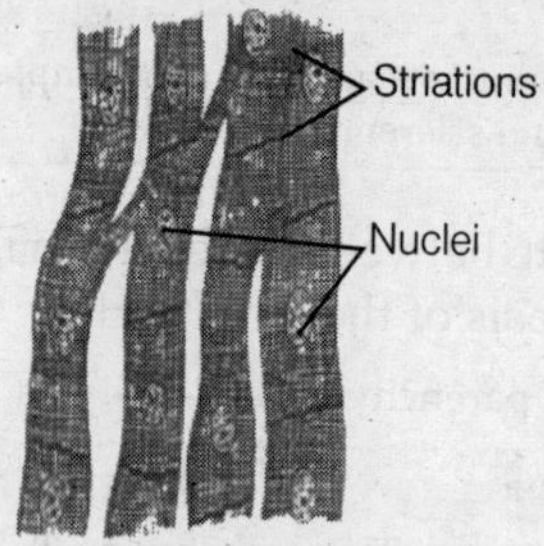

▲ Cardiac muscle

Question 7 What is the specific function of the cardiac muscles?

Sol. The function of cardiac muscles is rhythmic contraction and relaxation throughout life, which allows the heart to pump blood continuously without tiring under normal conditions.

Question 8 Differentiate between striated, unstriated and cardiac muscles on the basis of their structure and site/location in the body.

Sol.

Features	Striated Muscles	Unstriated Muscles	Cardiac Muscles
Structure	These are made up of long, cylindrical, unbranched and multinucleate cells. These show alternate light and dark striations.	These muscles are made up of long uninucleate cells with pointed ends. These do not show striations.	These are made up of cells which are cylindrical, branched and uninucleate. These muscles show faint striations.
Site/ Location	These are located in limbs and are mostly attached to bones to help in body movement.	These are mostly present in walls of alimentary canal, blood vessels, ureters, bronchi of the lungs and in the iris of eyes.	These are present only in the walls of heart.

Question 9 Draw a labelled diagram of a neuron.

Sol.

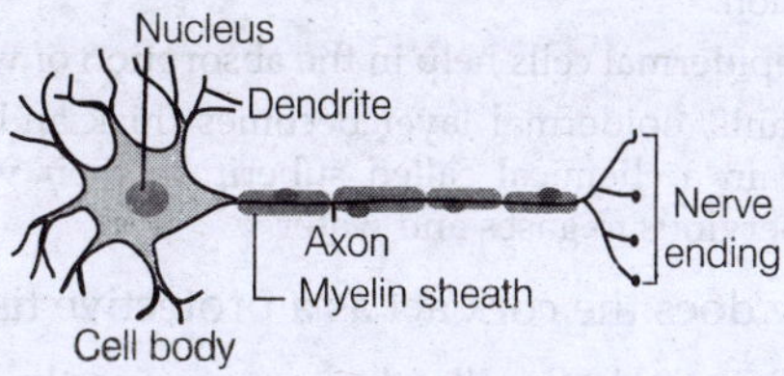

Question 10 Name the following.

(a) Tissue that forms the inner lining of our mouth.
(b) Tissue that connects muscle to bone in humans.
(c) Tissue that transports food in plants.
(d) Tissue that stores fat in our body.
(e) Connective tissue with a fluid matrix.
(f) Tissue present in the brain.

Sol. (a) Squamous epithelium (b) Tendons
(c) Phloem (d) Adipose tissue
(e) Blood (f) Nervous tissue

Question 11 Identify the type of tissue in the following skin, bark of tree, bone, lining of kidney tubule and vascular bundle.

Sol. (a) Skin—Squamous epithelium.
(b) Bark of tree—cork.
(c) Bone—Connective tissue.
(d) Lining of kidney tubule—Cuboidal epithelium.
(e) Vascular bundle—Complex permanent tissue (xylem and phloem).

Question 12 Name the regions in which parenchyma tissue is present.

Sol. Parenchyma tissue is mainly found in all soft parts of the plant such as root, stem, leaves, flowers, fruits, etc. It helps in storage, photosynthesis.

Question 13 What is the role of epidermis in plants?

Sol. Role of epidermis in plants are as follows.

(i) It is protective in function. It acts as a barrier against mechanical injury, pathogen and water loss.
(ii) It becomes thick and prevent water loss in plants living in very dry habitats.
(iii) These cells secrete a waxy, water-resistant layer on the outer surface which protect against loss of water, mechanical injury and infections.

(iv) Leaf epidermis have stomata which help in gas exchange and transpiration.

(v) In roots, epidermal cells help in the absorption of water.

(vi) In old plants, epidermal layer becomes thick and forms cork. Cork cells contain a chemical called suberin in their walls which makes them impervious to gases and water.

Question 14 How does the cork act as a protective tissue?

Sol. The cork cells are dead cells that are compactly arranged without intercellular spaces. This tight arrangement forms a barrier against external factors, while the presence of suberin in the cell wall makes cork impermeable to gases and water. This impermeability also prevent the entry of pathogens and insects, providing an additional layer of protection to the plant.

Question 15 Complete the following chart.

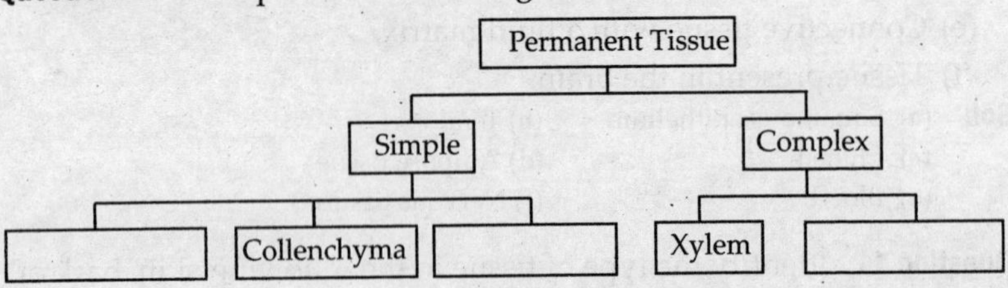

Sol.

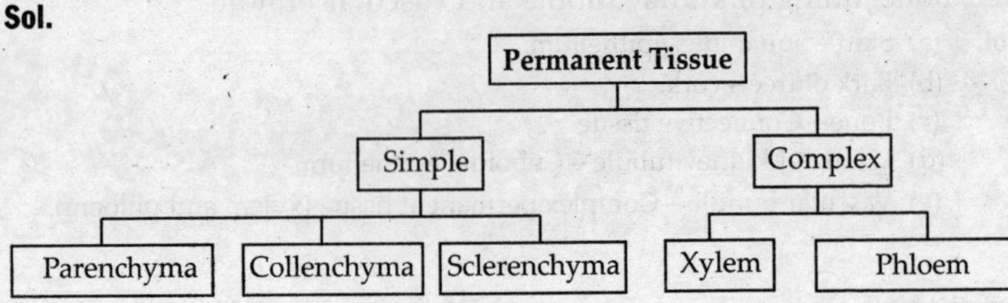

DIKSHA APP Questions

☐ Multiple Choice Questions

Q.1 The tissue that lines and covers the body is

(a) epithelial (b) connective

(c) nervous (d) muscle

Sol. (a) Epithelial tissue covers he external surfaces of the body and lines the internal cavities, organs, an passageways. They acts as a protective barrier and involved in abso ption, secretion, and sensation.

Q.2 The tissue that is thin enough to allow diffusion is

(a) simple cuboidal epithelium

(b) simple squamous epithelium

(c) areolar connective tissue

(d) hyaline cartilage

Sol. (b) Simple squamous epithelium consists of a single layer of flat cells that facilitate the diffusion of gases, nutrients, and waste products. This type of tissue is commonly found in the alveoli of lungs and the lining of blood vessels.

Q.3 Choose the wrong statement

(a) The nature of matrix differs according to the function of the tissue.

(b) Fats are stored below the skin and in between the internal organs

(c) Epithelial tissues have intercellular spaces between them.

(d) Cells of striated muscles are multinucleate and unbanked.

Sol. (c) The epithelial tissues have very little to no intercellular spaces between them. The cells are tightly packed, forming a continuous sheet that acts as a protective barrier.

Q.4 Survival of plants in terrestrial environments has been made possible by the presence of

(a) intercalary meristem (b) conducting tissue

(c) apical meristem (d) parenchymatous tissue

Sol. (b) Conducting tissues, such as xylem and phloem, are crucial for the transport of water, minerals, and nutrients throughout the plant, enabling it to survive in terrestrial environments.

Q.5 Flexibility in plants is due to

(a) collenchyma (b) sclerenchyma

(c) parenchyma (d) chlorenchyma

Sol. (a) Collenchyma cells have thickened cell walls that provide structural support while still allowing flexibility. This flexibility helps the plant to withstand various mechanical stresses, such as wind and bending.

☐ Very Short Answer Type

Q.1 Which kind of epithelium is found on the skin? State its function.

Sol. Stratified squamous epithelium is found on the skin. Its function is to protect underlying tissues from abrasion and to prevent wear and tear.

Q.2 Why are voluntary muscles called skeletal muscles?

Sol. Voluntary muscles are called skeletal muscles because they are primarily attached to bones and help in body movement.

Q.3 In desert plants, how does the rate of water loss gets reduced?

Sol. In desert plans the rate of water loss is reduced by the presence of a cuticle on the surface.

Q.4 Tissue *A* and tissue *B* constitute tissue *C*. *A* carries water, while *B* carries food for the plant. Identify *A*, *B* and *C*.

Sol. *A* is Xylem, *B* is Phloem, and C is Vascular bundles.

☐ Short Answer Type

Q.1 The root tips of a plant were cut and the plant was replanted, What will happen to the plant and why?

Sol. The plant is likely to die within a few days after replanting. This is because the root tips contain meristematic tissue, which are responsible for root growth. When the root tips are cut, the meristematic tissues are removed, preventing further root growth. Without growing roots, the plant cannot absorb water and minerals effectively, leading to its death.

Q.2 How are the messages conveyed from one place to another within the body?

Sol. Messages in the body are conveyed through nervous tissue, which consists of neurons. Neurons are specialised cells that receive stimuli and conduct electrical impulses. These impulses travel rapidly along the axon of the neuron, allowing the quick transmission of information from one part of the body to another.

Q.3 What is the lining of blood vessels made up of?

Sol. The lining of blood vessels is composed of squamous epithelium, which provides a smooth surface to reduce friction as blood flows through the vessels.

Q.4 What is the lining of the small intestine made up of?

Sol. The lining of the small intestine is made up of columnar epithelium, which is adapted for absorption and secretion, facilitating nutrient absorption from digested food.

Q.5 What is the lining of kidney tubules made up of?

Sol. The lining of kidney tubules is composed of cuboidal epithelium, which is specialized for secretion and absorption, crucial for the kidney's filtration functions.

Q.6 Differentiate between tendon and ligament.

Sol.

	Tendon	Ligament
1.	Helps to connect bone to muscles.	Helps to connect bone to bone.
2.	It is strong and non-flexible.	It is elastic and flexible.

Q.7 "Blood is the river of life". Justify the statement.

Sol. Blood helps in the transportation of oxygen, nutrients, waste products and hormones throughout the body. As the primary circulatory fluid, it ensures the delivery of essential substances to the cells and remove waste supporting overall bodily functions and maintaining homeostasis.

☐ Long Answer Type

Q.1 Create a flow chart to classify animal tissues.

Sol.

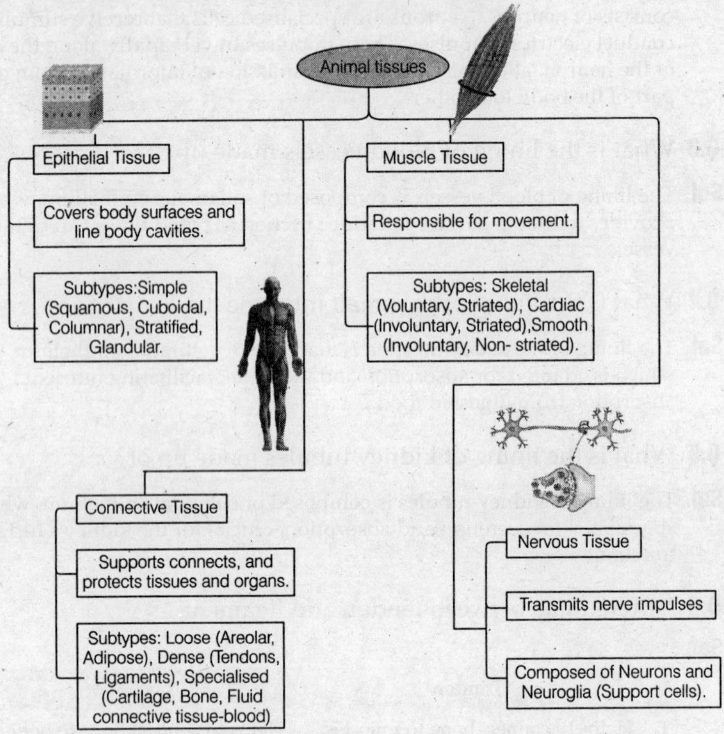

Q.2 What is a permanent tissue? Classify permanent tissue and describe them.

Sol. Permanent tissues are those tissues that originate from meristematic tissues. After a certain period, meristematic tissues lose their ability to divide and specialise to perform specific functions. Once cells in these tissues have differentiated, they attain a definite shape, size, and function.

Permanent tissues are classified into two main types:

1. **Simple Permanent Tissue**

   These tissues are composed of only one type of cell that is structurally and functionally similar.

Some types of simple permanent tissue are given below.

(i) **Parenchyma**

- Parenchyma cells are living, thin-walled, and usually isodiametric (having equal dimensions in all directions). They often have large central vacuoles.
- It forms the bulk of plant organs and plays major roles in storage, photosynthesis (in chlorenchyma), and providing buoyancy (in aerenchyma).

(ii) **Collenchyma**

- Collenchyma cells are living cells characterised by uneven thickening of cell walls, particularly at the corners. This thickening is primarily due to the deposition of cellulose and pectin.
- Provides mechanical support and flexibility to growing parts of the plant, such as stems and leaves, allowing them to bend without breaking.

(iii) **Sclerenchyma**

- They are dead cells with very thick, lignified walls. These cells lack protoplasm and are typically found in areas where plants need maximum support.
- It provides rigidity and structural support to the plant. It is commonly found in regions requiring extra strength, such as seed coats, bark, and vascular bundles.

2. **Complex Permanent Tissue**

Complex tissues consist of more than one type of cell. Which, work together to perform a common function.

Types of Complex Permanent Tissue

(i) **Xylem** Xylem is a vascular tissue responsible for the conduction of water and minerals from roots to different parts of the plant. It is composed of

- **Tracheids** Long, tapering cells that help in the transport of water and provide structural support.
- **Vessels** Tube-like structures that form a continuous channel for the movement of water.
- **Xylem Parenchyma** Living cells that store nutrients and assist in the lateral conduction of water.
- **Xylem Fibres** Dead, elongated cells that provide additional mechanical support.

(ii) **Phloem** Phloem transports organic nutrients, particularly sucrose, from the leaves (where it is synthesised during photosynthesis) to other parts of the plant. Phloem is composed of:

- **Sieve Tubes** Elongated, tube-like structures that are responsible for the transport of sugars.
- **Companion Cells** Living cells closely associated with sieve tubes, aiding in the maintenance and function of the sieve tubes.
- **Phloem Parenchyma** Living cells that help in the storage and lateral transport of food.
- **Phloem Fibres** Provide structural support and strength to the phloem tissue.

Xylem and phloem are collectively known as vascular tissues and together form vascular bundles, which are essential for the conduction of water, minerals, and nutrients throughout the plant.

Q.3 Why are plants and animals made up of different types of tissues? Why does an organism-plant or animal-require different types of cells in the body?

Sol. Plants and animals are fundamentally different in their structure and function, leading to the need for diverse tissue.

Differences in Tissue Composition

- **Plants** are autotrophic organisms, meaning they can produce their own food through photosynthesis. Because plants are stationary and do not require much energy for movement, most of their tissues are supportive in nature. Tissues such as xylem, phloem, sclerenchyma, and cork are often composed of dead cells, which provide structural support and transport functions without the need for living protoplasm.
- **Animals** are heterotrophic organisms that must move in search of food, mates, and shelter. This mobility requires higher energy levels, so most animal tissues consist of living cells. These tissues are involved in various active processes such as movement, digestion, and sensory perception, requiring a high level of cellular activity and energy consumption.

Need for Specialised Cells

In both plants and animals, a wide variety of cell types is essential for the organism's overall functioning:

- **In Plants** Specialised cells are required for processes such as photosynthesis, water and nutrient transport, and structural support. The diversity of cell types ensures that each function is carried out efficiently.

- **In Animals** Animals require a range of specialised cells to perform complex functions like movement, respiration, digestion, and immune response. For example, muscle cells facilitate movement, nerve cells transmit signals, and blood cells transport oxygen and nutrients.

Q.4 Explain with the help of a diagram, the location and function of meristematic tissue.

Sol. Meristematic tissues are regions of active cell division, responsible for the growth of plants. There are three types:

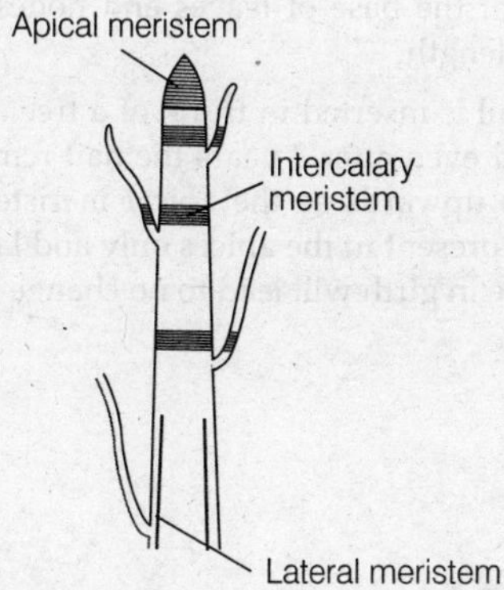

1. **Apical Meristem**
   - **Location** At the growing tips of roots and shoots.
   - **Function** Increases the length of the plant (primary growth).
2. **Intercalary Meristem**
   - **Location** At the base of leaves or internodes.
   - **Function** Increases the length of leaves and internodes.
3. **Lateral Meristem**
   - **Location** Along the sides of stems and roots (cork cambium, vascular cambium).
   - **Function** Increases the girth of the plant (secondary growth).

Q.5 Answer the following question.

(i) A person met with an accident in which two long bones of the hand were dislocated. What could be the reason?

(ii) If a tip of a sugarcane plant is removed from the field, even then it keeps on growing in length. Why?

(iii) A nail is inserted in the trunk of a tree at a height of 1 meter from the ground level. After 3 years, where will the nail be present?

Sol. (i) The dislocation of bones is due to the breakage or damage of ligaments. Ligaments are connective tissues that connect bones and stabilise joints.

(ii) Even after the removal of the tip (apical meristem), the sugarcane plant continues to grow because of the presence of intercalary meristem at the base of leaves and nodes. This meristem facilitates growth in length.

(iii) When a nail is inserted in trunk of a tree at a height of 1 metre from the ground even after 3 years the nail remains at same level. It does not moves upwards as the apical meristem responsible for growth (length) is present in the apices only and lateral meristem responsible for increase in girth will lead to no change in length.

Motion

CHAPTER 07

Important Points

01 Motion An object is said to be in motion if its position changes with time. Motion is a relative term, an object may appear to be moving for one person but can be stationary for other person.

02 Describing Motion Motion of an object is always described with respect to a reference point which is called origin.

03 Terms Required to Describe Motion

(i) **Distance** The total length of the path covered by a moving object is called distance.

- Distance is a scalar quantity, it requires only magnitude for representation.
- SI unit of distance is 'metre (m)'.
- Distance covered by a moving object can never be zero.

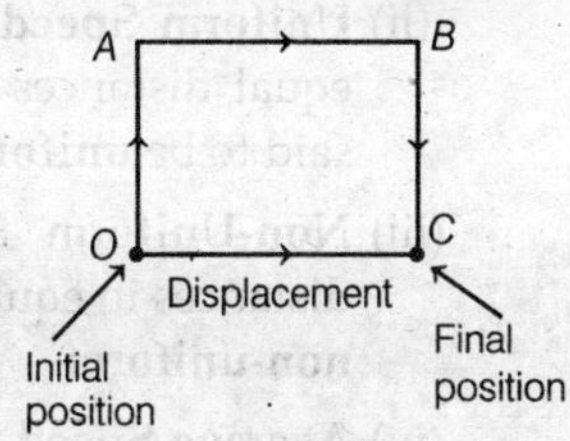

e.g., An object starts from point O and reaches C through A and B.
In this case, distance travelled by the object $= OA + AB + BC$

(ii) **Displacement** The shortest distance between the initial and final position of the moving object is called the **displacement** of the object.

- Displacement is a vector quantity.
- SI unit of displacement is 'metre (m)'.
- Displacement of the object can be both positive and negative.
- In the given figure displacement $= OC$

Note Displacement of a moving object can never be greater than the distance travelled by it.
$\therefore$ *i.e.,* ratio of displacement and distance is always less than or equal to 1.

04 Uniform Motion and Non-Uniform Motion

(i) If an object covers equal distances in equal intervals of time, then its motion is said to be **uniform motion**.

(ii) If an object covers unequal distance in equal intervals of time, then its motion is said to be **non-uniform motion**.

05 Rate of Motion

The ratio of distance travelled by an object and time taken is called the **rate of motion**.

Different objects may take different amounts of time to cover a given distance and so they will have different rates of motion.

06 Terms Required to Measure the Rate of Motion

(i) **Speed** Speed of an object is defined as the distance travelled by it per unit time.

$$\text{Speed} = \frac{\text{Distance}}{\text{Time}} \text{ or } s = \frac{D}{t}$$

- SI unit of speed is metre per second (ms^{-1} or m/s). Other units of speed are cms^{-1}, kmh^{-1} etc.
- Speed of a moving object can never be zero.
- Speed is always positive.

(ii) **Uniform Speed** (Constant Speed) If a moving object covers equal distances in equal intervals of time, then its speed is said to be **uniform speed**.

(iii) **Non-Uniform Speed** If a moving object covers unequal distances in equal intervals of time, then its speed is said to be **non-uniform**.

(iv) **Average Speed** It is defined as the ratio of the total distance travelled by the object and total time taken.

$$\text{Average speed} = \frac{\text{Total distance travelled}}{\text{Total time taken}}$$

(v) **Instantaneous Speed** The speed of an object at any instant during its motion is called **instantaneous speed**.

Note The speedometer of a vehicle indicates the instantaneous speed of the vehicle.

(vi) **Velocity** Velocity of an object is defined as the displacement of the object per unit time.

$$\text{Velocity} = \frac{\text{Displacement}}{\text{Time}} \Rightarrow v = \frac{D}{t}$$

- Velocity is a vector quantity.
- SI unit of velocity is ms^{-1}.
- Velocity of an object can be zero, positive or negative.
- Velocity of an object can be changed by changing the object's speed, direction of motion or both.

(vii) **Uniform or Constant Velocity** If an object covers equal displacements in equal intervals of time, then its velocity is said to be uniform or constant velocity.

(viii) **Non-Uniform or Variable Velocity** If an object covers unequal displacement in equal intervals of time, then its velocity is said to be non-uniform or variable velocity.

(ix) **Average Velocity** It is defined as the ratio of total displacement of the object and total time taken.

$$\text{Average velocity} = \frac{\text{Total displacement}}{\text{Total time taken}}$$

If velocity of an object changes at a uniform rate, then

$$\text{Average velocity} = \frac{\text{Initial velocity} + \text{Final velocity}}{2}$$

Or, $$v_{av} = \frac{u + v}{2}$$

where, u is the initial velocity and v is the final velocity.

Note • If a body is moving in a single straight line, then the magnitude of its speed and velocity will be equal.

• Average speed of an object can never be zero, but the average velocity of a moving object can be zero.

07 Rate of Change of Velocity : Acceleration

The change in velocity per unit time is called acceleration

$$\text{Acceleration} = \frac{\text{Change in velocity}}{\text{Time taken}}$$

If a body starts with velocity u and after time t its velocity become v, then acceleration $a = \frac{v - u}{t}$

Acceleration is a vector quantity. Its SI unit is ms^{-2}.

(i) **Positive Acceleration** If the velocity of an object increases with time in the direction of motion, then the acceleration of the object is said to be positive.

(ii) **Negative Acceleration** If the velocity of an object decreases with time, then the acceleration of the object is said to be negative. Negative acceleration is also called **retardation**.

Note If only the direction of motion (not the magnitude of velocity) of the object changes, then also the object has acceleration.

08 Graphical Representation of Motion

Motion of an object can be described using line graphs. Following graphs can be drawn for motion of an object.

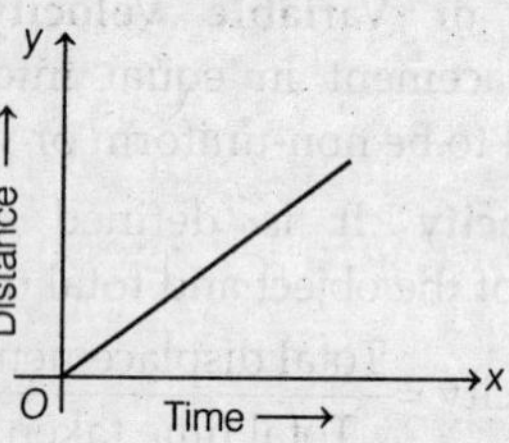

(i) **Distance-Time Graph**

- If an object moves with uniform speed, then distance-time graph is a straight line.
- Distance-time graph of a body can be used to calculate the speed/velocity of the body, slope of distance-time graph indicates speed.

If an object moves with non-uniform speed, then distance-time graph is a curved line. Some distance-time graphs for objects moving with non-uniform speeds are shown below

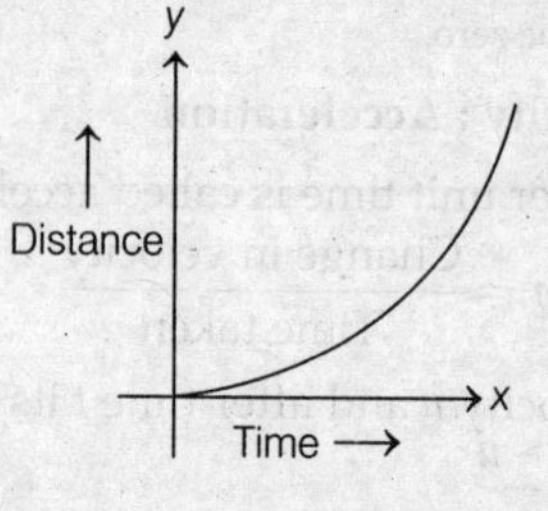

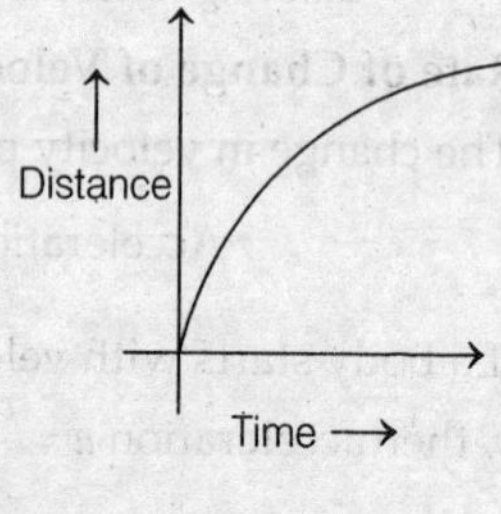

(ii) **Velocity-time graph**

- If object moves with uniform velocity, velocity-time graph will be a straight line parallel to X-axis.

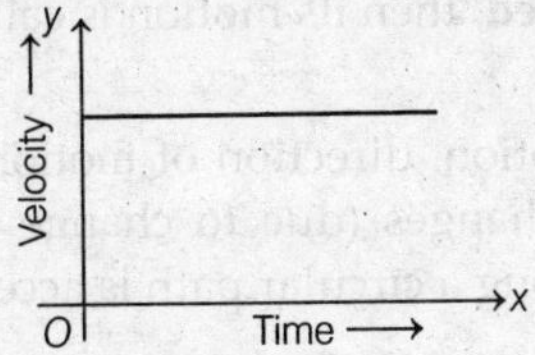

- The area enclosed by velocity-time graph and time axis will be equal to the magnitude of the displacement.
- For uniformly accelerated motion, velocity-time graph is a straight line.
- In case of non-uniformly accelerated motion, velocity-time graph can have any shape other than a straight line

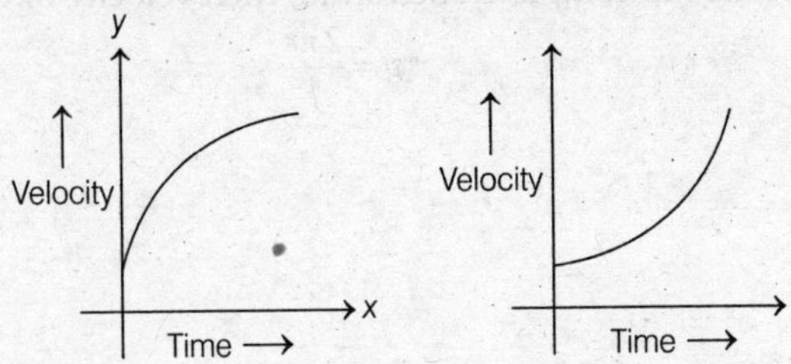

09 Equations of Motion

When an object moves along a straight line **with uniform acceleration**, then its velocity, acceleration and distance covered in given time can be related by a set of equations, which are known as **equations of motion**.

If an object starts with velocity u and after time t its velocity becomes v and during time t the distance covered is s.

The equations of motion are

(i) $v = u + at$ Ist equation of motion.

(ii) $s = ut + \frac{1}{2}at^2$ IInd equation of motion.

(iii) $v^2 = u^2 + 2as$ IIIrd equation of motion.

10 Circular Motion If an object moves around a fixed point in a circular path, then its motion is called circular motion.

11 Uniform Circular Motion If an object moves in a circular path **with uniform speed**, then its motion is called uniform circular motion.

(i) In circular motion, direction of motion changes continuously *i.e.*, velocity changes (due to change in direction), therefore the motion along a circular path is accelerated.

(ii) The acceleration present in circular motion is called **centripetal acceleration**.

It is given by

$$a = \frac{V^2}{r}$$

(iii) If an object is moving in a circular path of radius r and it takes time t to complete one round, then velocity of the object.

$$v = \frac{2\pi r}{t}$$

Intext Questions

On Page 74

Question 1 An object has moved through a distance. Can it have zero displacement? If yes, support your answer with an example.

Sol. An object can have zero displacement, yet it covers some distance, in the conditions if it comes back to its initial position.

If a boy starts from point A and comes back to the same point A then his displacement is zero because its initial and final position are same.

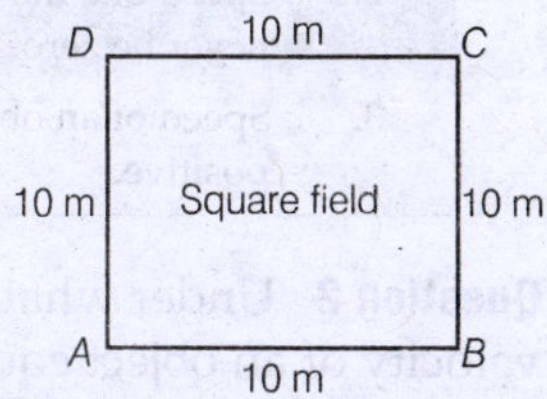

Question 2 A farmer moves along the boundary of a square field of side 10 m in 40 s. What will be the magnitude of displacement of the farmer at the end of 2 minutes 20 seconds, from his initial position?

Sol. Farmer takes 40 s to move along the boundary of the square field, *i.e.*, after 40 s farmer is again at initial position. So his displacement is zero.

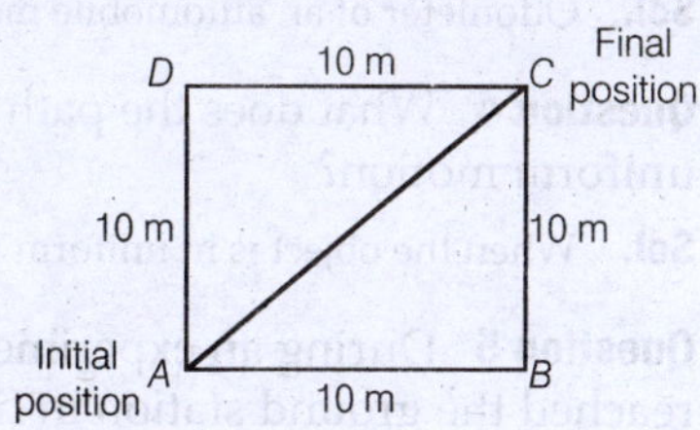

Time given = 2 min 20 s

$$= (2 \times 60 + 20) \text{ s} = 140 \text{ s}$$
$$= (40 \times 3 + 20) \text{ s}$$

Displacement of farmer after 2 min 20 s *i.e.*, after 140 s

$$= \text{Displacement after } (3 \times 40 + 20) \text{ s} = 0 + \text{displacement after 20 s}$$

($\because$ after each 40 s, displacement is zero)

Farmer completes one round in 40 s, so he will complete 1/2 round in 20 s, *i.e.*, after 20 s, final position of farmer is C.

Displacement of farmer = AC

$$= \sqrt{AB^2 + BC^2} = \sqrt{10^2 + 10^2}$$
$$= 10\sqrt{2} = 10 \times 1.414 = 14.14 \text{ m}$$

Question 3 Which of the following is true for displacement?

(a) It cannot be zero.

(b) Its magnitude is greater than the distance travelled by the object.

Sol. (a) Statement (a) is false because displacement of a moving object can be zero.

(b) Statement (b) is false because magnitude of displacement can never be greater than the distance travelled by the object.

On Page 76

Question 1 Distinguish between speed and velocity.

Sol.

S.N.	Speed	Velocity
1.	Speed is a scalar quantity.	Velocity is a vector quantity.
2.	Speed of a moving object can never be zero.	Velocity of a moving object can be zero.
3.	Speed of an object is always positive.	Velocity of an object can be positive or negative.

Question 2 Under what condition(s) is the magnitude of average velocity of an object equal to its average speed?

Sol. When an object moves in a straight line, then the magnitude of average velocity is equal to the average speed.

Question 3 What does the odometer of an automobile measure?

Sol. Odometer of an automobile measures the distance travelled by it.

Question 4 What does the path of an object look like when it is in uniform motion?

Sol. When the object is in uniform motion then its path is a straight line.

Question 5 During an experiment, a signal from a spaceship reached the ground station in five minutes. What was the distance of the spaceship from the ground station? The signal travels at the speed of light, that is, $3 \times 10^8 \text{ ms}^{-1}$.

Sol. Speed of signal = $3 \times 10^8 \text{ms}^{-1}$

Time taken by the signal in reaching the earth = 5 min = $5 \times 60 = 300$ s

Distance of spaceship from ground station

= Distance travelled by the signal in 5 min.

= Speed × Time = $3 \times 10^8 \times 300 = 9 \times 10^{10}$ m

On Page 77

Question 1 When will you say a body is in

(i) uniform acceleration? (ii) non-uniform acceleration?

Sol. (i) A body has uniform acceleration, if its velocity changes by equal amount in equal intervals of time.

(ii) A body has non-uniform acceleration, if its velocity changes by unequal amount in equal intervals of time.

Question 2 A bus decreases its speed from 80 kmh^{-1} to 60 kmh^{-1} in 5 s. Find the acceleration of the bus.

Sol. Initial speed $u = 80 \text{ km h}^{-1} = 80 \times \frac{5}{18} \text{ ms}^{-1} = \frac{200}{9} \text{ ms}^{-1}$

Final speed $v = 60 \text{ km h}^{-1} = 60 \times \frac{5}{18} = \frac{150}{9} \text{ ms}^{-1}$

$$\text{Acceleration } a = \frac{v-u}{t} = \frac{\frac{150}{9} - \frac{200}{9}}{5} = -\frac{50}{9 \times 5} = \frac{-10}{9} \text{ ms}^{-2}$$

Acceleration is negative because speed decreases.

Question 3 A train starting from a railway station and moving with uniform acceleration attains a speed 40 kmh^{-1} in 10 minutes. Find its acceleration.

Sol. Train starts from railway station, so initial speed, $u = 0$.

Final speed, $v = 40 \text{ kmh}^{-1}$

$= 40 \times \frac{5}{18} = \frac{100}{9} \text{ ms}^{-1}$

Time $t = 10$ min

$= 10 \times 60 = 600$ s

$$\text{Acceleration, } a = \frac{v-u}{t} = \frac{\frac{100}{9} - 0}{600} = \frac{100}{9 \times 600} = \frac{1}{54} \text{ ms}^{-2}$$

On Page 81

Question 1 What is the nature of the distance-time graphs for uniform and non-uniform motion of an object?

Sol. (i) For uniform motion of an object, its distance-time graph is a straight line with constant slope.

(ii) For non-uniform motion of an object, its distance-time graph is a curved line with increasing or decreasing slope.

Question 2 What can you say about the motion of an object whose distance-time graph is a straight line parallel to the time axis?

Sol. Distance-time graph is parallel to time axis, it means that the distance of the object is not changing with time *i.e.,* the object is at rest.

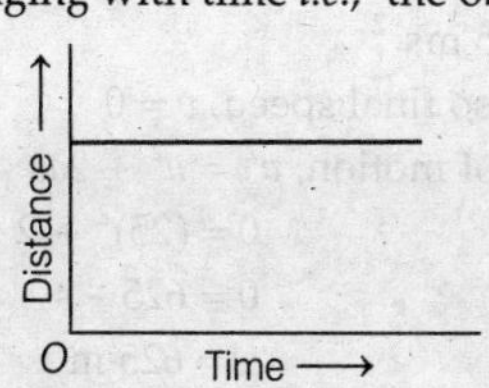

Question 3 What can you say about the motion of an object if its speed-time graph is a straight line parallel to the time axis?

Sol. Speed-time graph is a straight line parallel to time axis it means that the speed of the object is not changing with time, *i.e.,* the object is in uniform motion.

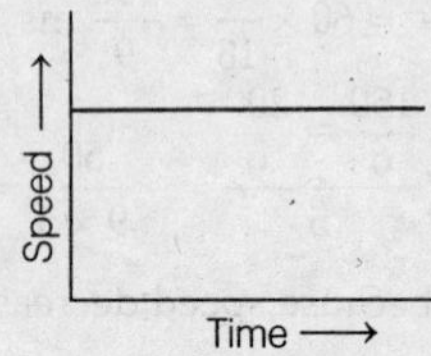

Question 4 What is the quantity which is measured by the area occupied below the velocity-time graph?

Sol. Area under the velocity-time graph gives the magnitude of displacement.

On Page 82

Question 1 A bus starting from rest moves with a uniform acceleration of 0.1 ms^{-2} for 2 minutes. Find

(a) the speed acquired,

(b) the distance travelled.

Sol. Here, acceleration, $a = 0.1\ ms^{-2}$

Time, $t = 2\ min = 2 \times 60 = 120\ s$

Initial speed, $u = 0$

(a) From Ist equation of motion, speed acquired, $v = u + at$

$= 0 + 0.1 \times 120 = 12\ ms^{-1}$

(b) From IInd equation of motion,

Distance travelled, $s = ut + \frac{1}{2}at^2 = 0 \times 120 + \frac{1}{2} \times 0.1 \times 120 \times 120$

$= 0.1 \times 60 \times 120 = 720\ m$

Question 2 A train is travelling at a speed of 90 kmh^{-1}. Brakes are applied so as to produce a uniform acceleration of $-0.5\ ms^{-2}$. Find how far the train will go before it is brought to rest?

Sol. Here, initial speed, $u = 90\ kmh^{-1} = 90 \times \frac{5}{18} = 25\ ms^{-1}$

Acceleration, $a = -0.5\ ms^{-2}$

Since, train is at rest, so final speed, $v = 0$

From third equation of motion, $v^2 = u^2 + 2as$

$0 = (25)^2 + 2 \times (-0.5) \times s$

$0 = 625 - s$

$s = 625\ m$

Question 3 A trolley, while going down an inclined plane, has an acceleration of 2 cm s^{-2}. What will be its velocity 3s after the start?

Sol. Here, initial velocity, $u = 0$

Acceleration, $a = 2 \text{ cm s}^{-2}$
Time, $t = 3 \text{ s}$
From, Ist equation of motion, $v = u + at$

$$= 0 + 2 \times 3 = 6 \text{ ms}^{-1}$$

Question 4 A racing car has a uniform acceleration of 4 ms^{-2}. What distance will it cover in 10 s after start?

Sol. Here $u = 0$, $a = 4 \text{ ms}^{-2}$, $t = 10$ s.

From 2nd equation of motion, distance travelled

$$s = ut + \frac{1}{2}at^2$$
$$= 0 + \frac{1}{2} \times 4 \times (10)^2$$
$$= \frac{1}{2} \times 4 \times 100$$
$$= 200 \text{ m}$$

Question 5 A stone is thrown in a vertically upward direction with a velocity of 5 ms^{-1}. If the acceleration of the stone during its motion is 10 ms^{-2} in the downward direction, what will be the height attained by the stone and how much time will it take to reach there?

Sol. Here $u = 5 \text{ ms}^{-1}$

$a = -10 \text{ ms}^{-2}$ (– ve sign is due to upward direction)
$v = 0$ (at maximum height velocity is zero)

Height attained $s = ?$, time taken $t = ?$.

(i) $v^2 = u^2 + 2as$

$$0 = (5)^2 + 2 \times -10 \times s$$
$$s = \frac{25}{20} = 1.25 \text{ m}$$

(ii) $v = u + at$

$$0 = 5 + (-10)\, t$$
$$t = \frac{5}{10} = 0.5 \, s$$

Note Whenever the speed of object decreases during its motion the acceleration is taken as negative.

Exercises

Question 1 An athlete completes one round of a circular track of diameter 200 m in 40 s. What will be the distance covered and the displacement at the end of 2 minutes 20 s?

◎ ***Thinking Process*** In this problem to find the distance covered by the athlete we will first calculate the distance covered in one second and then find the distance covered in 2 min 20 second and to find the displacement, first determine the final positions of the athlete and then calculate the displacement.

Sol. (i) Diameter of circular track = 200 m

$\therefore$ Radius of circular track $= \dfrac{200}{2} = 100$ m

Circumference of circular track $= 2\pi r = 2 \times \dfrac{22}{7} \times 100 = \dfrac{4400}{7}$ m

Total time given = 2 min 20 s = $2 \times 60 + 20 = 140$ s

According to question, athlete takes 40 s to complete one round.

$\therefore$ Distance covered in 40 s $= \dfrac{4400}{7}$ m

($\because$ Distance covered in one round is equal to the circumference of the track.)

Distance covered in 1 s $= \dfrac{4400}{7 \times 40}$

or distance covered in 140 s $= \dfrac{4400}{7 \times 40} \times 140 = 2200$ m $= 2.2$ km

(ii) As per the question, athlete completes one round in 40 s *i.e.*, after 40 s. athlete comes back to its initial position or after 40 s his displacement is zero. Similarly after 120 s (40×3), his displacement is also zero.

$\therefore$ Displacement after 2 min 20 s or 140 s = Displacement after 20 s.

($\because$ After 120 s, displacement is zero.)

In 20 s athlete will cover half the circular track from *A* to *B* (in 40 s one complete round is taken, so in 20 s half round will be taken.)

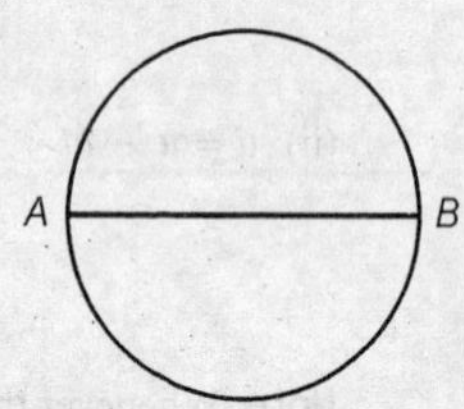

Displacement after 20 s = *AB*

(Initial position is *A* and after half round, final position is *B*)

$\Rightarrow$ displacement = Diameter of circular track

= 200 m

Question 2 Joseph jogs from one end A to the other end B of a straight 300 m road in 2 minutes 30 seconds and then turns around and jogs 100 m back to point C in another 1 min. What are Joseph's average speeds and velocities in jogging (a) from A to B and (b) from A to C?

Sol. Distance covered from A to B = 300 m

Displacement from A to B = 300 m

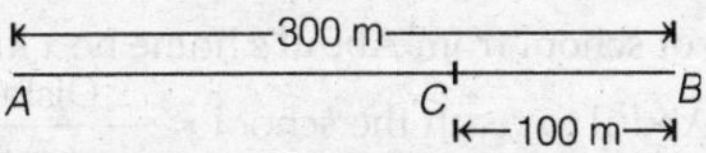

Time taken by Joseph to move from A to B

$$t = 2\text{min } 20\text{ s} = 2 \times 60 + 30$$
$$= 120 + 30 = 150\text{ s} \qquad (\because 1\text{ min} = 60\text{ s})$$

(a) Average speed in jogging from A to B

$$= \frac{\text{Distance from } A \text{ to } B}{\text{Time taken from } A \text{ to } B}$$
$$= \frac{300}{150} = 2\text{ ms}^{-1}$$

Average velocity in jogging from A to B

$$= \frac{\text{Displacement from } A \text{ to } B}{\text{Time taken from } A \text{ to } B} = \frac{300}{150} = 2\text{ ms}^{-1}$$

(b) Distance covered from A to C = $AB + BC$

$$= 300 + 100 = 400\text{ m}$$

Displacement from A to C = Minimum distance from A to C

$$= 300 - 100 = 200\text{ m}$$

Time taken in jogging from A to C = 2 min 30 s + 1min

$$= 2 \times 60 + 30 + 60 = 210\text{ s}$$

Average speed in jogging from A to C

$$= \frac{\text{Displacement from } A \text{ to } C}{\text{Time taken from } A \text{ to } C} = \frac{400}{210} = 1.9\text{ ms}^{-1}$$

Average velocity in jogging from A to C

$$= \frac{\text{Displacement from } A \text{ to } C}{\text{Time taken from } A \text{ to } C} = \frac{200}{210} = 0.95\text{ ms}^{-1}$$

Mistake Alert It is important to check the units of physical quantities given in the question. If the units are different from the SI units, then they must be converted in SI before using in the formulae. In this question, time is given in minute. So, it must be converted for calculations.

Question 3 Abdul, while driving to school, computes the average speed for his trip to be 20 kmh^{-1}. On his return trip along the same route, there is less traffic and the average speed is 30 kmh^{-1}. What is the average speed for Abdul's trip?

Thinking Process Average speed for a round trip depends on total distance and total time, not just the average of two speeds, as each speed is held for different times.

Sol. Let the distance of school from Abdul's home be x km.

$$\text{Time taken by Abdul to reach the school} = \frac{\text{Distance}}{\text{Average speed}} = \frac{x}{20}\ \text{h}$$

Similarly, time taken by Abdul to reach the home from school

$$= \frac{\text{Distance}}{\text{Average speed}} = \frac{x}{40}\ \text{h}$$

$$\text{Average speed for Abdul's trip} = \frac{\text{Total distance}}{\text{Total time}} = \frac{x + x}{\frac{x}{20} + \frac{x}{40}}$$

$$= \frac{2x}{\frac{4x + 2x}{80}} = \frac{2x \times 80}{6x}$$

$$= \frac{80}{3}\ kmh^{-1}$$

Mistake Alert Some students use $v_{av} = \frac{u + v}{2}$ to calculate the average speed which is incorrect. This formula is only valid when an object moves with speeds u and v for equal intervals of time. In this question, the time intervals are not equal.

Also, the formula

$\text{Average speed} = \frac{\text{Total distance}}{\text{Total time}}$ is a general formula and works in every situation.

Question 4 A motorboat starting from rest on a lake accelerates in a straight line at a constant rate of 3.0 ms^{-2} for 8.0 s. How far does the boat travel during this time?

Sol. The motorboat starts from rest, so initial velocity, $u = 0$

Time taken $t = 8$ s, acceleration, $a = 3\ ms^{-2}$

Distance covered during the given time

$$s = ut + \frac{1}{2}at^2 \quad \text{(From second equation of motion)}$$

$$= 0 \times 8 + \frac{1}{2} \times 3 \times (8)^2 = \frac{1}{2} \times 3 \times 64 = 0.96\ \text{m}$$

Question 5 A driver of a car travelling at 52 kmh^{-1} applies the brakes and accelerates uniformly in the opposite direction. The car stops in 5 s. Another driver going at 3 kmh^{-1} in another car applies his brakes slowly and stops in 10 s. On the same graph paper, plot the speed *versus* time graphs for the two cars. Which of the two cars travelled farther after the brakes were applied?

Sol. Initial speed of car $A = 52 \text{ km h}^{-1}$

$$= 52 \times \frac{5}{18} = 14.44 \text{ ms}^{-1}$$

The car stops in 5 s *i.e.*, final speed of car $v = 0$, time $t = 5$ s.

For speed-time graph of car *A*.

s	14.44 ms^{-1}	0
t	0	5

Initial speed of car $B = 3 \text{ kmh}^{-1} = 3 \times \frac{5}{18} = 0.83 \text{ ms}^{-1}$

The car stops in 10 s *i.e.*, final speed of car $v = 0$, time $t = 10$ s.

For speed-time graph of car *B*

s	0.83 ms^{-1}	0
t	0	10

The speed-time graphs of both cars *A* and *B* are shown below.

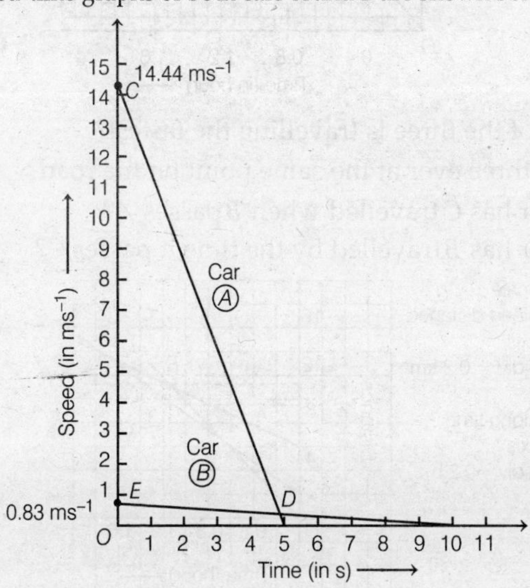

Car A

Distance travelled = Area under v - t graph

$$= \frac{1}{2} \times b \times h = \frac{1}{2} \times 5 \times \frac{130}{9} = 36.11 \text{ m}$$

Car B

Distance travelled = Area under v - t graph

$$= \frac{1}{2} \times b \times h = \frac{1}{2} \times 10 \times \frac{5}{6} = 4.166 \text{ m}$$

So, car A travelled farther when brakes where applied.

Note The speed-time graphs are straight line graphs as the cars have uniform retardation.

Question 6 Figure shows the distance-time graph of three objects A, B and C. Study the graph and answer the following questions

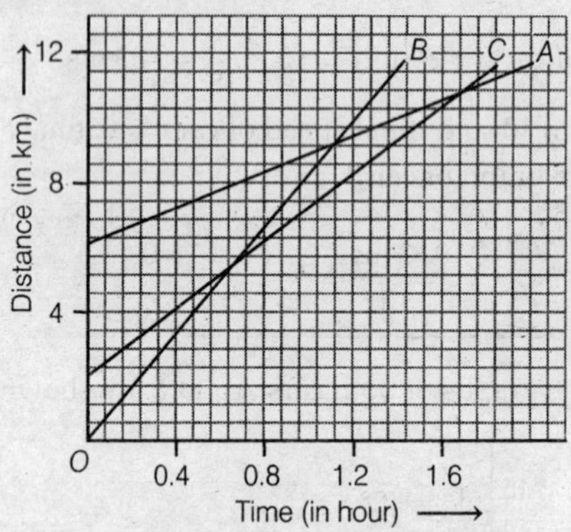

(a) Which of the three is travelling the fastest?

(b) Are all three ever at the same point on the road?

(c) How far has C travelled when B passes A?

(d) How far has B travelled by the time it passes C?

Sol. Scale :
Along distance axis :
1 div = 0.2 km

Along time axis
1 div =0.2 h

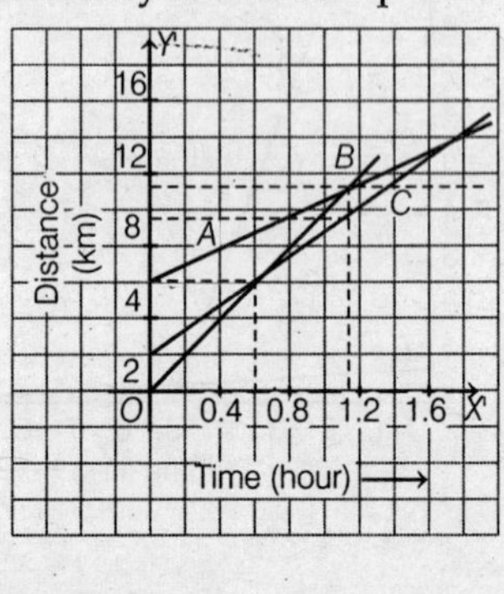

(a) The object for which slope of speed-time graph is maximum will have maximum speed *i.e.*, will travel the fastest. Here for object *B*, slope is maximum so it is travelling the fastest.

(b) All the three objects will ever be at the same point on the road if the distance-time graph intersect each other at any point. Here all the three graphs do not intersect each other at a single point, so these three will never be at the same point on the road.

(c) When *B* passes *A*, distance travelled by C = 9.6 − 2 = 7.6 km.

(d) Distance travelled by *B* by the time it passes C = 6 km.

Question 7 A ball is gently dropped from a height of 20 m. If its velocity increases uniformly at the rate of 10 ms^{-2}, with what velocity will it strike the ground? After what time will it strike the ground?

Thinking Process In this problem, the ball is dropped from a 20 m height with initial velocity zero. Using equations of motion under gravity (acceleration = 10 m / s^2), we first find the time to reach the ground, then calculate the impact velocity.

Sol. The ball is dropped from height *i.e.*, it starts from rest, so initial velocity, $u = 0$.

Height, $h = 10$ m; acceleration, $g = 10\ ms^{-2}$

(In the motion under gravity, acceleration is taken as *g*, acceleration due to gravity.)

From equation of motion, $h = ut + \frac{1}{2}gt^2$

$$20 = 0 \times t + \frac{1}{2} \times 10 \times t^2 \Rightarrow 20 = 5t^2 \Rightarrow t^2 = 4 \Rightarrow t = \sqrt{4} = 2\text{ s}$$

i.e., the ball will take 2 s to strike the ground.

Again from equation of motion $v = u + gt$, $v = 0 + 10 \times 2 = 20\ ms^{-1}$

i.e., the ball will strike the ground with velocity of 20 ms^{-1}.

Question 8 The speed-time graph for a car is shown in figure.

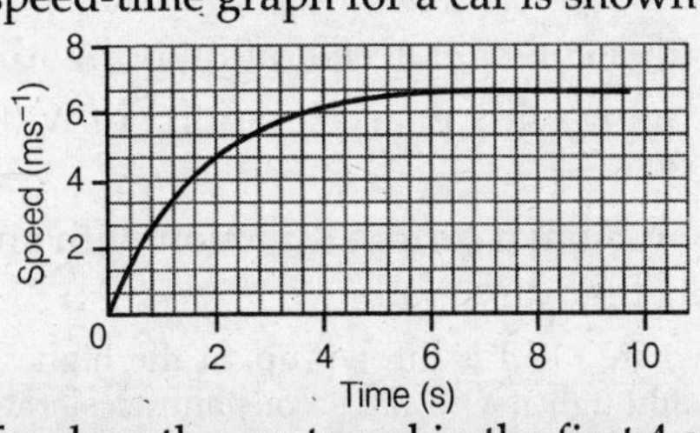

(a) Find how far does the car travel in the first 4 seconds. Shade the area on the graph that represents the distance travelled by the car during the period.

(b) Which part of the graph represents uniform motion of the car?

Sol. (a) Distance travelled in 4s = Area under the speed-time graph from 0 to 4s as shown in graph.

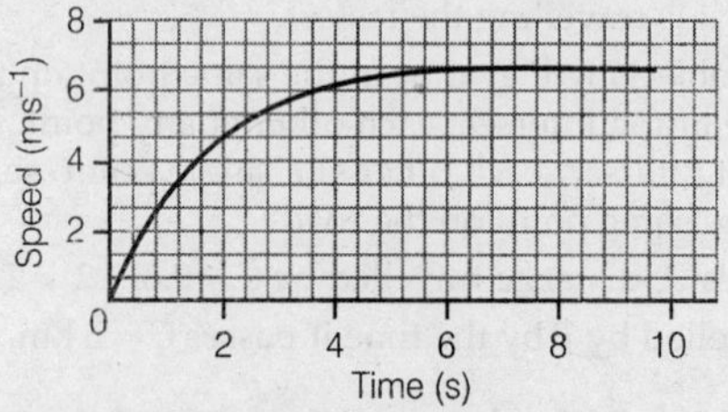

Since, this area cannot be calculated directly, we will count the number of small boxes and will multiply it with the area of 1 box to find out the total area.

$\because$ 5 div. on X- axis = 2s

1 div. on X- axis = $\frac{2}{5}$s

Similarly, 3 div. on Y-axis = 2 ms^{-1}

1 div. on Y axis = $\frac{2}{3}$ ms^{-1}

Area of 1 box = $\frac{2}{5} \times \frac{2}{3} = \frac{4}{15}$ m

Number of boxes under the graph between 0 to 4 s

= 56 complete boxes + $\frac{1}{2} \times$ (11 half boxes)

$\frac{113}{2}$ = boxes

Area = distance covered = $\frac{113}{2} \times \frac{4}{15}$ = 15.1 m

(b) For uniform motion, the speed-time graph is a straight line parallel to time axis. So, the straight part of the curve parallel to time axis represents the uniform motion of the car. This means that the car is in uniform motion of the 4 s.

Question 9 State which of the following situations are possible and give an example for each of these

(a) an object with a constant acceleration but with zero velocity.

(b) an object moving with an acceleration but with uniform speed.

(c) an object moving in a certain direction with an acceleration in the perpendicular direction.

Sol. (a) Possible when a ball is thrown up, at the highest point, it has zero velocity, although it will have constant acceleration due to gravity, which is equal to 9.8 m/s^2.

(b) Possible when a car is moving in a circular track with constant speed, it is accelerating due to change in direction of motion.

(c) Possible a car is moving in a circular track, its acceleration is perpendicular to the direction of motion.

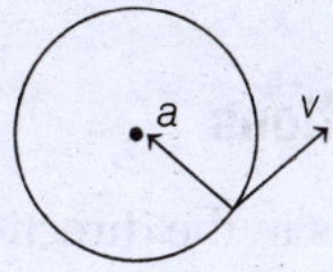

Note The direction of motion of an object is given by the direction of its velocity.

Question 10 An artificial satellite is moving in a circular orbit of radius 42250 km. Calculate its speed if it takes 24 hours to revolve around the earth.

Sol. Radius of the orbit, $r = 42250$ km

Distance covered in one revolution

$$s = 2\pi r \quad \text{(Circumference of the orbit)}$$

$$= 2 \times \frac{22}{7} \times 42250 = 265571.43 \text{ km}$$

Time taken in one revolution $t = 24$ h

$$\therefore \quad \text{Speed of satellite} = \frac{\text{Distance}}{\text{Time}}$$

$$= \frac{265571.43}{24}$$

$$= 11065.48 \text{ km h}^{-1}$$

Note In this question, we are not working with SI units. The distance is in km, time is in h and the speed calculated is in km/h.

DIKSHA APP Questions

☐ Multiple Choice Questions

Q.1 A force that always acts in the direction opposite to the direction of motion is:-

(a) Gravitational force
(b) Muscular force
(c) Friction
(d) Electrostatic force

Sol. (c) Frictional force opposes motion and arises when two object comes in contact against each other during motion. Hence, it act opposite to the direction of motion.

Q.2 Which one of the following is true for distance and displacement

(a) Displacement can be equal to or less than distance but never greater distance
(b) Displacement is always greater than distance
(c) Displacement cannot be zero
(d) Displacement and distance are always equal

Sol. (a) Displacement is the shortest distance between initial and final position of an object. Distance is the actual path taken by the object.

Hence, displacement can not be greater that the distance.

☐ Short Answer Type

Q.1 Ashi went on her bike from Delhi to Chandigarh. The odometer of her bike read 4200 km at the start of the trip and 4460 km at the end of the trip. If Ashi took 4 h 20 min to complete her trip, find the average speed both in m/s and km/h.

Sol. Here, $u = 4200$ km, $v = 4460$ km,

$t = 4$ h 20 min $t = 4\text{h} + 1/3\text{h} = 13/3\text{h}$

Therefore, Average speed = distance/time

$$d = 4460 - 4200 = 260 \text{ km}$$

$$t = \frac{13}{3} \text{ h}$$

That implies, $260/13/3 = 260/13 \times 3 = 20 \times 3 = 60$ km/h

Now, $1\text{km/h} = \frac{5}{18}$ m/s

Therefore, 60 km/h $= 60 \times 5/18 = 16.66$ m/s

Q.2 Sanket went on his bike from Delhi to Gurugram at 40 km/h and in the evening returned back at a speed of 60 km/h. What is the average speed for the entire journey?

Sol. Distance between Gurgaon and Delhi = s km

Time taken to go from Delhi to Gurgaon = $\frac{s}{60}$ h

Time taken to return = $\frac{s}{40}$ h

Total time = $s\left[\frac{1}{40}+\frac{1}{60}\right]=\frac{s}{24}$ h

Average speed for the entire journey = total distance/total time duration

= $2s/(s/24) = 48$ km/h

Q.3 A train moves with a speed of 30 km/h in the first 15 minutes, with another speed of 40 km/hr in the next 15 minutes and then with a speed of 60 km/hr in the last 30 minutes. Calculate the average speed of the train for this journey.

Sol. Distance 1 = $30 \times \frac{15}{60} = 7.5$ km

Distance 2 = $40 \times \frac{15}{60} = 10$ km

Distance 3 = $60 \times \frac{30}{60} = 30$ km

Total distance = 47.5 km

Total time = $\frac{15}{60}+\frac{15}{60}+\frac{30}{60} = 1$ hour

Average speed = total distance/total time = 47.5 km/hr

Q.4 A train starting from rest attains a velocity of 72 km/h in 5 minutes. Assuming the acceleration is uniform, find

(i) The acceleration

(ii) The distance travelled by the train for attaining this velocity 1.

Sol. Given, Initial velocity = $u = 0$ m/s

Final velocity = v = 72 km/h = $72 \times 5/18 = 20$ m/s

Time = 5 min = $5 \times 60 = 300$ sec

(i) As we know that, $a = v - u/t$

$\Rightarrow \quad a = v - u/t = 20 - 0/300 = 1/15\ \text{m/s}^2$

(ii) Distance travelled = $s = ut + 1/2at^2$

$= 0 \times 1/12 + 1/2(1/15)(300)^2$

= 3000 m

Distance travelled by the train for attaining this velocity 3 km.

☐ Long Answer Type

Q.1 (i) Define inertia

(ii) Give one daily life example of each- inertia of rest, inertia of motion and inertia of direction.

Sol. Inertia is a tendency of a body by the virtue of which it resist a change in its state of motion, direction, or rest. Here are some examples of inertia in daily life:

Inertia of rest When you beat a carpet with a stick, the dust particles remain at rest and separate. This is because of the dust particles' inertia or rest, which is their tendency to remain at rest.

Inertia or motion When a train stops suddenly, you fall forward. This is because of your inertia of motion, which is your tendency to remain in a state of uniform motion.

Inertia of direction A bike tends to move in a straight line unless you turn the handle. This is because of the bike's inertia of direction, which is its tendency to remain in a particular direction.

Force and Laws of Motion

CHAPTER 08

Important Points

01 In our everyday life, we observe that some effort is required to put a stationary object into motion or to stop a moving object, this effort is called **force**. In this chapter, we will study about force, its effect, types and concerned laws etc.

02 **Force** Force is a push or pull which can change the state of rest or state of motion of an object.

- Force cannot be seen but its effect on an object can be felt.
- Force can bring a stationary object into motion.
- Force can stop a moving object.
- Force can change the direction of motion of an object.
- Force can change the shape and size of object.
- Force is a vector quantity and its SI unit is newton.

$$1 \text{ newton} = 1 \text{ kg ms}^{-2}$$

03 **Balanced and Unbalanced Forces**

- **Balanced Forces** If the net effect of all the forces acting on an object is zero, then the forces are called balanced forces.
  - If balanced forces are acting on an object, then it appears as no force is acting on it.
  - An object under the effect of balanced forces cannot change its state of motion or rest.
  - If balanced forces are acting on an object in uniform motion, then the object remains in the state of uniform motion.
- **Unbalanced Forces** If the net effect of all the forces acting on an object is non zero, then these forces are called unbalanced forces.
  - Unbalanced forces can move a stationary object or can stop a moving object.

04 Newton's Laws of Motion

(a) **First Law of Motion** According to first law of motion, "If a body is in rest or in uniform motion along a straight line, then it will remain in same state until and unless an external force is applied on it".

- **Inertia** The property of an object to resist any change in its state of motion or rest is called inertia. If an object is at rest, it tends to remain at rest and if it is moving, it tends to keep moving with a uniform velocity.
  - The mass of an object is a measure of its inertia. Heavier objects have higher inertia than lighter objects.
  - If an object resists the change in its state of rest, its inertia is called inertia of rest.
  - If an object resists the change in its state of motion, its inertia is called inertia of motion.
  - If an object resists the change in its direction of motion, its inertia is called inertia of direction.

  Some Daily Life Examples of Inertia

  (i) When a bus suddenly starts, the passenger in the bus falls backward.

  (ii) When a moving bus stops suddenly, the passenger is pushed forward.

  (iii) When a bus turns to a corner sharply, passenger tends to fall sideways.

  (iv) A bullet fired from a gun makes a small hole in the window pane while a stone striking a window pane breaks it into pieces.

  (v) When a tree is vigorously shaken, then some leaves fall from it.

- **Momentum** The amount of motion possessed by an object is called the momentum of the object.
  - Momentum of an object is equal to the product of its mass (m) and velocity (v).

$$\text{Momentum, } p = m \times v$$

  - It is a vector quantity. Its SI unit is kg ms^{-1} and CGS unit is g cm s^{-1}.

- Momentum of an object is directly proportional to
  (i) mass of the object.
  (ii) velocity of the object.
- Direction of momentum is same as that of velocity.

Example What is the momentum of a motorbike having mass 125 kg, moving with a velocity of 54 km h^{-1}?

Sol. Mass, $m = 125$ kg

$$\text{Velocity, } v = 54 \text{ km h}^{-1} = 54 \times \frac{5}{18} = 15 \text{ ms}^{-1}$$

Momentum of motorbike, $p = mv = 125 \times 15 = 1875$ kg ms^{-1}

(b) **Second Law of Motion** According to second law of motion, "The rate of change of momentum of an object is directly proportional to the force applied on it". The change in momentum takes place in the direction of force.

According to second law of motion,

$$F \propto \frac{\Delta p}{\Delta t} \qquad \text{...(i)}$$

Here, Δp = change in momentum

Δt = time taken in change

If an object of mass m is moving with velocity u and after time t its velocity becomes v, then

Initial momentum, $p_1 = mu$

Final momentum, $p_2 = mv$

Change in momentum $\Delta p = p_2 - p_1 = mv - mu = m(v - u)$

$$\text{Rate of change of momentum} = \frac{\Delta p}{\Delta t}$$

$$= m\left(\frac{v-u}{t}\right)$$

From Eq. (i),

$$F \propto m\left(\frac{v-u}{t}\right)$$

We know that

$$\frac{v-u}{t} = a \text{ (acceleration of the object)}$$

$$\therefore \qquad F \propto ma \quad \text{or } F = kma$$

where, k is a constant of proportionality.

It has been found that the value of this constant of proportionality (k) is 1.

$$\therefore \qquad F = ma$$

i.e., force applied on an object is equal to the product of mass of the body and acceleration produced in it.

If $m = 1$ kg, $a = 1$ m s^{-2}

$$\therefore \qquad F = 1 \times 1 = 1 \text{ kg ms}^{-2} = 1 \text{ N}$$

"1 newton is defined as the amount of force which, when applied to an object of mass 1 kg, produces on acceleration of 1 ms^{-2} in it."

Example Velocity of a car increases from 10 m s^{-1} to 20 ms^{-1}. If the mass of the car is 1500 kg, calculate change in momentum of the car. If time taken in changing the velocity is 10 s, also find the force applied on the car.

Sol. Mass, $m = 1500$ kg

Initial velocity, $u = 10$ m s^{-1}

Final velocity, $v = 20$ m s^{-1}

Time taken, $t = 10$ s

Change in momentum = Final momentum – Initial momentum

$$= mv - mu = m(v - u)$$

$$= 1500\,(20 - 10) = 1500 \times 10 = 15000$$

$$= 1.5 \times 10^4 \text{ kg ms}^{-1}$$

Force applied on the car,

$$F = \text{Rate of change of momentum}$$

$$= \frac{\text{Change in momentum}}{\text{Time taken}}$$

$$= \frac{1.5 \times 10^4}{10} = 1.5 \times 10^3 \text{ N}$$

Some Daily Life Examples of Newton's Second Law

(i) A cricket fielder lowers his hands while catching a ball.

(ii) A high jumping athlete is provided either a cushion or heap of sand on the ground to fall upon.

(iii) Vehicles are provided with shockers.

(iv) If a moving train collides with a stationary train, then huge damage takes place.

(c) **Third Law of Motion** According to this law, "To every action there is always an equal and opposite reaction." It means that if a body '*X*' exerts force *F* on another body '*Y*', then body '*Y*' also exerts the same force *F* on body '*X*'.

Action and reaction always act on different bodies.

Some Daily Life Examples of Newton's Third Law

(i) Recoiling of a gun on firing the bullet.
(ii) Flying of jet planes.
(iii) Rebounding of a ball after striking the floor.
(iv) Motion of boat.

05 Law of Conservation of Momentum According to this law, "The total momentum of a system remains constant, till an external force is applied on it."

$$\text{Momentum of the system, } p = \text{constant, if } F = 0$$

We can say that total initial momentum of the system is equal to the total final momentum of the system, if there is no external force acting on the system.

If two objects collide with each other, then we can say,

Total momentum before collision = Total momentum after collision.

Intext Questions

On Page 91

Question 1 Which of the following has more inertia:

(a) a rubber ball and a stone of the same size?

(b) a bicycle and a train?

(c) a five-rupees coin and a one-rupee coin?

Sol. Inertia of an object is the measurement of its mass.

(a) A stone of same size as that of rubber ball will have greater mass, so stone will have more inertia.

(b) A train has much greater mass than that of a bicycle, so the train will have more inertia.

(c) A five-rupees coin has more mass than a one-rupee coin, so five-rupees coin will have greater inertia.

Question 2 In the following example, try to identify the number of times the velocity of the ball changes

"A football player kicks a football to another player of his team who kicks the football towards the goal. The goalkeeper of the opposite team collects the football and kicks it towards a player of his own team."

Also identify the agent supplying the force in each case.

Sol. Given below are the number of times velocity of the ball changes.

Whenever a force is applied on the ball, the velocity of the ball changes.

(i) When first player kicks the ball towards another player of his team then the velocity of ball changes because first player applies some force on the ball.

(ii) When another player kicks the ball towards the goal, then the velocity of ball changes, again as a force is applied on the ball.

(iii) When goalkeeper of the opposite team collects the ball, then the velocity of ball changes to zero. Here the goalkeeper applies some force on the ball to stop it.

(iv) When the goalkeeper kicks the ball towards his own team, the velocity of the ball changes again because goalkeeper applies some force on the ball.

Question 3 Explain why some of the leaves may get detached from a tree if we vigorously shake its branch?

Sol. When a tree is vigorously shaken, the branches of the tree come in the state of motion but the leaves tend to maintain their state of rest because of inertia of rest, so leaves get detached from the tree and fall down.

Question 4 Why do you fall in the forward direction when a moving bus brakes to a stop and fall backwards when it accelerates from rest?

Sol. When a moving bus brakes suddenly to stop, the lower part of the body which is in contact with the bus comes in the state of rest, but the upper part of the body tends to maintain its state of motion because of inertia of motion due to which we fall in the forward direction.

Exercises

Question 1 An object experiences a net zero external unbalanced force. Is it possible for the object to be travelling with a non-zero velocity? If yes, state the conditions that must be placed on the magnitude and direction of the velocity. If no, provide a reason.

Sol. As per Newton's 1st law of motion, no force is needed to move an object which is moving with a constant (non-zero) velocity. So, when an object experiences a net zero external unbalanced force, then it can move with a non-zero velocity. Also, an object may not move at all, if it experiences a net zero external unbalanced force, if the object is initially at rest.

Question 2 When a carpet is beaten with a stick, dust comes out of it. Explain.

Sol. When a carpet is beaten with a stick, the fibres of the carpet attain the state of motion while the dust particles remain in rest due to inertia of rest. Therefore, the dust particles fall down.

Question 3 Why is it advised to tie any luggage kept on the roof of a bus with a rope?

Sol. It is advised to tie any luggage kept on the roof of a bus because when the bus stops suddenly then bus comes in the state of rest but the luggage remains in the state of motion due to inertia of motion. So, the luggage moves forward and falls down from the roof of the bus. Also, if the bus suddenly starts, then bus comes in the state of motion but luggage remains in the state of rest due to inertia of rest. So, the luggage moves in the backward direction and falls down.

Question 4 A batsman hits a cricket ball which then rolls on a level ground. After covering a short distance, the ball comes to rest. The ball slows to a stop because

(a) the batsman did not hit the ball hard enough.
(b) velocity is proportional to the force exerted on the ball.
(c) there is a force on the ball opposing the motion.
(d) there is no unbalanced force on the ball, so the ball would want to come to rest.

Sol. (c) The ball slows down to rest because the force of friction acting between the ground and the ball opposes the motion of the ball.

Question 5 A truck starts from rest and rolls down a hill with a constant acceleration. It travels a distance of 400 m in 20 s. Find its acceleration. Find the force acting on it if its mass is 7 tonnes. (Hint: 1 tonne = 1000 kg).

Sol. The truck starts from rest, so initial velocity, $u = 0$, distance, $s = 400$ m, $t = 20$ s, $m = 7$ tonnes $= 7 \times 1000 = 7000$ kg.

From 2nd equation of motion,

$$s = ut + \frac{1}{2}at^2$$

$$400 = 0 \times 20 + \frac{1}{2} \times a \times (20)^2$$

$$400 = 200\,a \Rightarrow a = 2 \text{ ms}^{-2}$$

From Newton's 2nd law of motion, force acting on the truck,

$$F = ma = 7000 \times 2 = 14000 \text{ N} = 1.4 \times 10^4 \text{ N}$$

Question 6 A stone of 1 kg is thrown with a velocity of 20 ms^{-1} across the frozen surface of a lake and comes to rest after travelling a distance of 50 m. What is the force of friction between the stone and the ice?

Sol. Mass of stone, $m = 1$ kg, initial velocity, $u = 20 \text{ ms}^{-1}$, final velocity, $v = 0$ ($\because$ the stone comes to rest), distance covered, $s = 50$ m.

From third equation of motion,

$$v^2 = u^2 + 2as$$

$$(0)^2 = (20)^2 + 2a\,(50)$$

$$100a = -400 \Rightarrow a = -4 \text{ ms}^{-2}$$

Here negative sign shows that there is retardation in the motion of stone.

Force of friction between stone and ice = Force required to stop the stone

$$= ma = 1 \times -4 = -4 \text{ N or } 4 \text{ N}$$

Question 7 A 8000 kg engine pulls a train of 5 wagons, each of 2000 kg, along a horizontal track. If the engine exerts a force of 40000 N and the track offers a friction force of 5000 N, then calculate

(a) the net accelerating force and

(b) the acceleration of the train.

◎ ***Thinking Process*** In this problem first calculate the net force by subtracting the frictional force from the engine's force. Then apply Newton's Second law to find the acceleration by dividing the net force by the total mass of the system.

Sol. (a) Net accelerating force = Force exerted by engine – Friction force

(Here frictional force is subtracted because it opposes the motion)

$$= 40000 - 5000$$
$$= 35000 \text{ N}$$
$$= 3.5 \times 10^4 \text{ N}$$

(b) From Newton's second law of motion,

Force = Mass of the train × Acceleration of train

$$a = \frac{F}{m}$$

Mass of train = Mass of engine + Mass of all wagons

$$= 8000 + 5 \times 2000$$
$$= 8000 + 10000 = 18000 \text{ kg}$$

$$\therefore \text{ Acceleration} = \frac{35000}{18000}$$
$$= \frac{35}{18} = 1.94 \text{ m s}^{-2}$$

Question 8 An automobile vehicle has a mass of 1500 kg. What must be the force between the vehicle and road if the vehicle is to be stopped with a negative acceleration of 1.7 ms^{-2}?

Sol. Mass, m = 1500 kg; Acceleration, $a = -1.7 \text{ ms}^{-2}$

From Newton's second law of motion,

$$F = ma = 1500 \times (-1.7) = -2550 \text{ N}$$

Question 9 What is the momentum of an object of mass m, moving with a velocity v?

(a) $(mv)^2$ (b) mv^2

(c) $\frac{1}{2} mv^2$ (d) mv

Sol. (d) The momentum of an object of mass m moving with a velocity v is

$$p = mv$$

Question 10 Using a horizontal force of 200 N, we intend to move a wooden cabinet across a floor at a constant velocity. What is the friction force that will be exerted on the cabinet?

Sol. The cabinet will move across the floor with constant velocity, if there is no net external force is acting on it. Here a horizontal force of 200 N is applied on the cabinet, so for the net force to be zero, an external force of 200 N must be exerted on the cabinet in opposite direction.

Thus, frictional force = 200 N

Note Frictional force always acts in the opposite direction of motion.

Question 11 According to the third law of motion, when we push on an object, the object pushes back on us with an equal and opposite force. If the object is a massive truck parked along the roadside, it will probably not move. A student justifies this by answering that the two opposite and equal forces cancel each other. Comment on this logic and explain why the truck does not move.

Sol. The logic given by the student is not correct because two equal and opposite forces cancel each other only in the case if they act on the same body. According to Newton's third law, action and reaction force always act on two different bodies, so they cannot cancel each other.

When a massive truck is pushed, then the truck may not move because the force applied is not sufficient to move the truck.

Note Newton's third law explains that action and reaction forces act on different objects and hence do not cancel each other. To move a massive object like a truck, the applied force must overcome the object's inertia and any opposing frictional forces.

Question 12 A hockey ball of mass 200 g travelling at 10 ms^{-1} is struck by a hockey stick so as to return it along its original path with a velocity at 5 ms^{-1}. Calculate the change of momentum occurred in the motion of the hockey ball by the force applied by the hockey stick.

Sol. Mass of hockey ball, $m = 200\text{ g} = 0.2\text{ kg}$

Initial velocity, $u = 10\text{ ms}^{-1}$

Final velocity, $v = -5\text{ ms}^{-1}$

($\because$ Final velocity of the ball is in the direction opposite to the direction of initial velocity.)

Change in momentum of the ball = Final momentum – Initial momentum

$$= mv - mu = m(v - u)$$

$$= 0.2(-5 - 10) = 0.2 \times -15 = -3\text{ kg ms}^{-1}$$

Question 13 A bullet of mass 10 g travelling horizontally with a velocity of 150 ms^{-1} strikes a stationary wooden block and comes to rest in 0.03 s. Calculate the distance of penetration of the bullet into the block. Also calculate the magnitude of the force exerted by the wooden block on the bullet.

Sol. Mass of bullet, $m = 10\text{ g} = \frac{10}{1000}\text{ kg} = 0.01\text{ kg}$

Initial velocity, $u = 150\text{ ms}^{-1}$

Final velocity, $v = 0$ ($\because$ The bullet comes to rest)

Time, $t = 0.03\text{ s}$

From equation of motion

$$v = u + at$$
$$0 = 150 + a \times 0.03$$
$$a = \frac{-150}{0.03} = -5000 \text{ ms}^{-2}$$

Distance covered by the bullet before coming to rest is given by

$$v^2 = u^2 + 2as$$
$$0 = (150)^2 + 2(-5000)s$$
$$s = \frac{(150)^2}{10000} = 2.25 \text{ m}$$

Magnitude of the force applied by the bullet on the block

$$F = ma = 0.01 \times -5000 = -50 \text{ N}$$

Mistake Alert Calculating force ($F = ma$), students might ignore the negative sign in acceleration resulting in +50 N instead of −50 N, which is incorrect. Since, the force is in the opposite direction of the bullets motion.

Question 14 An object of mass 1 kg travelling in a straight line with a velocity of 10 ms^{-1} collides with, and sticks to, a stationary wooden block of mass 5 kg. Then they both move off together in the same straight line. Calculate the total momentum just before the impact and just after the impact. Also, calculate the velocity of the combined object.

Thinking Process This question uses the law of conservation of momentum. Before the collision, only the smaller object is moving. After the collision, both objects stick together and move with the same velocity. So, total momentum before collision = total momentum after collision. Use this to find the common velocity.

Sol. Mass of object, $m_1 = 1$ kg,

Velocity, $u = 10 \text{ ms}^{-1}$

Mass of wooden block, $m_2 = 5$ kg

Velocity, $u_2 = 0$ ($\because$ Wooden block is at rest)

Total momentum just before the impact

= Momentum of object + Momentum of block

$= 1 \times 10 + 5 \times 0 = 10 \text{ kg ms}^{-1}$

According to law of conservation of momentum

Momentum after impact = Momentum before impact

$$(m_1 + m_2)\,v = 10$$

where, v = velocity of combined object

$$\Rightarrow \quad (1 + 5)\,v = 10$$
$$\Rightarrow \quad v = \frac{10}{6} = 1.67 \text{ ms}^{-1}$$

Question 15 An object of mass 100 kg is accelerated uniformly from a velocity of 5 ms^{-1} to 8 ms^{-1} in 6 s. Calculate the initial and final momentum of the object. Also, find the magnitude of the force exerted on the object.

Sol. Mass of the object, $m = 100$ kg

Initial velocity, $u = 5\ ms^{-1}$

Final velocity, $v = 8\ ms^{-1}$

(i) Initial momentum $= mu = 100 \times 5 = 500$ kg ms^{-1}

Final momentum $= mv$

$= 100 \times 8 = 800$ kg ms^{-1}

(ii) From Newton's second law, force exerted on the object = Rate of change of momentum,

$$\Rightarrow \quad F = \frac{\text{Change in momentum}}{\text{Time}}$$

$$= \frac{\text{Final momentum} - \text{Initial momentum}}{\text{Time}}$$

$$= \frac{800 - 500}{6} = \frac{300}{6} = 50\text{ N}$$

Question 16 Akhtar, Kiran and Rahul were riding in a motorcar that was moving with a high velocity on an expressway when an insect hit the windshield and got stuck on the windscreen. Akhtar and Kiran started pondering over the situation. Kiran suggested that the insect suffered a greater change in momentum as compared to the change in momentum of the motorcar (because the change in the velocity of the insect was much more than that of the motorcar). Akhtar said that since the motorcar was moving with a larger velocity, it exerted a larger force on the insect. And as a result the insect died. Rahul while putting an entirely new explanation said that both the motorcar and the insect experienced the same force and a change in their momentum. Comment on these suggestions.

Sol. Rahul's explanation is correct. This is because in absence of external force, the total momentum of the system remains conserved. So,

$$p^i_{insect} + p^i_{insect} = p^t_{car} - p^t_{car}$$

p^i stands for initial momentum and p^t stands for final momentum.

$$\Rightarrow \quad p^i_{insect} - p^t_{insect} = p^t_{car} - p^i_{car}$$

$\Rightarrow$ – Change in momentum of insect = change in momentum of car (– sign indicates that the difference of momentum of car and insect are opposite

Also, since change in momentum is same, they experience same force.

Question 17 How much momentum will a dumb-bell of mass 10 kg transfer to the floor if it falls from a height of 80 cm? Take its downward acceleration to be 10 ms^{-2}?

Sol. $m = 10$ kg, $u = 0$ (because it falls from rest)

Distance covered, $s = 80$ cm $= 0.8$ m

$$a = 10 \text{ ms}^{-2}$$

From equation of motion, $v^2 = u^2 + 2as$

$$v^2 = 0 + 2 \times 10 \times 0.8 = 16$$

$$\Rightarrow \quad v = \sqrt{16} = 4 \text{ ms}^{-1}$$

Momentum of dumb-bell just before it touches the floor,

$$p = mv = 10 \times 4 = 40 \text{ kg ms}^{-1}$$

When the dumb-bell touches the floor, its velocity becomes zero and hence, the momentum. Thus, the total momentum of the dumb-bell is transfered to the floor.

$\therefore$ The momentum transferred to floor = 40 kg ms^{-1}

Additional Exercises

Question 1 The following is the distance-time table of an object in motion.

Time (in seconds)	Distance (in metres)
0	0
1	1
2	8
3	27
4	64
5	125
6	216
7	343

(a) What conclusion can you draw about the acceleration? Is it constant, increasing, decreasing or zero?

(b) What do you infer about the force acting on the object?

Sol. (a) Here $u = 0$

Using $$s = ut + \frac{1}{2}at^2 = \frac{1}{2}at^2 \quad (\because u = 0)$$

We get $$a = \frac{2s}{t^2}$$

Time (in seconds)	Distance (in metres)	$a = 2s/t^2$
0	0	0
1	1	2
2	8	4
3	27	6
4	64	8
5	125	10
6	216	12
7	343	14

Thus, acceleration is increasing.

(b) Since, acceleration is increasing, so net unbalanced force is acting on the object.

Question 2 Two persons manage to push a motorcar of mass 1200 kg at a uniform velocity along a level road. The same motorcar can be pushed by three persons to produce an acceleration of 0.2 ms^{-2}. With what force does each person push the motorcar? (Assume that all persons push the motorcar with the same muscular effort.)

Sol. Mass of motorcar, $m = 1200$ kg

Acceleration produced, $a = 0.2 \text{ m s}^{-2}$

$\therefore$ Force applied on the car by three persons

$$F = ma$$

$$= 1200 \times 0.2 = 240 \text{ N}$$

Force applied on the car by one person $= \dfrac{240}{3} = 80$ N

Question 3 A hammer of mass 500 g, moving at 50 ms^{-1}, strikes a nail. The nail stops the hammer in a very short time of 0.01 s. What is the force of the nail on the hammer?

Sol. Mass of the hammer = 500 g = 0.05 kg

Initial velocity of hammer, $u = 50 \text{ ms}^{-1}$

Final velocity of hammer, $v = 0$ (Because the hammer stops)

Time $t = 0.01$ s

Force of the nail on the hammer

= Rate of change of momentum of hammer

$$= \frac{mv - mu}{t}$$

$$= \frac{0.5 \times 0 - 0.5 \times 50}{0.01}$$

$$= -\frac{25}{0.01} = -2500 \text{ N}$$

Question 4 A motorcar of mass 1200 kg is moving along a straight line with a uniform velocity of 90 kmh^{-1}. Its velocity is slowed down to 18 kmh^{-1} in 4 s by an unbalanced external force. Calculate the acceleration and change in momentum. Also calculate the magnitude of the force required.

Sol. Mass, $m = 1200$ kg

Initial velocity, $u = 90 \text{ km h}^{-1}$

$$= 90 \times \frac{5}{18} = 25 \text{ ms}^{-1}$$

Final velocity, $v = 18 \text{ kmh}^{-1} = 18 \times \frac{5}{18} = 5 \text{ ms}^{-1}$

Time, $t = 4$ s

(i) Acceleration $= \frac{v-u}{t} = \frac{5-25}{t} = -\frac{20}{4} = -5 \text{ m s}^{-2}$

(Here negative sign indicates that the velocity decreases)

(ii) Change in momentum = Final momentum – Initial momentum

$$= mv - mu$$
$$= m(v-u) = 1200\,(5-25)$$
$$= 1200 \times -20$$
$$= -24000 \text{ kg ms}^{-1}$$

(iii) Magnitude of the force required = Rate of change of momentum

$$= \frac{\text{Change in momentum}}{\text{Time}}$$
$$= \frac{-24000}{4} = -6000 \text{ N}$$

DIKSHA APP Questions

☐ Multiple Choice Questions

Q.1 To accelerate an object, which of the following is required

(a) Unbalanced force
(b) Balanced force
(c) Velocity
(d) Speed

Sol. (a) The produce an acceleration, net force on the object must be non-zero. Thus, an unbalance force is required.

Q.2 A boy applies a force of 15 N on a tree, the tree does not move. What is the amount of force applied by the tree on the boy?

(a) 10 N
(b) 20 N
(c) 8 N
(d) 15 N

Sol. (d) According to Newton's third law of motion, the force applied by the tree on the boy will be equal and opposite to the force applied by the boy on the tree which is 15 N.

☐ Very Short Answer Type

Q.1 A body of mass 5 kg is moving with an acceleration of 5 m/s^2. What is the rate of change of momentum?

Sol. According to Newton's 2nd law of motion,

Rate of change of momentum of an object = Force applied

$$\Rightarrow \quad \frac{\Delta p}{\Delta t} = ma$$

$$= 5 \times 5$$

$$= 25 \text{ N}$$

Q.2 Heavier bodies require greater force to put them in motion as compared to lighter bodies. Why?

Sol. According to Newton's second law of motion, $F = ma$, more the mass, more will be the inertia and hence, a greater force will be required to move the object.

Q.3 What is the principle of working of a rocket.

Sol. It is based on the principle of conservation of momentum.

□ Short Answer Type

Q.1 Two trucks of mass equal to 5000 kg are moving on a road. One is moving with velocity of 50 m/s while the other is moving with a velocity of 2 m/s. Calculate the force required to stop them in 20 seconds? Which one of them requires more force and why?

Sol. Initial momentum of truck 1 = Mass × Velocity = 5000 × 50 = 250000 kg ms^{-1}

Final momentum of truck 1 = 0 (∵ It is coming to rest)

Change in momentum, Δp = Final momentum – Initial momentum

$$= 0 - 250000 = -250000$$

$$\text{Force} = \frac{\text{Change in momentum}}{\text{Time}} \Rightarrow F = \frac{-250000}{20} = -12500 \text{ N (Time} = 20 \text{ s)}$$

(Negative sign indicates that it is a stopping force)

Similarly, initial momentum of truck 2 = 5000 × 2 = 10000 kg ms^{-1}

Final momentum of truck 2 = 0

$$\text{Force} = \frac{0 - 10000}{20} = -500 \text{ N}$$

Therefore, to stop truck 1 we need a greater force as we need to change its momentum by a larger amount as compared to truck 2.

Q.2 (i) State the law of conservation of momentum.

(ii) A man throws a ball of mass 0.4 kg vertically upwards with a velocity of 15 m/s. What will be its momentum at maximum height?

Sol. (i) The sum of momenta of two objects before collision is equal to the sum of momenta after collision provided there is no external unbalanced force acting on them. This is known as the law of conservation of momentum.

(ii) At maximum height, $v = 0 \Rightarrow p = mv = 0$.

Q.3 A target of mass 400 g moving with a horizontal speed of 10 m/s is hit by a bullet of mass 0.01 kg moving in opposite direction. If both the bullet and the target come to rest after the collision, calculate the velocity of the bullet at the time of striking the target.

Sol. Mass of target, m_1 = 400 g = 0.4 kg

Velocity of target, $u_1 = 10\ ms^{-1}$

Mass of bullet, $m_2 = 0.01\text{kg}$

Velocity of bullet, u_2 = ?

As no external force is acting on the system, total momentum of the system remains conserved.

$\Rightarrow \quad m_1u_1 + m_2u_2 = m_1v_1 + m_2v_2 \Rightarrow 0.4 \times 10 + 0.01 \times u_2 = 0$

(Since, bullet and target both comes to rest $v_1 = v_2 = 0$)

$\Rightarrow \quad u_2 = \dfrac{-4}{0.01} = -400 \text{ ms}^{-1}$

Here, negative sign represents that the direction of motion of bullet is opposite to the direction of motion of target.

☐ Long Answer Type

Q.1 The velocity-time graph of a car is shown in figure. The car weight 1000 kg.

(a) What is the distance travelled by the car in the first two seconds?

(b) What is the braking force applied at the end of 5 s to bring the car to a stop with in one second?

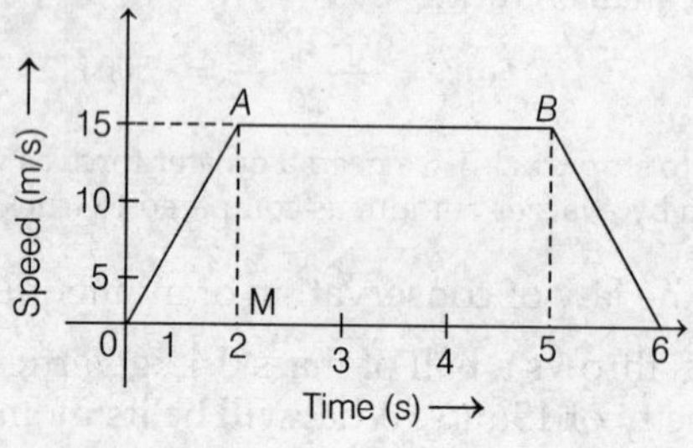

Sol. (a) Distance travelled by the car in the first two seconds = Area under the v-t graph between 0 to 2 s.

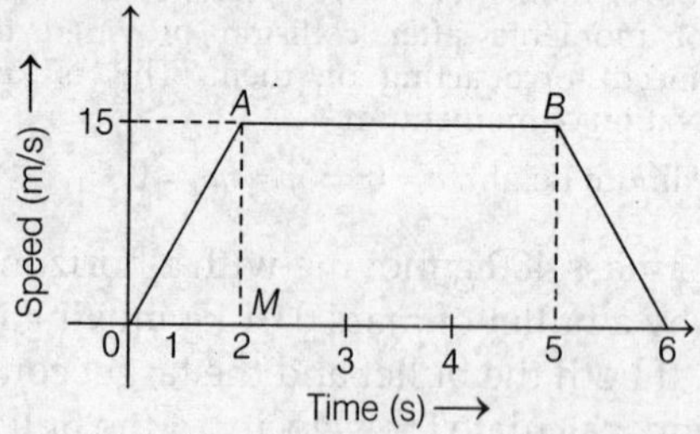

$\Rightarrow \quad s = \text{Area of } \Delta OAM$ (see figure)

$\Rightarrow \quad s = \dfrac{1}{2} \times OM \times AM \Rightarrow s = \dfrac{1}{2} \times 2 \times 15 = 15 \text{ m}$

(b) Retardation = Slope of BC

$\Rightarrow \quad a = \dfrac{0-15}{6-5} = -15 \text{ ms}^{-2}$

Force needed to stop the car $= ma \Rightarrow F = 1000 \times 15 = 15000$ N

Gravitation

CHAPTER 09

Important Points

01 Gravitation The force with which earth pulls everything towards itself is called gravitational force or gravity. Due to gravitational force

(i) all objects fall down when released from a height.

(ii) we can stand.

(iii) moon revolves around the earth, etc.

02 Newton's Universal Law of Gravitation "Every object in the universe attracts every other object with a force which is directly proportional to the product of their masses and inversely proportional to the square of distance between them."

This force acts along the line joining the centres of the two objects.

According to Newton's law of gravitation, force of attraction (F) between two objects of mass m_1 and m_2 having a distance r between their centres is

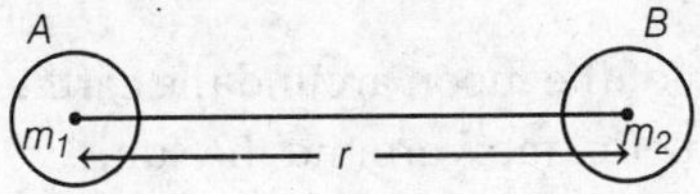

$$F = G\frac{m_1 m_2}{r^2}$$

where, G is called universal gravitational constant and its value is 6.67×10^{-11} Nm^2 kg^{-2}.

- Newton's gravitational law is said to be universal law because it is applicable to all bodies, whether the bodies are big or small, whether they are celestial or terrestrials.

- Though different object on earth attract one another but they do not cause any motion because the gravitational force acting between them is very small.
- Due to gravitation, earth keeps moving around the sun.
- Gravitational force holds the solar system together.
- Gravitational force applied by earth on a body of mass m placed on its surface is

$$F = G\frac{m_e m}{R_e^2}$$

where, m_e = mass of earth, R_e = radius of earth.

03 Characteristics of Gravitational Force

(i) Gravitational force is action at a distance *i.e.*, it does not need any contact between the two bodies.

(ii) Gravitational force is an **inverse square force** because it is inversely proportional to the square of the distance between the two bodies.

(iii) Gravitational force between two bodies form **action-reaction** pair.

(iv) Gravitational force is always attractive

(v) Gravitational force between two small bodies is very small. On the other hand, gravitational force between two large bodies (say the sun and the earth) is large.

04 Importance of Universal Law of Gravitation

Universal law of gravitation successfully explains several phenomena like:

(i) The motion of the moon around the earth.

(ii) The motion of planets around the sun.

(iii) The tides due to the moon and the sun.

05 Free Fall Whenever objects fall towards the earth under the earth's gravitational force alone, such object are called freely falling objects and such fall is called **Free Fall**.

- Whenever an object falls towards the earth, an acceleration is involved, this acceleration is due to the earth's gravitational pull and is called **acceleration due to gravity**.
- The acceleration with which an object falls towards the earth due to earth's gravitational pull is called acceleration due to gravity.

- Acceleration due to gravity is represented by g and its value at earth's surface is 9.8 ms^{-2}.

$$g = \frac{GM}{R^2}$$

Its SI unit is ms^{-2}. Here G = Universal gravitational constant. M = Mass of earth, R = Radius of earth.

- The value of g decreases with the height from the surface of earth.
- The value of g decreases with the depth into the crust of the earth.
- The value of g is more at poles and less at equator.
- The value of g does not depend on the mass of the object.

06 Equations of Motion for An object under the influence of gravitational Force of the Earth.

Equations of motion for the object moving under the influence of gravitational force of the earth are:

(i) $v = u + gt$ (ii) $h = ut + \frac{1}{2}gt^2$ (iii) $v^2 = u^2 + 2gh$

Note The only difference between the equations of motion for object moving in straight line is that in place of acceleration (a), we take acceleration due to gravity (g).

- If an object falls vertically downward then acceleration due to gravity is taken as positive ($\because$ its velocity increases while falling.)
- If an object is thrown vertically upward then acceleration due to gravity is taken as negative ($\because$ its velocity decreases as it moves upward.)
- If an object is dropped freely from a height, its initial velocity u is zero.
- If an object is thrown vertically upwards, its final velocity (v) becomes zero.
- Time taken by an object to fall from a height is same as that taken by it to rise to the same height.

07 Mass The total amount of matter contained in an object is called its mass.

- SI unit of mass is kilogram (kg).
- Mass of a body does not change from time to time, it remains constant.
- The mass of a body cannot be zero.

08 **Weight** The weight of an object on earth is the force with which it is attracted towards the earth.

Weight of an object $w = mg$

where, m = mass, g = acceleration due to gravity

or $$w = \frac{GMm}{R^2}$$

Here, M = mass of the earth, R = radius of the earth.

Note From the above formula it is clear that weight of object will change at same planet other than earth.

09 Weight of an object on the moon is 1/6th of the weight on the earth (because on the moon, the acceleration due to gravity is 1/6th that of earth's).

10 Weight is a vector quantity, it acts in vertically downward direction and its SI unit is newton (N). Weight of 1 kg mass is 9.8 newton.

11 Weight of an object is not constant, it changes from place to place.

12 In the space where $g = 0$, weight of an object is zero. At the centre of earth, weight of an object is zero.

13 **Thrust and Pressure**

- **Thrust** The force acting on an object perpendicular to its surface is called thrust.
- **Pressure** It is defined as the 'Normal force acting per unit surface area' or the thrust on unit area is called pressure.

$$\text{Pressure} = \frac{\text{Thrust}}{\text{Surface area}} \quad \text{or} \quad P = \frac{F}{A}$$

- Pressure is a scalar quantity, its SI unit is N m^{-2} or pascal (Pa).
- One pascal is defined as the pressure exerted on a unit surface area by a thrust of one newton.

14 **Some Daily Life Applications of Pressure**

- The handles of bags and suitcase etc, are made broad so that the small pressure is exerted on the hand.
- Building are provided with **broad foundations** so that the pressure exerted on the ground becomes less.
- Railway tracks are laid on cement or iron sleepers so that the pressure exerted by train is spread over a large area and thus becomes less.
- Pins, needles and nails are provided sharp pointed ends.
- Cutting tools have sharp edges.

15 Pressure in Fluids The substances which can flow are called fluids. Fluids have weight, so they exert pressure on the base and walls of the container in which they are enclosed. Pressure exerted in any confined mass of fluid is transmitted undiminished in all directions.

16 Buoyancy When an object is immersed in a liquid, then liquid exerts an upward force on the object, this phenomena is called buoyancy.

The upward force exerted by the liquid on the object immersed in it, is called upthrust or buoyant force. The magnitude of buoyant force depend on the density of the fluid.

- If the buoyant force applied by a liquid on an object is greater than the weight of the object then the object will float in that liquid.
- If buoyant force is less than the weight of the object then the object will sink in that liquid.
- The magnitude of buoyant force depends on the density of the liquid.

17 Floating or Sinking of Objects in Liquid Objects having density less than that of the liquid in which they are immersed, float on the surface of the liquid. If the density of the object is more than the density of the object in which it is immersed then it sinks in the liquid.

18 Archimedes' Principle When a body is immersed fully or partially in a fluid, it experiences an upward force that is equal to the weight of the fluid displaced by it.

Archimedes' principle is used in

(i) designing ships and submarines.

(ii) lactometer (used to determine density of liquid) is based on Archimedes' principle.

(iii) hydrometer (used for determining density of liquid) is based on Archimedes' principle.

19 Relative Density The relative density of a substance is the ratio of its density to that of water.

$$\text{Relative density} = \frac{\text{Density of a substance}}{\text{Density of water}}$$

Relative density is a ratio, so it has no unit.

Intext Questions

On Page 102

Question 1 State the universal law of gravitation.

Sol. According to universal law of gravitation, the force of attraction between two objects is directly proportional to the product of their masses and inversely proportional to the square of the distance between them.

Force of attraction between two objects of mass m_1 and m_2 placed at distance d apart is given by

$$F = G\frac{m_1 m_2}{d^2}$$

where, G = universal gravitational constant.

Question 2 Write the formula to find the magnitude of the gravitational force between the earth and an object on the surface of the earth.

Sol. The force of attraction between the earth and an object on its surface is given by

$$F = \frac{GMm}{R^2}$$

where, G = Universal gravitational constant,
M = Mass of earth,
m = Mass of object,
R = Radius of earth.

(Here we have considered that the whole mass of earth is concentrated at its centre.)

On Page 104

Question 1 What do you mean by free fall?

Sol. When an object falls towards the earth under the effect of earth's gravitational pull alone, then the object is said to be in free fall.

Question 2 What do you mean by acceleration due to gravity?

Sol. The acceleration that an object has in its free fall towards earth is called acceleration due to gravity. For earth, the value of acceleration due to gravity is $9.8\ \text{m-s}^{-2}$.

On Page 106

Question 1 What are the differences between the mass of an object and its weight?

Sol. The differences between mass and weight of an object are given below:

S.No.	Mass	Weight
1.	The quantity of matter contained in a body is called the mass of the body.	The force with which the earth attracts a body towards its centre is called the weight of the body.
2.	Mass of a body remains constant.	Weight of a body changes from place to place.
3.	Mass of a body is never zero.	Weight of a body at the centre of the earth is zero.
4.	Mass is a scalar quantity.	Weight is a vector quantity.
5.	Mass is measured in kg.	Weight is measured in kgf or N.
6.	Mass is measured by a beam balance.	Weight is measured by a weighing machine or a spring balance.

Question 2 Why is the weight of an object on the moon $\frac{1}{6}$ th its weight on the earth?

◎ ***Thinking Process*** The weight difference between the earth and the moon is due to their different gravitational accelerations.

Sol. Weight of an object on earth,

$$W_e = \frac{GM_e m}{R_e^2} \text{ and } W_e = mg_e \Rightarrow g_e = \frac{GM_e}{R_e^2}$$

Here, M_e is not mass of earth, M is mass of object and R_e is radius of earth.

Now weight of an object on Moon,

$$W_m = \frac{GM_m m}{R_m^2} \text{ and } W_m = mg_m \Rightarrow g_m = \frac{GM_m}{R_m^2}$$

Here, M_m is mass of moon, m is mass of the object and R_m is radius of moon.

Now, $$\frac{w_e}{w_m} = \left(\frac{GM_e}{R_e^2}\right) \times \left(\frac{R_m^2}{GM_m}\right) = \frac{g_e}{g_m}$$

As, acceleration due to gravity on earth is 6 times that on moon, $g_e = 6\,\text{gm}$

$$\Rightarrow \frac{g_e}{g_m} = 6$$

On substituting, we get $\frac{W_e}{W_m} = 6$ or $W_m = \frac{1}{6} w_e$.

On Page 109

Question 1 Why is it difficult to hold a school bag having a strap made of a thin and strong string?

Sol. It is difficult to hold a school bag having a strap made of a thin and strong string because the area of contact between strap and skin is small. Hence, large pressure is exerted by the strap on the fingers or shoulders.

Due to the large pressure, the strap tends to cut the skin and hence pain is caused.

Question 2 What do you mean by buoyancy?

Sol. The tendency of an object to float in a liquid or the ability of liquid to make an object float in it, is called buoyancy.

Question 3 Why does an object float or sink when placed on the surface of water?

Sol. When an object is placed on the surface of water, two forces acts on the object.

(i) The weight of the object, acting vertically downward.

(ii) The upthrust of the water, acting vertically upward.

The object will float on the surface of water if the upthrust is greater than the weight of the object. The object will sink if the weight of the object is more than the upthrust of the water.

On Page 110

Question 1 You find your mass to be 42 kg on a weighing machine. Is your mass more or less than 42 kg?

Sol. A weighing machine measures the mass of the object by calculating its weight. Which we stand on a weighing machine, we all experience a buoyant force due to air in the upward direction due to which our apparent weight decreases. Thus, the reading of the mass calculated by the machine using the formula $m = \frac{W}{g}$ will be less than the actual mass.

So, we can say the person's mass is more than 42 kg.

Question 2 You have a bag of cotton and an iron bar, each indicating a mass of 100 kg when measured on a weighing machine. In reality, one is heavier than other. Can you say which one is heavier and why?

Sol. Cotton bag has a larger area than an iron bar and therefore experiences greater upthrust (buoyant force). So the weighing machine shows less mass of a cotton bag as compared to an iron bar.

Therefore, if the machine is showing equal mass for both cotton bag and iron bar, this means that cotton bag is heavier than an iron bar in reality.

Exercises

Question 1 How does the force of gravitation between two objects change when the distance between them is reduced to half?

Sol. Force of gravitation between two objects, $F = G\frac{m_1 m_2}{r^2}$

If distance is reduced to half *i.e.*, $r' = r/2$

Then new force of gravitation, $F' = \frac{Gm_1 m_2}{r'^2}$

$$= \frac{Gm_1 m_2}{(r/2)^2}$$

$$= 4\frac{Gm_1 m_2}{r^2} = 4F$$

i.e., the force of gravitation becomes 4 times than the original value.

Question 2 Gravitational force acts on all objects in proportion to their masses. Why then, a heavy object does not fall faster than a light object?

Sol. Each object falls towards the earth with an acceleration, equal to acceleration due to gravity, which is approximately constant (9.8 ms^{-2}) and does not depend on the mass of the object. So, heavy object does not fall faster than the light object.

Question 3 What is the magnitude of the gravitational force between the earth and a 1 kg object on its surface? (Mass of the earth is 6×10^{24} kg and radius of the earth is 6.4×10^6 m.)

Sol. Gravitational force between the earth and an object,

$$F = \frac{GMm}{R^2}$$

where, G = Gravitational constant = $6.67 \times 10^{-11} \text{ Nm}^2 \text{ kg}^{-2}$

M = Mass of earth = 6×10^{24} kg,

R = Radius of earth = 6.4×10^6 m

m = Mass of object = 1 kg

$$\therefore \quad F = \frac{6.67 \times 10^{-11} \times 6 \times 10^{24} \times 1}{(6.4 \times 10^6)^2}$$

$$= 9.8 \text{ N}$$

Mistake Alert A common mistake in this calculation is to incorrectly square the radius or forget the exponent rules during multiplication. Be cautions with each power of 10 in the calculations to avoid errors.

Question 4 The earth and the moon are attracted to each other by gravitational force. Does the earth attract the moon with a force that is greater or smaller or the same as the force with which the moon attracts the earth? Why?

Sol. When two objects attract each other then gravitational force of attraction applied by first object on the second object is same as the force applied by the second object on the first object as a consequence of Newton's third law of motion. So, both earth and moon attract each other by the same gravitational force of attraction.

Question 5 If the moon attracts the earth, why does the earth not move towards the moon?

Sol. The earth and the moon attract each other with the same force. However, since $a = \frac{F}{M}$, this means that for the same force, greater the mass, less is the acceleration. The mass of the earth is very large in comparison to the moon and so the acceleration produced is very small and so the earth does not seem to move towards the moon.

Question 6 What happens to the force between two objects, if

(i) the mass of one object is doubled?

(ii) the distance between the objects is doubled and tripled?

(iii) the masses of both objects are doubled?

Sol. Force of attraction between two objects, $F = \frac{Gm_1 m_2}{r^2}$

where, m_1, m_2 = masses of the objects,

r = distance between the objects, G = gravitational constant.

(i) If mass of one object is doubled, then the new force

$$F' = \frac{G(2m_1)\, m_2}{r^2}$$

$$= 2\frac{Gm_1 m_2}{r^2} = 2F$$

i.e., force becomes double.

(ii) If the distance between the objects is doubled, then the new force

$$F' = \frac{Gm_1 m_2}{(2r)^2} = \frac{Gm_1 m_2}{4r^2}$$

$$= \frac{1}{4}\frac{Gm_1 m_2}{r^2}$$

$$= \frac{1}{4}(F)$$

$$= \frac{F}{4}$$

i.e., force becomes one-fourth.

If the distance between the objects is tripled, then

$$\text{new force } F' = \frac{Gm_1 m_2}{(3r)^2} = \frac{Gm_1 m_2}{9r^2}$$

$$= \frac{1}{9}\left(\frac{Gm_1 m_2}{r^2}\right)$$

$$= \frac{1}{9}F = \frac{F}{9}$$

i.e., force becomes one-ninth.

(iii) If masses of both objects are doubled, then

$$\text{new force } F' = \frac{G(2m_1)(2m_2)}{r^2}$$

$$= 4\frac{Gm_1 m_2}{r^2} = 4F$$

i.e., force becomes four times.

Mistake Alert Be careful with distance changes. Remember that the gravitational force varies with the square of the distance, so any change in distance will have a squared effect on the force.

Question 7 What is the importance of universal law of gravitation?

Sol. The importance of universal law of gravitation can be understood from the following points:

(i) All the planets revolve around the sun due to gravitational force between the sun and planets. Hence gravitational force is responsible for the existence of solar system.

(ii) Tides in oceans are formed due to the gravitational force between the moon and water in oceans.

(iii) Artificial satellites revolve around the earth due to gravitational force of earth.

(iv) The atmosphere of the earth is attached with it due to gravitational force of earth.

(v) We can stand on the surface of earth due to gravitational force of earth.

Question 8 What is the acceleration of free fall?

Sol. The acceleration of free fall is the acceleration experienced by an object when it falls fieely towards the earth. It is also called acceleration due to gravity. Its value on earth's surface is 9.8 m s^{-2}.

Question 9 What do we call the gravitational force between the earth and an object?

Sol. The gravitational force between the earth and an object is called force of gravity.

Question 10 Amit buys few grams of gold at the poles as per the instruction of one of his friends. He hands over the same when he meets him at the equator. Will the friend agree with the weight of the gold bought. If not, why?
[**Hint** The value of g is greater at the poles than at the equator.]

Sol. Weight of an object, $w = mg$

where, g = acceleration due to gravity
The value of g is greater at the poles than at the equator. So, the weight of the gold at the equator will be less than the weight of the gold at poles. So, Amit's friend will find the weight of the gold less than the weight told by Amit.

Question 11 Why will a sheet of paper fall slower than one that is crumpled into a ball?

Sol. The sheet of paper falls slower than one that is crumpled into a ball because the area of the sheet is more so it experiences large opposing force due to air. While the sheet crumpled into a ball experience less opposing force due to its small area.

Question 12 Gravitational force on the surface of the moon is only $\frac{1}{6}$ as strong as gravitational force on the earth. What is the weight in newtons of a 10 kg object on the moon and on the earth?

Sol. Mass of the object $m = 10$ kg

Weight on the earth $w = mg = 10 \times 9.8 = 98$ N

Weight on the moon $= \frac{1}{6}$ of the weight on the earth

$$= \frac{1}{6} \times 98 = 16.33 \text{ N}$$

Question 13 A ball is thrown vertically upwards with a velocity of 49 ms^{-1}. Calculate

(i) the maximum height to which it rises,

(ii) the total time it takes to return to the surface of the earth.

Sol. Initial velocity, $u = 49 \text{ ms}^{-1}$

(i) At the maximum height velocity becomes zero,

[$a = -g$ as speed is decreasing]

$\therefore$ Final velocity, $v = 0$

From 3rd equation of motion, $v^2 = u^2 - 2gh$

$$0 = (49)^2 - 2 \times 9.8 \times h$$

$$\therefore \quad h = \frac{(49)^2}{2 \times 9.8} = 122.5 \text{ m}$$

Maximum height attained = 122.5 m

(ii) Time taken by the ball to reach the maximum height.

[$a = -g$ as speed is decreasing]

From 1st equation of motion, $v = u - gt$

$$0 = 49 - 9.8 \times t$$

$$t = \frac{49}{9.8} = 5\text{ s}$$

In the motion against gravity, the time of descent is same as the time of ascent.

So, time taken by the ball to fall from maximum height = 5 s

$\therefore$ Total time taken by the ball to return to surface of the earth

$$= 5 + 5 = 10\text{ s}$$

Question 14 A stone is released from the top of a tower of height 19.6 m. Calculate its final velocity just before touching the ground.

Sol. Given, $h = 19.6$ m

Initial velocity, $u = 0$ ($\because$ It starts from rest)

From equation of motion, $v^2 = u^2 + 2gh$

$$v^2 = 0 + 2 \times 9.8 \times 19.6 = 19.6 \times 19.6$$

$$\therefore \quad v = \sqrt{19.6 \times 19.6}$$

$$= 19.6\text{ ms}^{-1}$$

Final velocity of stone just before touching the ground = 19.6 m s^{-1}

Question 15. A stone is thrown vertically upward with an initial velocity of 40 ms^{-1}. Taking $g = 10\text{ ms}^{-2}$, find the maximum height reached by the stone. What is the net displacement and the total distance covered by the stone?

Sol. Initial velocity, $u = 40\text{ ms}^{-1}$

At maximum height, final velocity becomes zero *i.e.*, $v = 0$

From equation of motion $v^2 = u^2 - 2gh$,

$$(0)^2 = (40)^2 - 2 \times 10 \times h$$

$$\Rightarrow \quad 0 = 1600 - 20h$$

$$\Rightarrow \quad h = \frac{1600}{20} = 80\text{ m}$$

$\therefore$ Maximum height reached by the stone = 80 m

After reaching the maximum height, the stone will fall towards the earth and will reach the earth surface covering the same distance.

So, distance covered by the stone = 80 + 80 = 160 m

Displacement of the stone = 0

(because the stone starts from the earth surface and finally reaches the earth surface again, *i.e.*, the initial and final position of the stone are same)

Question 16 Calculate the force of gravitation between the earth and the sun, given that the mass of the earth $= 6 \times 10^{24}$ kg and of the sun $= 2 \times 10^{30}$ kg. The average distance between them is 1.5×10^{11} m.

Sol. The force of attraction between the earth and the sun

$$F = \frac{G M_s M_e}{r^2}$$

where, $G = 6.67 \times 10^{-11}$ Nm^2 kg^{-2}

Given, mass of the sun, $M_s = 2 \times 10^{30}$ kg

Mass of the earth, $M_e = 6 \times 10^{24}$ kg

Average distance between the earth and the sun $= 1.5 \times 10^{11}$

$$\therefore \quad F = \frac{6.67 \times 10^{-11} \times 2 \times 10^{30} \times 6 \times 10^{24}}{(1.5 \times 10^{11})^2}$$

$$= 3.6 \times 10^{22} \text{ N}$$

Question 17 A stone is allowed to fall from the top of a tower 100 m high and at the same time another stone is projected vertically upwards from the ground with a velocity of 25 ms^{-1}. Calculate when and where the two stones will meet.

◎ *Thinking Process* In this question, we need to find the time when two stones, one dropped from a height and another projected upwards, will meet. To approach this, we can use $S = ut + \frac{1}{2} gt^2$ to calculate the distance travelled by each stone until they meet

Sol. Let after time t both stone meet and s be the distance travelled by the stone dropped from the top of tower to the point where the stones will meet.

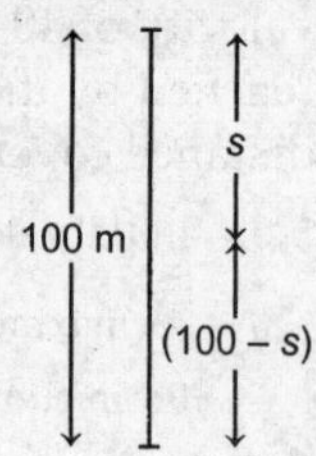

Distance travelled by the stone dropped = s

$\therefore$ Distance travelled by the stone projected upwards $= (100 - s)$

For the stone dropped from the tower,

$$s = ut + \frac{1}{2} gt^2$$

$$\Rightarrow \quad s = 0 + \frac{1}{2}(10)t^2$$

($u = 0$, because stone is dropped *i.e.*, it starts from rest)

$$\Rightarrow \quad s = 5t^2 \quad \ldots \text{(i)}$$

For the stone projected upward, $s' = ut - \frac{1}{2} gt^2$

(Due to upward motion negative sign of acceleration is taken)

$$(100 - s) = 25t - \frac{1}{2} \times 10t^2$$

$$\Rightarrow \quad 100 - s = 25t - 5t^2$$

From Eq. (i)

$$100 - 5t^2 = 25\,t - 5t^2$$

$$\Rightarrow \quad 25t = 100$$

$$\Rightarrow \quad t = 4\text{ s}$$

$\therefore$ The stones will meet after 4 s

$$s = 5t^2 = 5 \times (4)^2 = 80\text{ m}$$

$\therefore$ The stones will be at a distance of 80 m from the top of tower or 20 m (100 m – 80 m) from the base of the tower.

Question 18 A ball thrown up vertically returns to the thrower after 6 s. Find

(a) the velocity with which it was thrown up,
(b) the maximum height it reaches, and
(c) its position after 4 s.

◎ ***Thinking Process*** In this question, the concept of vertical motion under gravity is applied. When a ball is thrown upwards it, decelerates until it reaches its maximum height and accelerates downward.

Sol. Total time taken = 6 s

$\therefore$ Time taken to reach the maximum height $= \frac{6}{2} = 3$ s

($\because$ time of ascent = time of descent)

(a) From equation of motion, $v = u - gt$

(Negative sign is taken due to upward motion)

$$0 = u - 9.8 \times 3 \quad (\because \text{At maximum height } v = 0)$$

$$u = 29.4\text{ ms}^{-1}$$

(b) From equation of motion,

$$v^2 = u^2 - 2gh$$

$$0 = (29.4)^2 - 2 \times 9.8 \times h$$

$$h = \frac{(29.4)^2}{2 \times 9.8} = 44.1\text{ m}$$

Maximum height attained by the ball is 44.1 m.

(c) In initial 3 s, the ball will rise then in next 3 s it falls toward the earth.

$\therefore$ The position after 4 s (3 + 1)

= Distance covered in 1 s in the downward motion

From equation of motion, $s = ut + \frac{1}{2}gt^2$

$$= 0 + \frac{1}{2} \times 9.8 \times (1)^2$$

$$= 4.9\text{ m}$$

i.e., the ball will be at 4.9 m from the top of the tower.

Question 19 In what direction does the buoyant force on an object immersed in a liquid act?

Sol. The buoyant force on an object immersed in a liquid always act in upward direction.

Question 20 Why does a block of plastic released under water come up to the surface of water?

Sol. The upthrust or buoyant force acting on the block of plastic by the water is greater than the weight of the plastic block. So, plastic block comes up to the surface of water.

Question 21 The volume of 50g of a substance is 20 cm^3. If the density of water is 1 g cm^{-3}, will the substance float or sink.

Sol. Mass of substance = 50 g

Volume of substance = 20 cm^3

$$\therefore \text{Density of substance, } d = \frac{\text{Mass}}{\text{Volume}}$$

$$= \frac{50}{20} = 1.25 \text{ g cm}^{-3}$$

i.e., the density of the substance is greater than the density of water, so it will sink in water.

Question 22 The volume of a 500 g sealed packet is 350 cm^3. Will the packet float or sink in water if the density of water is 1 gcm^{-3}? What will be the mass of the water displaced by this packet?

Sol. Mass of packet = 500 g

Volume of packet = 350 cm^3

$$\therefore \text{Density of packet, } d = \frac{\text{Mass}}{\text{Volume}}$$

$$= \frac{500}{350} = 1.43 \text{ g cm}^{-3}$$

i.e., the density of packet is greater than density of water, so it will sink in water.

Mass of water displaced by the packet

= Volume of packet × Density of water

= 350 × 1 = 350 g

DIKSHA APP Questions

☐ Multiple Choice Questions

Q.1 The relation between g/cm^3 and kg/m^3 unit of density is

(a) 1,000 kg/m^3 equals 1 g/cm^3

(b) 2.1 kg/m^3 equals 1000 g/cm^3

(c) 1,000 kg/m^3 equals 10 g/cm^3

(d) 141,000 kg/m^3 equals 100 g/cm^3

Sol. (a) $$1\ kg/m^3 = \frac{1\ kg}{1\ m^3} = \frac{1000\ g}{(100\ cm)^3} = \frac{1000\ g}{1000000\ cm^3} = 10^{-3}\ \frac{g}{cm^3}$$

or $$1\frac{g}{cm^3} = 1000\ \frac{kg}{m^3}$$

Q.2 An object weighing 5N in air, weighs 4.5 N in a liquid. The buoyant force experienced by the object is

(a) 0.05 N (b) 4.5 N (c) 0.5 N (d) 1.5 N

Sol. (c) Weight in liquid = Weight in air – Buoyant force

$\Rightarrow$ $$w_L = w_a - F_B$$

Given, $w_a = 5$ N, $w_L = 4.5$ N

$\Rightarrow$ $$4.5 = 5 - F_B$$

$\Rightarrow$ $$F_B = 0.5\ N$$

Q.3 The value of acceleration due to gravity 'g'.

(a) Is same on equator and poles (b) Is least on poles

(c) Is least on equator (d) Increases from pole to equator

Sol. (c) The value of acceleration due to gravity 'g' is lowest on equator and highest at poles.

☐ Very Short Answer Type

Q.1 The density of gold is 19300 kg/m^3 and that of water is 1000 kg/m^3. What is the relative density of gold?

Sol. $$\text{Relative density} = \frac{\text{Density of substance}}{\text{Density of water}}$$

Here, density of gold = 19300 kg m^{-3}

and, density of water = 1000 kg m^{-3}

$$\therefore \text{Relative density of gold} = \frac{19300}{1000} = 19.3$$

Q.2 A force of 20 N distributed uniformly over an area of 20 cm^2, find pressure in Pascal.

Sol. Force, $F = 20$ N

Area, $A = 20\ cm^2 = 20 \times (10^{-2}\ m)^2$ $\quad (\because 1\ cm = 10^{-2}\ m)$

$= 20 \times 10^{-4}\ m^2$

Pressure, $P = \frac{F}{A} = \frac{20}{20 \times 10^{-4}} = 10^4$ Pa

☐ Short Answer Type

Q.1 Two bodies of mass 10 kg and 100 kg respectively dropped from the same height 4.9 m in vacuum. Calculate and compare their final velocities just before hitting the ground.

Sol. For object 1

$m = 10$ kg, $u = 0$, $s = 4.9$ m, $a = 9.8\ ms^{-2}$

Using 3rd equation of motion,

$v^2 = u^2 + 2as \Rightarrow v^2 = 0^2 + 2 \times 4.9 \times 9.8$

$\Rightarrow \quad v = \sqrt{9.8 \times 9.8} \Rightarrow v = 9.8\ ms^{-1}$

For object 2

$M = 100$ kg, $u = 0$, $s = 4.9$ m, $a = 9.8\ ms^{-2}$

Using 3rd equation of motion, $v^2 = u^2 + 2as$

On putting the values, we will get, $v = 9.8\ ms^{-1}$

Thus, both the objects reach the ground with same velocity.

This velocity is independent of mass and so a lighter and heavier object when dropped from a certain height reach with the same velocity.

Q.2 Find the volume of stone immersed in the liquid in the given figure.

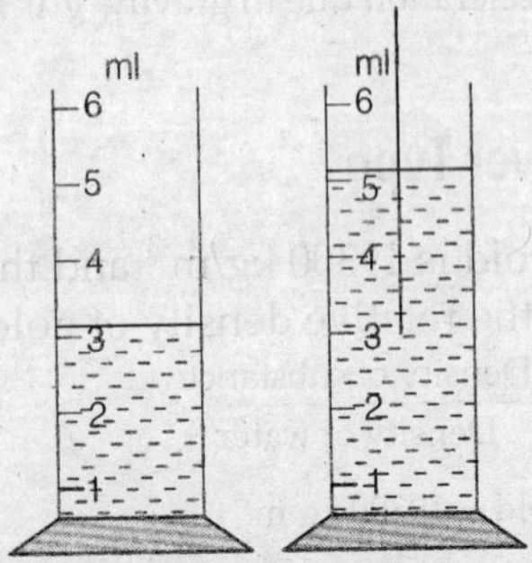

Sol. Volume of stone = Rise in water level

$\Rightarrow \quad V$ = Final reading – Initial reading $= 5 - 3 = 2$ ml

Q.3 When a body is thrown vertically upwards, what will be its velocity at maximum height?

Sol. The body's kinetic energy is completely converted into potential energy at maximum height. This means that the velocity at this point is zero because at the maximum height the body momenterity comes to rest betore it starts falling back down.

☐ Long Answer Type

Q.1 A man is standing at the top of a 60 m high tower. He throws a ball vertically with a velocity of 20 m/s. After what time, will the ball pass him going downwards? How long after its release, will the ball reach the ground?

Sol. Initial velocity, $u = 20$ m/s

Final velocity at maximum height, $v = 0$

Acceleration, $a = -10\ \text{m/s}^2$ (negative sign indicates that the velocity is decreasing)

Time taken to reach the maximum height can be calculated by using first equation of motion, $v = u + at$

$$\Rightarrow \qquad 0 = 20 - 10t \quad \Rightarrow \quad t = \frac{20}{10} = 2\text{ s}$$

Time taken by the ball to pass the man = $2 \times t = 2 \times 2 = 4$

At the point where the ball passes the man, velocity, $u = 20$ m/s

(Since, the upward motion and downward motion is symmetric, at all points the upward velocity is same as downward velocity)

distance covered, $s = 60$ m (Since, height of tower is 60 m)

Acceleration, $a = 10\ \text{m/s}^2$

Using second equation of motion to calculate the time required by the ball to hit the ground from the point when the man is standing,

$$s = ut + \frac{1}{2}at^2$$

$$\Rightarrow \qquad 60 = 20t + \frac{1}{2}(10) \times t^2 \Rightarrow 60 = 20t + 5t^2$$

$$\Rightarrow \qquad t^2 + 4t - 12 = 0 \Rightarrow t^2 + 6t - 2t - 12 = 0$$

[Using method of factorisation to solve the quadratic equation]

$$\Rightarrow \qquad t(t+6) - 2(t+6) = 0$$

$$\Rightarrow \qquad (t+6)(t-2) = 0$$

$$\Rightarrow \qquad t = -6 \text{ or } t = 2$$

Since, $t = -6$ is not possible. Therefore, time taken to hit the ground after passing the man is 2s.

Q.2 (i) Define relative density.

(ii) Relative densities of two substances A and B are 2.5 and 0.9 respectively. Find densities of A and B. Also find whether they will sink or float in water. (Density of water $= 1000\ kg/m^3$).

Sol. (i) The relative density of a substance is the ratio of its density to that the water.

(ii) Relative density (RD) $= \dfrac{\text{density of substance}}{\text{density of water}}$

RD of $A = 2.5 = \dfrac{\text{density of } A}{1000\ kg/m^3}$

$\Rightarrow$ density of $A = 2.5 \times 10^3\ kg/m^3$

Similarly, RD of $B = 0.9 = \dfrac{\text{density of } B}{1000\ kg/m^3}$

$\Rightarrow$ density of $B = 0.9 \times 10^3\ kg/m^3$

Substance A will sink in water as it is denser then water whereas substance B will float in water as it is lighter than water.

Work and Energy

CHAPTER 10

Important Points

01 Work is said to be done if on applying a force on an object, displaces it.

If a constant force F acts on an object and object is displaced through a distances in the direction of force, then work,

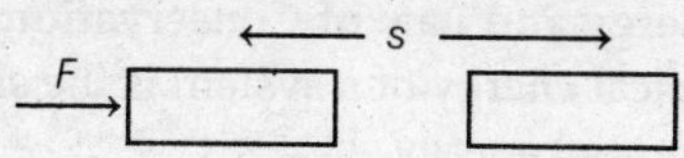

$$W = F \cdot s$$

- SI unit of work is joule and it is a scalar quantity.
- If there is an angle θ between the direction of force and direction of displacement, then

$$\text{Work, } W = Fs \cos \theta$$

- If the direction of displacement is perpendicular to the direction of force, then work done by the force on the object is zero, $w = 0$.

02 Energy The ability of a body to do some work is called energy. It is a scalar quantity and its SI unit is joule.

Larger unit of energy is kilojoule (kJ).

$$1 \text{ kJ} = 1000 \text{ J}$$

There are many forms of energies like mechanical energy (kinetic energy + potential energy), heat energy, chemical energy, light energy etc.

03 Kinetic energy The energy possessed by a moving body by virtue of its motion is called kinetic energy.

Kinetic energy possessed by an object of mass (m), moving with velocity (v), is

$$E_k = \frac{1}{2} mv^2$$

04 Potential Energy The energy possessed by an object by virtue of its position or configuration is called potential energy.

If an object of mass (m) is placed at height (h) above the earth surface, then the work done in lifting the object is stored in the form of gravitational potential energy.

The potential energy of an object at a height (h) depends on the ground level or the zero level. An object in a given position can have a certain potential energy with respect to another level.

05 Law of Conservation of Energy According to law of conservation of energy, energy can only be converted from one form to another, it can neither be created nor be destroyed. The total energy before and after the transformation remains same. This law is valid in all situations and for all kinds of transformations.

06 Mechanical energy and Law of Conservation of Mechanical energy Mechanical energy of a system is the sum of its kinetic energy and potential energy.

Law of conservation of mechanical energy states that in absence of frictional forces, the total mechanical energy of a system remains constant *i.e.*, $mgh + \frac{1}{2}mv^2 = \text{constant}$.

07 Power : Rate of Doing work Power is defined as the rate of doing work or the rate of transfer of energy. If an object does a work W in time t, then the power is given by

$$\text{Power} = \frac{\text{Work}}{\text{Time}} = \frac{W}{t}$$

Its SI unit is watt (W)

08 Average Power Average power is obtained by dividing the total energy consumed by the total time taken.

09 Commercial Unit of Energy The unit joule is too small. So, it is inconvenient to express large quantity of energy in kilo joule. A bigger unit called kWh is used to express large quantity of energies. It is called commercial unit of energy.

$$1 \text{ kWh} = 3.6 \times 10^6 \text{ J}$$

The energy used in house holds, industries and commercial establishment are usually expressed in kilowatt hour. (1 kWh) and it is also called 1 unit.

Intext Questions

On Page 115

Question 1 A force of 7 N acts on an object. The displacement is, say 8 m, in the direction of the force as shown in figure. Let us take it that the force acts on the object through the displacement. What is the work in this case?

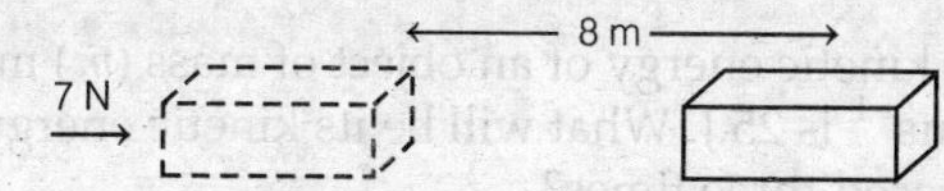

Sol. Given, Force, $F = 7$ N

Displacement, $s = 8$ m

$\therefore$ Work done, $W = F \cdot s$

$= 7 \times 8 = 56$ N-m or 56 J

On Page 116

Question 1 When do we say that work is done?

Sol. Work is said to be done when force acts on an object and displaces it from its initial position.

Question 2 Write an expression for the work done when a force is acting on an object in the direction of its displacement.

Sol. Expression for the work done when the displacement is along the direction of the force, is

$$W = Fs$$

where, F = force applied, s = displacement.

Question 3 Define 1 J of work.

Sol. Work is said to be 1 J, if 1 N force displaces an object through 1 metre in its own direction.

Question 4 A pair of bullocks exerts a force of 140 N on a plough. The field being ploughed is 15 m long. How much work is done in ploughing the length of the field?

Sol. Given, applied force, $F = 140$ N

Displacement, $s = 15$ m

Work done in ploughing the field, $W = F \cdot s$

$= 140 \times 15 = 2100 \text{ J} = 2.1 \times 10^3$ J

On Page 119

Question 1 What is the kinetic energy of an object?

Sol. The energy possessed by an object by virtue of its motion is known as the kinetic energy of the object.

Question 2 Write the expression for the kinetic energy of an object.

Sol. The expression for the kinetic energy of an object, $K = \frac{1}{2} mv^2$

where, m = mass of the object, v = velocity of the object.

Question 3 The kinetic energy of an object of mass (m) moving with a velocity of 5 ms^{-1} is 25 J. What will be its kinetic energy when its velocity is increased three times?

Sol. Kinetic energy, $K = \frac{1}{2} mv^2$

where, m = mass of object, v = velocity of the object.

Here, mass (m) is same in both cases ($\because$ object is same).

$$\therefore \quad \frac{K_1}{K_2} = \left(\frac{v_1}{v_2}\right)^2$$

Initial kinetic energy (K_1) = 25 J,

Initial velocity (v_1) = 5 ms^{-1},

New kinetic energy (K_2) = ?

New velocity (v_2) = $3v_1 = 3 \times 5 = 15$ ms^{-1}

$$\therefore \quad \frac{25}{K_2} = \left(\frac{5}{15}\right)^2 \Rightarrow \frac{25}{K_2} = \frac{1}{9} \Rightarrow K_2 = 225 \text{ J}$$

On Page 123

Question 1 What is power?

Sol. Power is defined as the rate of doing work. If the work done by an object in time (t) is W. Then,

$$\text{Power } P = \frac{W}{t}$$

Its unit is J/s or watt.

Question 2 Define 1 watt of power?

Sol. Power, $$P = \frac{W}{t}$$

If $$W = 1 \text{ J}, t = 1 \text{ s}$$

then $$P = \frac{1}{1} = 1 \text{ W}$$

Power of an object is said to be 1 watt if it does 1 joule of work in 1 second.

Question 3 A lamp consumes 1000 J of electrical energy in 10 s. What is its power?

Sol. Energy = 1000 J, *i.e.*, work, $W = 1000$ J

Time, $t = 10$ s

$$\text{Power of lamp, } P = \frac{W}{t} = \frac{1000}{10} = 100 \text{ W}$$

Question 4 Define average power.

Sol. Average power is defined as the ratio of total work done by a force on an object to the total time taken.

Exercises

Question 1 Look at the activities listed below. Reason out whether or not work is done in the light of your understanding of the term 'work'.

(a) Suma is swimming in a pond.
(b) A donkey is carrying a load on its back.
(c) A wind-mill is lifting water from a well.
(d) A green plant is carrying out photosynthesis.
(e) An engine is pulling a train.
(f) Food grains are getting dried in the sun.
(g) A sail boat is moving due to wind energy.

Sol. (a) Work is being done by Suma because she displaces the water by applying the force.

(b) No work is being done by the donkey because the direction of force *i.e.,* weight is vertically downward and displacement is horizontal. If displacement and force are perpendicular, then no work is done.

(c) Work is done, because wind mill is lifting the water *i.e.,* it is changing the position of water.

(d) No work is done, because there is no force and displacement.

(e) Work is done, because engine is changing the position of train.

(f) No work is done, because there is no force and no displacement.

(g) Work is done, because the force acting on the boat is moving it.

Question 2 An object thrown at a certain angle to the ground moves in a curved path and falls back to the ground. The initial and the final points of the path of the object lie on the same horizontal line? What is the work done by the force of gravity on the object?

Sol. Work done by the force of gravity, $W = mgh$.

where, h = difference in height of initial and final positions of the object.

According to question, the initial and final positions of the object lie on the same horizontal line, so $h = 0$

$\therefore$ Work done, $W = mg \times 0 = 0$

Question 3 A battery lights a bulb. Describe the energy changes involved in the process.

Sol. The battery has chemical energy which is converted into electrical energy. The electrical energy provided to the bulb gets further converted into light energy.

Question 4 Certain force acting on a mass 20 kg mass changes its velocity from 5 ms^{-1} to 2 ms^{-1}. Calculate the work done by the force?

Sol. Given, mass, $m = 20$ kg

Initial velocity, $u = 5\ ms^{-1}$

Final velocity, $v = 2\ ms^{-1}$

Work done by the force = Change in kinetic energy

= Final kinetic energy – Initial kinetic energy

$$= \frac{1}{2} mv^2 - \frac{1}{2} mu^2$$

$$= \frac{1}{2} m (v^2 - u^2)$$

$$= \frac{1}{2} \times 20 [(2)^2 - (5)^2]$$

$$= 10 (4 - 25) = 10 \times - 21 = - 210 \text{ J}$$

Question 5 A mass of 10 kg is at a point A on a table. It is moved to a point B. If the line joining A and B is horizontal, what is the work done on the object by the gravitational force? Explain your answer.

Sol. Work done by gravitational force, $W = mgh$

where h = difference in the heights of initial and final positions of the object.

Here, both the initial and final positions are on the same horizontal line. So, there is no difference in height *i.e.*, $h = 0$

$\therefore$ Work done, $W = mg \times 0 = 0$

Question 6 The potential energy of a freely falling object decreases progressively. Does this violate law of conservation of energy? Why?

Sol. It is true that the potential energy of freely falling object decreases progressively.

But as the object falls down, its speed increases progressively *i.e.*, the kinetic energy of the object increases progressively. The potential energy is converted in to kinetic energy, hence, total energy during free fall is conserved. So, we can say that the law of conservation of energy is not violated, because the decrease in potential energy results in the increase of kinetic energy.

Question 7 What are the various energy tansformations that occur when you are riding on a bicycle?

Sol. In case of bicycle, the muscular energy is converted into the kinetic energy of the bicycle.

Question 8 Does the transfer of energy take place when you push a huge rock with all your might and fail to move it? Where is the energy you spend going?

Sol. When we push a huge rock, then the rock also exerts a huge force on us (according to Newton's third law of motion). The muscular energy spent by us in the process is used to oppose the huge force acting on us by the rock.

Question 9 A certain household has consumed 250 units of energy during a month. How much energy is this in joules?

Sol. Energy consumed = 250 units

$$= 250 \text{ kWh} = 250 \times 1000 \text{ W} \times 3600 \text{ s}$$
$$= 250 \times 1000 \text{ J/s} \times 3600 \text{ s} = 9 \times 10^8 \text{ J}$$

Question 10 An object of mass 40 kg is raised to a height of 5 m above the ground. What is its potential energy? If the object is allowed to fall, find its kinetic energy when it is half-way down.

◎ ***Thinking Process*** In energy conservation, potential energy decreases while kinetic energy increases as the object falls, but their sum remains constant.

Sol. Given, mass, $m = 40$ kg; height, $h = 5$ m

Potential energy, PE = $mgh = 40 \times 9.8 \times 5 = 1960$ J

KE at half-way down = PE at half-way down

($\because$ total mechanical energy remains conserved)

$$\Rightarrow \quad k = mg\frac{h}{2} = 40 \times 9.8 \times \frac{5}{2} = 980 \text{ J}$$

Question 11 What is the work done by the force of gravity on a satellite moving round the earth? Justify your answer.

Sol. The satellite round the earth moves in a circular orbit.

Here, the force of gravity acts towards the centre of the earth and displacement of the satellite is along there tangent of circular path. That means the force and displacement are perpendicular to each other.

So, Work done, $W = F \cdot s \cos \theta$

$$= F \cdot s \cos 90° = F \cdot s \times 0 = 0$$

i.e., no work is done by the force of gravity.

Question 12 Can there be displacement of an object in the absence of any force acting on it? Think, discuss this question with your friends and teacher.

Sol. If an object moves with a constant velocity, (*i.e.*, there is no acceleration) then no force acts on it. Thus, there will be displacement of an object moving with constant velocity in the absence of force.

Question 13 A person holds a bundle of hay over his head for 30 minutes and gets tried. Has he done some work or not? Justify your answer.

Sol. The person has no movement *i.e.*, his displacement is zero, so the person has done no work ($\because$ work is done only when the object is displaced).

Question 14 An electric heater is rated 1500 W. How much energy does it use in 10 hours?

Sol. Power = 1500 W

$$\text{Time} = 10\text{ h} = 10 \times 60\text{ min} = 10 \times 60 \times 60\text{ s}$$

$$\text{Power} = \frac{\text{Energy or work}}{\text{Time}}$$

$$\therefore \quad \text{Energy} = \text{Power} \times \text{Time}$$

$$= 1500 \times 10 \times 60 \times 60 = 5.4 \times 10^7\text{ J}$$

Question 15 Illustrate the law of conservation of energy by discussing the energy changes which occur when we draw a pendulum bob to one side and allow it to oscillate. Why does the bob eventually come to rest? What happens to its energy eventually? Is it a violation of the law of conservation of energy?

◎ ***Thinking Process*** In this problem, when the pendulum bob is drawn to one side, it gains potential energy due to its height. As it is released, this potential energy converts into kinetic energy as it moves downward.

Sol.

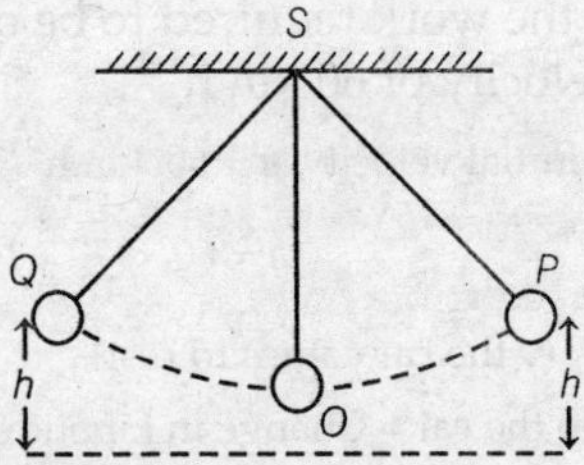

When bob of pendulum is release from height h at point P (where it has height value of potential energy due to its position), It start oscillating be fueen point P and Q. As shown in figure.

At position O, whole of the potential energy of the pendulum is converted into its kinetic energy and at point Q, whole of the kinetic energy is converted into potential energy. Thus, we find that the potential energy gets converted into kinetic energy and *vice-versa* during the motion of the pendulum. But the total mechanical energy remains constant.

When the pendulum oscillates in air, the air friction opposes its motion. So, some part of kinetic energy of pendulum is used to overcome this friction. With the passage of time, kinetic energy of the pendulum goes on decreasing and finally becomes zero. The kinetic energy of the pendulum is transferred to the atmosphere. So, energy is being transferred *i.e.*, is converted from one form to another. So, here is no violation of law of conservation of energy.

Note In a pendulum, energy continuously transforms between potential and kinetic forms, but due to air resistance and friction, some energy eventully dissipates as heat.

Question 16 An object of mass $m$is moving with a constant velocity v. How much work should be done on the object in order to bring the object to rest?

Sol. The work done on the object to bring the object to rest

= Change in kinetic energy

= Final kinetic energy – Initial kinetic energy

Here, final kinetic energy is zero because the object is brought to rest.

$$= 0 - \frac{1}{2} mv^2$$

$$= -\frac{1}{2} mv^2$$

Question 17 Calculate the work required to be done to stop a car of 1500 kg moving at a velocity of 60 km h^{-1}.

Sol. Given, $m = 1500$ kg, initial velocity, $u = 60$ km h^{-1}

$$\Rightarrow \quad u = 60 \times \frac{5}{18} = 16.67 \text{ ms}^{-1}$$

Final velocity, $v = 0$ ($\because$ the car comes to rest)

$\therefore$ Work done to stop the car = Change in kinetic energy

$$= \text{Final kinetic energy} - \text{Initial kinetic energy}$$
$$= \frac{1}{2} mv^2 - \frac{1}{2} mu^2$$
$$= \frac{1}{2} \times 1500 \times (0)^2 - \frac{1}{2} \times 1500 \times (16.67)^2$$
$$= -\frac{1}{2} \times 1500 \times (16.67)^2 = -208333.33 \text{ J}$$

Question 18 In each of the following, a force F is acting on an object of mass, m. The direction of displacement is from west to east shown by the longer arrow. Observe the diagrams carefully and state whether the work done by the force is negative, positive or zero.

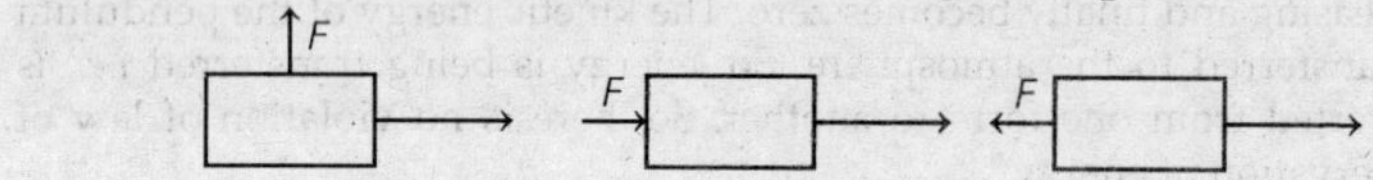

◎ ***Thinking Process*** We know that, the work W done by a force is given by the formula:

$$W = F.d.\cos\theta$$

The sign of work depends on the angle θ between the force and the displacement.

Sol. **Case I** The force and displacement are perpendicular to each other, so $\theta = 90°$.

$$\text{Work done, } W = Fs\cos\theta = Fs\cos 90°$$
$$= Fs \times 0 = 0 \qquad (\because \cos 90° = 0)$$

i.e., the work done is zero.

Case II The force and displacement are in the same direction, so $\theta = 0°$

$$\therefore \quad \text{Work done, } W = Fs\cos\theta = Fs\cos 0°$$
$$= Fs \times 1 = Fs \qquad (\because \cos 0° = 1)$$

i.e., the work done is positive.

Case III The force and displacement in opposite directions,

so $\theta = 180°$

$$\therefore \quad \text{Work done, } W = Fs\cos\theta = Fs\cos 180°$$
$$= Fs \times -1 \qquad (\because \cos 180° = -1)$$
$$= -Fs$$

i.e., the work done is negative.

Question 19 Soni says that the acceleration in an object could be zero even when several forces are acting on it. Do you agree with her? Why?

Sol. Yes, I agree with Soni. The acceleration in an object can be zero even when several forces are acting on it, if the resultant of all the forces acting on object is zero.

Question 20 Find the energy in joule consumed in 10 h by four devices of power 500 W each.

Sol. Total power, $P = 500 \text{ W} \times 4 = 2000 \text{ W}$

$$\text{Time, } t = 10 \text{ h}$$

$$\begin{aligned}\text{Energy consumed} &= \text{Power} \times \text{Time} \\ &= 2000 \text{ W} \times 10 \text{ h} \\ &= 2 \text{ kW} \times 10 \text{ h} = 20 \text{ kWh}\end{aligned}$$

Question 21 A freely falling object eventually stops on reaching the ground. What happens to its kinetic energy?

Sol. When freely falling object strikes the earth then some sound and heat is produced. So, the kinetic energy of the object gets converted into sound energy and heat energy.

DIKSHA APP Questions

☐ Multiple Choice Questions

Q.1 The commercial unit of energy is

(a) joule (b) Newton
(c) watt (d) kilowatt hour

Sol. (d) The SI unit of energy is joule but its commercial unit is kilowatt hour (kWh)

Q.2 What kind of energy is possessed by water stored in a dam:

(a) no energy
(b) potential energy
(c) kinetic energy
(d) electrical energy

Sol. (b) A dam holds a large amount of water at some height. So, the energy stored is potential energy. This potential energy of the water gets converted to kinetic energy which rotates the turbines in a power plant to produce electricity.

Q.3 If kinetic energy of a body of mass 2 kg is 9J. Its speed is

(a) 3 m/s
(b) 4 m/s
(c) 9 m/s
(d) 5 m/s

Sol. (a) Mass, $m = 2\,\text{kg}$,

Kinetic energy, $k = 9\,\text{J}$

Speed, $v = ?$

$$\because \quad k = \frac{1}{2} m v^2$$

$$\Rightarrow \quad 9 = \frac{1}{2} \times 2 \times v^2$$

$$\Rightarrow \quad v^2 = 9$$

$$\Rightarrow \quad v = 3$$

☐ Very Short Answer Type

Q.1 Evaluate kinetic energy in terms of momemtum.

Sol. If an object of mass, m moves with velocity v, then momentum,

$$p = mv$$

$$\Rightarrow \quad v = \frac{p}{m}$$

and kinetic energy, $K = \frac{1}{2}mv^2$

$$\Rightarrow \quad K = \frac{1}{2}m\left(\frac{p}{m}\right)^2$$

$$\Rightarrow \quad K = \frac{p^2}{2m}$$

This is the expression of kinetic energy in terms of momentum.

Q.2 List two conditions which need to be satisfied for the work to be done.

Sol. The two conditions are

(i) Force must produce a displacement in an object.

$\because \quad W = Fs\cos\theta$, if $s = 0$, then $W = 0$

(ii) The displacement produced by force must not be perpendicular to force. *i.e.* if $\theta = 90°$,

then $\quad W = Fs\cos 90° = 0 \quad (\because \cos 90° = 0)$

Q.3 When an object is dropped from a certain height, what kind of energy transformation takes place?

Sol. When the object is dropped from a height, the potential energy of the object gets converted into its kinetic energy.

Q.4 A body of mass 10 kg is displaced through a distance of 2 m under acceleration of 5 m/s^2. Calculate the work done.

Sol. Mass, $m = 10$ kg,

displacement, $s = 2$ m,

acceleration, $a = 5$ m/s^2

$\therefore \quad$ Force, $F = ma$

$$\Rightarrow \quad F = 10 \times 5 = 50 \text{ N}$$

Now, work done, $W = Fs$

$$\Rightarrow \quad W = 50 \times 2 = 100 \text{ J}$$

☐ Short Answer Type

Q.1 Two bodies of equal masses move with uniform velocities 'v' and '$3v$' respectively. Find the ratio of their kinetic energies.

Sol. Using $K = \frac{1}{2}mv^2$, we get

$$\frac{K_1}{K_2} = \frac{\frac{1}{2}m_1v_1^2}{\frac{1}{2}m_2v_2^2}$$

$$\Rightarrow \quad \frac{K_1}{K_2} = \frac{m_1v_1^2}{m_2v_2^2}$$

Given, masses of objects are equal *i.e,* $m_1 = m_2 = m$ (let)

and, $v_1 = v, v_2 = 3v$

On substituting these values,

$$\frac{K_1}{K_2} = \frac{mv^2}{m(3v)^2} = \frac{1}{9}$$

$$\therefore \quad K_1 : K_2 = 1:9$$

Q.2 (i) Can any object have mechanical energy even if its momentum is zero?

(ii) Can any object have momentum even if its mechanical energy is zero?

Justify the above two statements.

Sol. (i) If the momentum of the particle is zero, then its kinetic energy is also zero ($K = 0$)

as $$K = \frac{p^2}{2m}.$$

But, the object can possess a non-zero potential energy. So, the total mechanical energy y which is the sum of kinetic energy and potential energy could be non-zero.

(ii) If the mechanical energy of an object is zero, then both its kinetic energy and potential energy is zero.

Since, $K = 0 \Rightarrow p = 0$ $\quad (\because p = \sqrt{2mK})$

Q.3 (i) Define gravitational potential energy and derive an expression for it.

(ii) A body of mass 5 kg is thrown vertically upwards with a speed of 10 m/s. What is its kinetic energy when it is thrown? Find its potential energy when it reaches at the highest point. Also find the maximum height attained by the body.

Sol. (i) Gravitation potential energy of an object at a point above the ground is defined as the work done is raising the object from the ground to that point against gravity.

If and object is raised to a height (h) then force

$F = mg$ (m is the mass of the object and g is the acceleration due to gravity)

$\therefore$ Work done, $W = Fs \Rightarrow W = mgh$

$\because$ Work done is equal to the potential energy, $U = mgh$

(ii) Initial speed, $u = 10$ m/s, Mass, $m = 5$ kg

Initial kinetic energy, $K = \frac{1}{2} mu^2$

$= \frac{1}{2} \times 5 \times 10^2$

$= 250$ J

At the highest point, $v = 0$. This means that $K = 0$ and on the kinetic energy has converted to potential energy.

$\therefore$ Potential energy at highest point, $U = 250$ J

To find the height attained by the object, we can use the expression for potential energy.

$U = mgh$ (let maximum height be h)

$\Rightarrow \quad 250 = mgh$

$\Rightarrow \quad h = \frac{250}{5 \times 10} \qquad (\because g = 10\,\text{m/s}^2)$

$\Rightarrow \quad h = 5$ m

Q.4 (i) Define power and specify its SI unit.

(ii) A household has a 100 W lamp lighted for 2 hours, two 60 W lamps lighted for 4 hours and an electric fan of 50 W working for 8 hours a day. Calculate the electric units consumed each day.

Sol. (i) Power is defined as the rate of doing work or the rate of transfer of energy. Its SI unit is watt (W).

(ii) $P_1 = 100$ W, $t_1 = 2$ h

Energy consumed, $E_1 = P_1 \times t_1 = 100 \text{ W} \times 2\text{h}$

$= 0.1 \text{ kW} \times 2 \text{ h} = 0.2 \text{ kWh}$

$$\Rightarrow \quad E_1 = 0.2 \text{ units}$$

Now, $P_2 = 60\text{ W}, t_2 = 4\text{ h}$

$$E_2 = P_2 \times t_2 = 60\text{ W} \times 4\text{ h}$$
$$= \frac{60}{1000}\text{ kW} \times 4\text{h} = 0.24\text{ kWh}$$

$$\Rightarrow \quad E_2 = 0.24 \text{ units}$$

Since, there are two lamps of 60 W,

Energy consumed, $E = 2 \times 0.24$ units $\Rightarrow E = 0.48$ units

Also, $P_3 = 50\text{ W}, t_3 = 8\text{ h}$

$$E_3 = P_3 \times t_3 = 50\text{ w} \times 8\text{ h}$$
$$= \frac{50}{1000}\text{ kW} \times 8\text{h} = 0.4\text{ kWh}$$

$$\Rightarrow \quad E_3 = 0.4 \text{ units}$$

Thus, total energy consumed each day = 0.2 + 0.48 + 0.4 = 1.08 units

☐ Long Answer Type

Q.1 An object of mass 20 kg is dropped from a height of 4 m. Evaluate its kinetic energy and potential energy at various heights and thus prove law of conservation of energy.

◎ *Thinking Process* In this problem, as the object falls, gravitational potential energy decreases while kinetic energy increases proportionally. This transformation shows that gravitational force conserves mechanical energy.

Sol. Let us consider three different points *A*, *B* and *C* to prove the law of conservation of energy as shown in the figure.

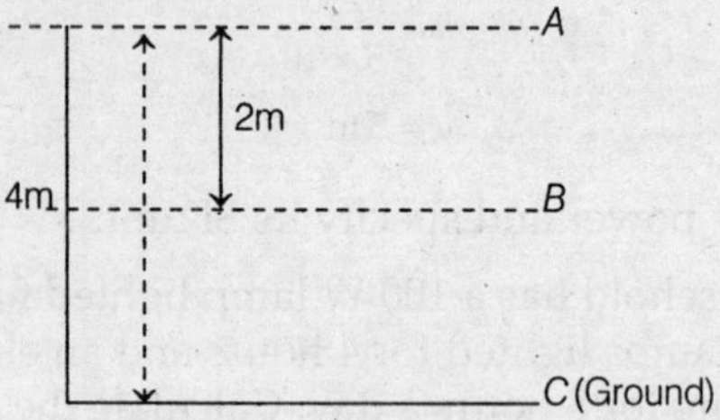

A is the point from where the object is dropped.

B is the point when the object reaches midway between *A* and ground

C is a point on the ground.

At point A

Initial velocity of the particle, $u = 0$

$$\therefore \quad K_A = \frac{1}{2} mu^2 = 0$$

Potential energy, $U = mgh$

$$= 20 \times 10 \times 4 = 800 \text{ J (Mass of object is 20 kg)}$$

Total mechanical energy, $E_A = K_A + U_A = 0 + 800 = 800$ J

At point B

In order to find out the kinetic energy of B, we need to find out the velocity at B using third equation of motion

initial velocity (at A), $u = 0$

distance covered (A to B), $s = 2$ m

$$v^2 = u^2 + 2as$$

$$\Rightarrow \quad v^2 = 0 + 2 \times 10 \times 2 \qquad (\because a = g = 10 \text{ m/s}^2)$$

$$\Rightarrow \quad v^2 = 40$$

$$\Rightarrow \quad v = \sqrt{40} \text{ m/s}$$

Kinetic energy at B, $K_B = \frac{1}{2} mv^2 = \frac{1}{2} \times 20 \times 40 = 400$ J

Also potential energy of B, $U_B = mgh$

$$= 20 \times 10 \times 2 \qquad (\because \text{at height at } B \text{ is 2 m above the ground})$$

$$= 400 \text{ J}$$

$\therefore$ Total mechanical energy, $E_B = K_B + U_B$

$$= 400 + 400 = 800 \text{ J}$$

At point C

Again, we need to find the velocity of which the object strikes the ground in order to find the kinetic energy.

Initial velocity (at A), $u = 0$

Distance covered (A to C), $s = 4$ m

$$v^2 = u^2 + 2as$$

$$\Rightarrow \quad v^2 = 0 + 2 \times 10 \times 4 \qquad (\because a = g = 10 \text{ m/s}^2)$$

$$\Rightarrow \quad v^2 = 80$$

$$\Rightarrow \quad v = \sqrt{80} \text{ m/s}$$

Kinetic energy at C, $K_C = \frac{1}{2} mv^2$

$$= \frac{1}{2} \times 20 \times 80 = 800 \text{ J}$$

Potential energy at C, $U_C = mgh$

$$= 0 \qquad (\because \text{height at } C \text{ is zero above the ground})$$

$\therefore$ Total mechanical energy, $E_C = K_C + U_C$

$$= 800 + 0$$
$$= 800 \text{ J}$$

Thus, we can say that the total mechanical energy of a freely falling object remains conserved.

Q.2 (i) A car of mass 1000 kg is moving with a speed of 90 km/h to stop it in 5 seconds, calculate the force applied by brakes and total work done.

(ii) State law of conservation of energy. Express it in mathematical equation.

Sol. (i) Mass of car, $m = 1000$ kg

Initial speed, $u = 90 \text{ km/h} = 90 \times \frac{5}{18} \text{ m/s} = 25 \text{ m/s}$

Final speed, $v = 0$ (As the car stops)

Time taken, $t = 5$ s

Using first equation of motion to find the acceleration,

$$v = u + at$$
$$\Rightarrow \quad 0 = 25 + a(5)$$
$$\Rightarrow \quad a = -5 \text{ m/s}^2$$

Here, negative sign represents that this is retardation as the speed of the car is reducing.

Force applied by brakes, $F = ma$

$$= 1000 \times (-5) = -5000 \text{ N}$$

Using third equation to motion to find the displacement,

$$v^2 = u^2 + 2as$$
$$\Rightarrow \quad 0 = (25)^2 + 2(-5)s$$
$$\Rightarrow \quad 10s = 625$$
$$\Rightarrow \quad s = 62.5 \text{ m}$$

Work done, $W = F \times s$

$$= -5000 \times 62.5 = -312500 \text{ J}$$

(ii) Law of conservation of energy states that the total mechanical energy of a system remains constant in absence of any frictional force.

i.e., $mgh + \frac{1}{2}mv^2 = \text{constant}$

Mistake Alert The force and work done should be negative, indicating the direction opposite to the motion.

Q.3 (i) What is work done when force is applied?

(a) Perpendicular to direction of motion.

(b) Opposite to direction of motion.

(c) Toward the direction of motion.

(ii) A boy of mass 50 kg runs up a staircase of 45 steps in 9 s. If the height of each step is 15 cm, find his power. (Given, $g = 10\ m/s^2$)

Sol. (i) The formula for work done (W) is

$$W = Fs\cos\theta$$

Where, F = applied force, s = displacement and

θ = angle between the force and the direction of motion.

(a) Force applied perpendicular to the direction of motion ($\theta = 90°$)

$\therefore \quad W = Fs\cos\theta = Fs\cos 90° = 0 \qquad [\because \cos 90° = 0]$

work done is zero in this case.

(b) Force applied opposite to the direction of motion ($\theta = 180°$)

$\therefore \quad W = Fs\cos\theta = Fs\cos 180° = -Fs \qquad [\because \cos 180° = -1]$

work done is negative and indicating that the force opposes the motion.

(c) Force applied towards the direction of motion ($\theta = 0°$)

$W = Fs\cos\theta = Fs\cos 0° = Fs \qquad [\because Cos\ 0° = 1]$

Work done is positive, as the force consists the motion.

(ii) $\text{Power} = \dfrac{\text{Work (or Energy)}}{\text{Time}}$

Work done by the boy = mgh

Height attained by the boy

= Number of steps × Height of each step

$= 45 \times 0.15 \qquad (\because \text{Height of step} = 15\,\text{cm} = 0.15\text{ m})$

$= 6.75$ m

$\Rightarrow$ Work done $= 50 \times 10 \times 6.75 \qquad (\because M = 50\,\text{kg and } g = 10\,\text{m/s}^2)$

$= 3375$ J

$\therefore \quad \text{Power} = \dfrac{3375}{9} \qquad (\because \text{Time taken} = 9\text{ s})$

$\Rightarrow \quad P = 375$ W

Sound

CHAPTER 11

Important Points

01 Sound is a form of energy which produces the sensation of hearing in our ears.

02 **Production of Sound** Sound is produced by vibrating objects. When an object vibrates, it sets the particles of the medium around it vibrating. The particles do not travel all the way from the vibrating object to the ear. A particle of the medium in contact with the vibrating object is first displaced from its equilibrium position. It then exerts a force on the adjacent particle. As a result of which the adjacent particle get displaced from its position.

After displacing, the particle comes back to its original position. This process continues in the medium till the sound reaches our ear.

Propagation of Sound

- Sound waves need a material medium like air, water or metal etc, for their propagation. Speed of sound in different media is different. The speed of sound in a medium depends primarily on the nature and temperature of the medium.
- Sound waves are longitudinal waves, *i.e.*, the individual particles of the medium oscillate in a direction parallel to the direction of propagation of the wave (disturbance).
- In transverse wave, the individual particles of the medium oscillate in a direction perpendicular to the direction of propagation of the wave (disturbance).

03 **Characteristics of a Sound Wave** The sound wave can be characterised by

(i) Frequency
(ii) Amplitude
(iii) Speed

04 A sound wave in graphic form is shown below, it represents how density and pressure change when the sound wave moves in a medium. The density as well as pressure of the medium at a given time vary with distance.

- **Compressions** are the regions where the particles are crowded together and are represented by the upper portion of the curve. The peak represents the region of maximum compression. At compressions, the density as well as pressure is high.
- **Rarefactions** are the regions of low pressure where particles are spread apart and are represented by the valley, *i.e.*, the lower portion of the curve. A peak is called the crest and a valley is called the trough of a wave.

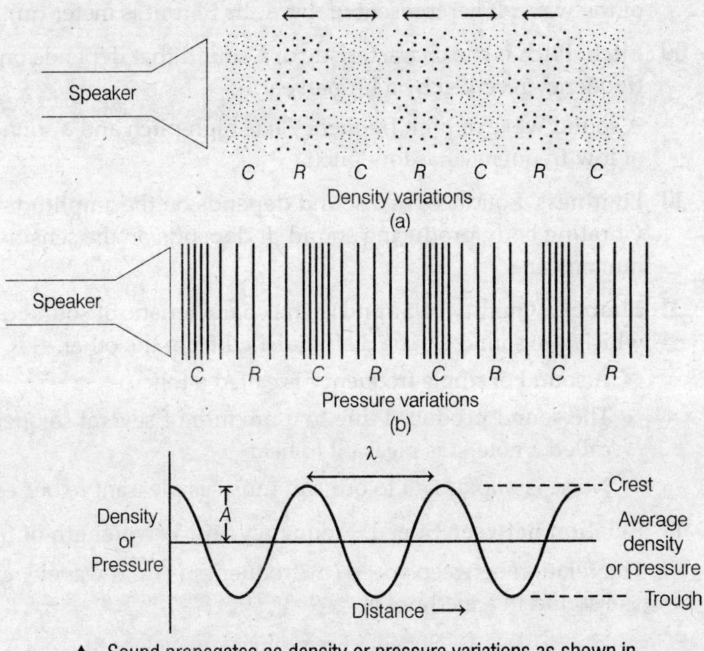

▲ Sound propagates as density or pressure variations as shown in (a) and (b), (c) represents graphically the density and pressure variations.

05 **Wavelength** The distance between two consecutive compressions or rarefactions is called the wavelength. It is represented by λ (lambda). Its SI unit is metre (m).

06 Frequency The number of oscillations per unit time is called frequency of the sound wave. The number of compressions or rarefactions occuring per unit time is equal to the frequency of sound wave. It is represented by ν (nu). Its SI unit is hertz (Hz).

07 Time Period The time taken in one complete oscillation is called the time period of the wave. It is represented by T. Its SI unit is second (s).

$$\text{Time period } (T) = \frac{1}{\text{Frequency}(\nu)}$$

08 Amplitude The magnitude of the maximum disturbance in the medium on either side of the mean value is called the amplitude of the wave. It is represented by A. Its SI unit is meter (m).

09 Pitch Pitch is the characteristic of a sound that depends on the frequency received by a human ear.

A sound wave of high frequency has high pitch and a sound wave of low frequency has low pitch.

10 Loudness Loudness of a sound depends on the amplitude of the vibrating body producing sound. It depends on the sensitivity of human ear.

11 Timber a Quality of Sound The characteristic of sound due to which one sound can be distinguished from the other.

- A sound of single frequency is called a tone.
- The sound produced due to a mixture of several frequencies is called a note, it is pleasant to hear.
- Noise is unpleasant to our ear, music is pleasant to our ear.

12 Relation Between Speed, Frequency and Wavelength of Sound

The relation between speed (v), frequency (ν) and wavelength (λ) of a sound in a medium is

$$\text{Speed} = \text{Frequency} \times \text{wavelength}$$

i.e., $$v = \nu\lambda$$

13 Reflection of Sound The bouncing back of sound wave travelling in a medium after striking the second medium is called reflection of sound.

14 Echo Echo is a repetition of sound due to the reflection of original sound by a large and hard obstacle.

15 Different conditions required for the production of echo are

(i) The echo will be heard if the original sound reflected by an obstacle reaches our ear after 0.1 s.

(ii) The echo will be heard only if the minimum distance between the source of sound and obstacle is 17.2 m.

(iii) The echo can be produced if the size of the obstacle reflecting sound is large compared to the wavelength of the sound wave.

16 **Reverberation** In big rooms or halls, echoes follow so closely behind the original sound that the original sound appears to be prolonged even when the source of sound stops producing sound. This effect is called reverberation. It occurs due to multiple reflection of sound.

17 Different practical uses of multiple reflection of sound are: megaphone, hearing aid, sound boards, stethoscope, etc.

18 **Range of Hearing** The audible range of sound for human beings is 20 Hz to 20000 Hz.

- The sound having frequency less than 20 Hz is called infrasound.
- The sound having frequency more than 20000 Hz are called ultrasound.
- Some animals can hear the sound above and less than the above frequency range.

19 **Applications of Ultrasound** Ultrasounds are high frequency waves. These are able to travel along well defined paths even in the presence of obstacles. These are used for

(i) cleaning the parts located in hard-to-reach places, *e.g.*, spiral tube, odd shaped parts, etc.

(ii) these are used to detect cracks and flaws in metal blocks.

(iii) these are used in echocardiography.

(iv) ultrasound scanner is an application of ultrasound waves.

(v) bats reach out prey and fly in dark night by emitting and detecting reflections of ultrasonic waves. This is known as echolocation.

20 SONAR stands for Sound Navigation And Ranging. It is a device that uses ultrasonic waves to measure the distance, direction and speed of under water objects.

Intext Questions

On Page 129

Question 1 How does the sound produced by a vibrating object in a medium reach your ear?

Sol. Sound is produced by vibrating objects. When an object vibrates, it sets the particles of the medium around it vibrating. The particles do not travel all the way from the vibrating object to the ear. A particle of the medium in contact with the vibrating object is first displaced from its equilibrium position. It then exerts a force on the adjacent particle. As a result of which the adjacent particle get displaced from its position. After displacing, the particle comes back to its original position. This process continues in the medium till the sound reaches our ear.

Question 2 Explain how sound is produced by your school bell?

Sol. The bell produces the sound when it is struck by a hammer. When the bell is struck by hammer, it starts vibrating. Since, the vibrating objects produce sound, so the bell produces sound.

Question 3 Why are sound waves called mechanical waves?

Sol. Sound waves are called mechanical waves because they require a material medium for their propagation. They cannot propagate in vacuum. Waves that required material medium for their propagation are called mechanical waves.

Question 4 Suppose you and your friend are on the moon. Will you be able to hear any sound produced by your friend?

Sol. I will not be able to hear any sound produced by my friend because the sound waves require some material medium like air to travel. There is no atmosphere or air on the moon, so the sound produced by my friend will not reach me, and I will not be able to hear.

On Page 132

Question 1 Which wave property determines (a) loudness, (b) pitch?

Sol. (a) Loudness of wave is determined by its amplitude.

(b) Pitch of the wave is determined by its frequency.

Question 2 Guess which sound has a higher pitch : guitar or car horn?

Sol. Pitch of guitar sound is higher because the frequency of sound produced by guitar is higher than that of car horn.

On Page 132

Question 1 What are wavelength, frequency, time period and amplitude of a sound wave?

Sol. (i) **Wavelength** The distance travelled by the wave during its one complete oscillation is called wavelength of the wave.

The distance between two consecutive regions of high pressure or high density (compression) or the distance between two consecutive regions of low pressure or low density (rarefaction) is equal to the wavelength. It is represented by λ. Its SI unit is meter (m).

(ii) **Frequency** The number of oscillations made by the wave in one second is called frequency of the wave. It is represented by ν. Its SI unit is s^{-1} or hertz.

(iii) **Time period** The time taken by the wave to complete one oscillation is called the time period of the wave. It is represented by *T*. Its SI unit is second(s).

(iv) **Amplitude** The maximum displacement of the wave from its mean or equilibrium position is called the amplitude of the wave. It is represented by *A*. Its SI unit is meter (m).

Question 2 How are the wavelength and frequency of a sound wave related to its speed?

Sol. The relation between wavelength (λ), frequency (ν) and speed of wave (v) is

$$v = \nu\lambda$$

Question 3 Calculate the wavelength of a sound wave whose frequency is 220 Hz and speed is 440 m s^{-1} in a given medium.

Sol. Frequency ν = 220 Hz, speed v = 440 ms^{-1},

wavelength λ = ?

From the relation, $v = \nu\lambda$

$\Rightarrow$ $440 = 220\,\lambda$

$\Rightarrow$ $\lambda = \frac{440}{220} = 2$ m

Mistake Alert If you accidentally divided the frequency by the speed (i.e., f / v), the answer would be incorrect. Always ensure you divide the speed by the frequency when calculating wavelength.

Question 4 A person is listening to a tone of 500 Hz sitting at a distance of 450 m from the source of the sound. What is the time interval between successive compressions from the source?

Sol. The time interval between two successive compressions or rarefactions is equal to the time period of the wave.

$\therefore$ Required time interval = Time period

$$= \frac{1}{\text{Frequency}}$$

$$= \frac{1}{500} = 0.002 \text{ s}$$

$$= 2 \times 10^{-3} \text{ s} = 2 \text{ ms}$$

On Page 133

Question 1 Distinguish between loudness and intensity of sound.

Sol. Differences between loudness and intensity of sound are given below.

S.N.	Loudness	Intensity
1.	It is a subjective quantity. A sound may be loud for one person but may be feeble for another person.	It is an objective physical quantity which does not change from person to person.
2.	It cannot be measured as it is just a sensation which can be only felt.	It can be measured as a physical quantity.

On Page 133

Question 1 In which of the three media, air, water or iron, does sound travel the fastest at a particular temperature?

Sol. Sound waves travel fastest in solid medium *i.e.,* out of the given media, sound wave will travel fastest in iron.

On Page 134

Question 1 An echo is heard in 3 s. What is the distance of the reflecting surface from the source, given that the speed of sound is 342 ms^{-1}?

Sol. Echo returns in 3 s. Therefore, time taken by sound to travel from the source to the reflecting surface, $t = \frac{3}{2} = 1.5$ s speed,

$$v = 342 \text{ ms}^{-1}.$$

$\therefore$ Distance of reflecting surface from the source = Speed × Time

$$= 342 \times 1.5 = 513 \text{ m}.$$

On Page 135

Question 1 Why are the ceilings of concert halls curved?

Sol. The ceilings of the concert halls are made curved so that the sound reflected from the ceilings reaches to all the corners of the hall.

On Page 136

Question 1 What is the audible range of the average human ear?

Sol. The audible frequency range for the average human ear is 20 Hz-20000 Hz.

Question 2 What is the range of frequencies associated with
(a) infrasound (b) ultrasound ?

Sol. (a) Sound waves having frequencies less than 20 Hz and greater than zero are called infrasound.

(b) Sound waves having frequencies more than 20000 Hz are called ultrasound.

Exercises

Question 1 What is sound and how is it produced?

Sol. Sound is a form of energy. It is produces when an object is set to vibrate or we can say that vibrating objects produce sound.

Question 2 Describe with the help of a diagram, how compressions and rarefactions are produced in air near a source of sound.

◎ *Thinking Process* Compression and rarefactions are produced when a vibrating sound source causes air particles to oscillate, pushing them together (compression) and pulling them apart (rarefaction), creating alternating high and low-pressure regions that travel through the medium.

Sol. The production of compression and rarefactions in air can be explained as When a vibrating object moves forward it pushes the air in front of it creating a region of high pressure. This region is called compression. This compression starts to move away from the vibrating object. When the vibrating object moves backwards, it creates a region of low pressure called rarefaction. As the object moves back and forth rapidly, a series of compressions and rarefactions are created.

These make the sound wave that propagates through the medium.

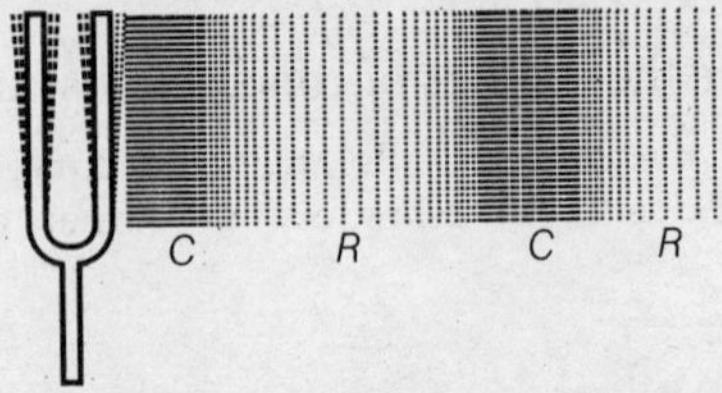

▲ A vibrating object creating a series of compressions (C) and rarefactions (R) in the medium.

Question 3 Why is sound wave called a longitudinal wave?

Sol. The sound wave is called longitudinal wave because when a sound wave propagates in a medium, the particles of the medium vibrate to and fro about their equilibrium positions parallel to the direction of propagation of the wave.

Question 4 Which characteristic of the sound helps you to identify your friend by his voice while sitting with others in a dark room?

Sol. Timber or quality of sound is the characteristic by which we can identify a person by their voice.

Question 5 Flash and thunder are produced simultaneously. But thunder is heard a few seconds after the flash is seen, why?

Sol. Thunder is heard few seconds later after the flash because speed of light in atmosphere (or air) is 3×10^8 ms^{-1} which is very high as compared to the speed of sound which is only 330 ms^{-1}. So, sound of thunder reaches us later than the flash.

Question 6 A person has a hearing range from 20 Hz to 20 kHz. What are the typical wavelengths of sound waves in air corresponding to these two frequencies? Take the speed of sound in air as 344 m s^{-1}.

Sol. Using the relation between speed (v), wavelength (λ) and frequency (ν) of a wave, we have

$$v = \nu\lambda \quad \text{or} \quad \lambda = \frac{v}{\nu}$$

(i) Here, $v = 344$ ms^{-1}, $\nu = 20$ Hz

$\therefore$ Corresponding wavelength $\lambda = \frac{v}{\nu} = \frac{344}{20} = 17.2$ m

(ii) Here, $v = 344$ ms^{-1}, $\nu = 20$ kHz $= 20 \times 10^3$ Hz

$\therefore$ Corresponding wavelength $\lambda = \frac{v}{\nu} = \frac{344}{20 \times 10^3} = 1.72 \times 10^{-2}$ m

Mistake Alert Mistakenly using $\lambda = v \times \nu$ instead of $\lambda = \frac{v}{\nu}$ is a common error, so use the correct formula. Be careful with conversion for kHz (1kHz = 1000Hz) to avoid calculation errors.

Question 7 Two children are at opposite ends of an aluminium rod. One strikes the end of the rod with a stone. Find the ratio of times taken by the sound wave in air and in the aluminium to reach the second child.

Sol. Let l = length of the rod

Time taken by the sound to travel through the aluminium rod

$$t_1 = \frac{\text{Distasnce}}{\text{Speed}} = \frac{l}{v_{Al}}$$

Similarily, time taken by the sound to travel through the air

$$t_2 = \frac{\text{Distance}}{\text{Speed}} = \frac{l}{v_{air}}$$

∴ Required ratio, $t_1 : t_2 = v_{air} : v_{Al}$

Question 8 The frequency of a source of sound is 100 Hz. How many times does it vibrate in a minute?

Sol. Frequency = 100 Hz

From the definition of frequency, we can say that

Number of oscillations in 1 s = 100

∴ Number of oscillations in 1 min or 60 s = $100 \times 60 = 6000 = 6 \times 10^3$

Question 9 Does sound follow the same laws of reflection as light does? Explain.

Sol. Yes, sound waves follow the same laws of reflection as light does.

These laws are

(i) The incident sound, reflected sound and normal at the point of the incidence lie on the same plane.

(ii) Angle of incidence is equal to the angle of reflection.

Question 10 When a sound is reflected from a distant object, an echo is produced. Let the distance between the reflecting surface and the source of sound production remains the same. Do you hear echo sound on a hotter day?

Sol. The time taken by echo to be heard, $t = \frac{2d}{v}$

where, d = distance between the reflecting surface and source of sound and v = speed of sound in air.

As we know that speed of sound increases with increase in temperature, so on a hotter day speed of sound will be higher, so the time after which echo is heard will decrease. If time taken by the reflected sound is less than 0.1 s after the production of original sound, then echo is not heard.

Question 11 Give two practical applications of reflection of sound waves.

Sol. The two practical application of reflection of sound are

(i) Megaphone (ii) Hearing aid

Question 12 A stone is dropped from the top of a tower 500 m high into a pond of water at the base of the tower. When is the splash heard at the top? Given, $g = 10\ ms^{-2}$ and speed of sound $= 340\ ms^{-1}$.

◎ *Thinking Process* This problem combines free fall (motion under gravity) and sound propagation. The key is to separate the motion of the falling stone and the travel of sound, solving each part independently using basic kinematic equations and the formula for constant speed.

Sol. Time after which the splash is heard

= Time taken by the stone to reach the pond

+ time taken by splash sound to reach the top of tower

(i) For the time taken by the stone to reach the pond.

Here, $u = 0$ ($\because$ Stone is dropped from rest)

From equation of motion under gravity, $h = ut + \frac{1}{2}gt^2$

$$\Rightarrow \quad 500 = 0 \times t + \frac{1}{2} \times 10\,(t)^2 \Rightarrow 500 = 5t^2$$

$$\Rightarrow \quad t^2 = 100$$

$$\Rightarrow \quad t = \sqrt{100} = 10\ s$$

(ii) Time taken by splash sound to reach the top of the tower

$$t' = \frac{\text{Distance}}{\text{Speed}} = \frac{500}{340} = 1.47\ s$$

$\therefore$ Time after which splash is heard = 10 + 1.47 = 11.47 s

Question 13 A sound wave travels at a speed of $339\ ms^{-1}$. If its wave length is 1.5 cm, what is the frequency of the wave? Will it be audible?

Sol. Given, speed, $v = 339\ ms^{-1}$, Wavelength, $\lambda = 1.5\ cm = 1.5 \times 10^{-2}\ m$

$$\therefore \quad \text{Frequency, } \nu = \frac{v}{\lambda} = \frac{339}{1.5 \times 10^{-2}} = 226 \times 10^2 = 22600\ Hz$$

This frequency is greater than 20000 Hz, so it will not be audible. The audible range for human ear is 20 Hz to 20000 Hz.

Question 14 What is reverberation? How can it be reduced?

Sol. The phenomenon of prolongation of original sound due to the multiple reflections of sound waves even after the source of sound stops producing sound is called reverberation. Reverberation can be reduced by covering the roofs and walls of the hall by absorbing materials.

Question 15 What is loudness of sound? What factors does it depend on?

Sol. Loudness is a measure of the response of the ear to the sound. It is a subjective quality. Loudness depends on (i) the amplitude of the vibrating body and (ii) the sensitivity of human ear.

Question 16 How is ultrasound used for cleaning?

Sol. Ultrasound is generally used to clean parts located in hard-to-reach places, for example, spiral tube, odd shaped parts, electronic components etc. Objects to be cleaned are placed in a cleaning solution and ultrasonic waves are sent into the solution. Due to the high frequency, the particles of dust, grease and dirt get detached and drop out. The objects thus get thoroughly cleaned.

Question 17 Explain how defects in a metal block can be detected using ultrasound?

Sol. Ultrasounds can be used to detect cracks and flaws in metal blocks. Metallic components are generally used in construction of big structures like buildings, bridges, machines and also scientific equipments. The cracks or holes inside the metal blocks, which are invisible from outside reduces the strength of the structure. Ultrasonic waves are allowed to pass through the metal block and detectors are used to detect the transmitted waves. If there is even a small defect, the ultrasound gets reflected back indicating the presence of the flaw or defect, as shown in the figure.

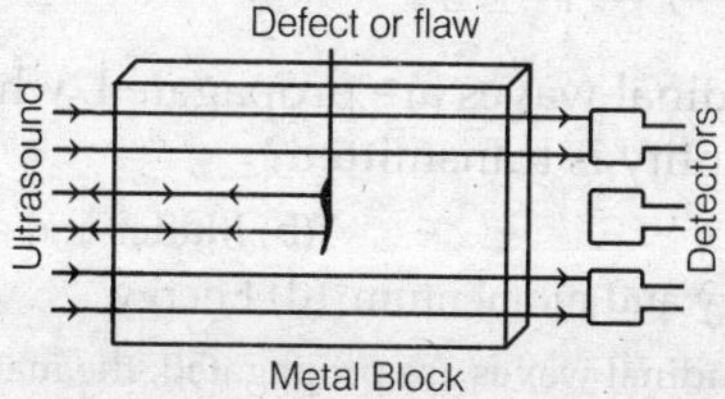

▲ Ultrasound is reflected back from the defective locations inside a metal block

DIKSHA APP Questions

☐ Multiple Choice Questions

Q.1 The speed of sound waves in air

(a) is independent of humidity
(b) is independent of temperature
(c) increases with increase in humidity
(d) decreases with increase in humidity

Sol. (c) We know that speed of sound increases from gases to liquids to solids. Thus, with increase in humidity, as a moisture in air increases, the speed of sound increases.

Q.2 Mechanical waves are those waves

(a) which can propagate through all mediums but not through vacuum
(b) which can propagate through vacuum
(c) which can propagate in solids only
(d) which cannot propagate in solids

Sol. (a) Mechanical waves are those waves that require a material for their propagation. So, they can propagate through all the mediums except vacuum.

Q.3 When longitudinal waves are propagated, which of the following quantity is transmitted?

(a) Matter (b) Matter and energy
(c) Matter,energy and momentum (d) Energy

Sol. (d) When longitudinal waves are propagated, the matter particles of the medium vibrate about their mean positions but are not transported from one place to other. Only energy is transmitted when a wave propagates.

☐ Very Short Answer Type

Q.1 Waves of frequency 100 Hz are produced in a string as shown in figure. Give its (i) amplitude, (ii) wavelength

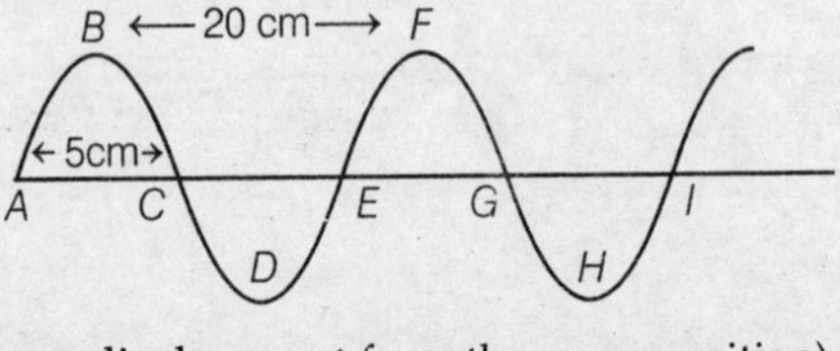

Sol. (i) 5 cm (maximum displacement from the mean position)

(ii) 20 cm (distance between two crests or two troughs)

Q.2 Discuss one point of difference between sound waves and light waves.

Sol. Sound waves are mechanical waves which are longitudinal in nature, whereas light waves are electromagnetic waves which are transverse in nature.

Q.3 Differentiate between roar of lion and buzzing of mosquito.

Sol. Roar of lion is a sound of low pitch and high loudness whereas the buzzing of a mosquito is a sound of high pitch but low loudness.

Q.4 Graphically show the difference between

(a) Loud and Soft sound

(b) High pitch and Low pitch sound

Sol. (a) Wave difference

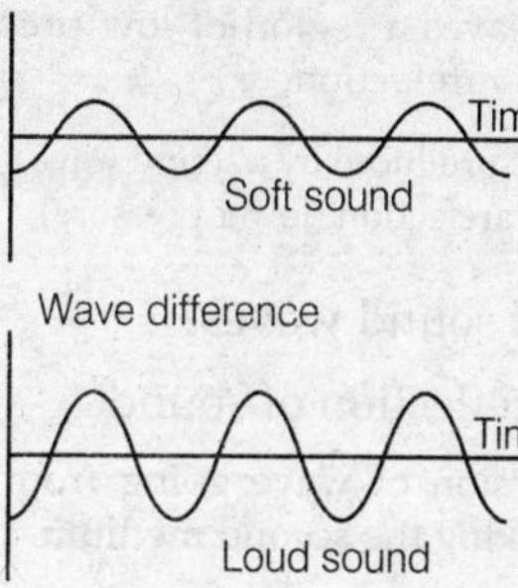

(b) Wave difference

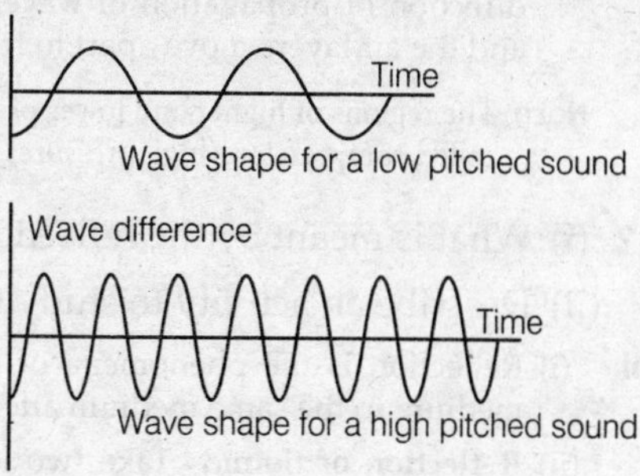

Q.5 (i) Establish the relationship between speed of sound, its wavelength and frequency.

(ii) If velocity of sound in air is 340 ms^{-1}, calculate wavelength when frequency is 256 Hz.

Sol. (i) Speed of sound, $v = \dfrac{\text{distance } (\lambda)}{\text{time } (T)}$

$$\therefore \quad v = \frac{\lambda}{T} = \left(\frac{1}{T}\right)\lambda$$

We know that, $\nu = \dfrac{1}{T}$

Where, ν is the frequency of the sound wave.

Thus, $v = \nu\lambda$ or $v = \lambda\nu$

i.e., speed is equal to frequency × wavelength.

(ii) $\lambda = \dfrac{v}{\nu} \Rightarrow \lambda = \dfrac{340}{256} \Rightarrow \lambda = 1.33$ m

□ Short Answer Type

Q.1 A loudspeaker cone oscillates to produce sound waves,

(i) As the sound wave passes a point, it produces regions of higher and lower pressure. State the names of these regions.

(ii) Describe how the movement of the loudspeaker cone produces these regions of different pressure.

Sol. (i) Regions of higher pressure are called compressions regions of lower pressure are called are rarefactions.

(ii) Production of the regions of higher pressure when the loudspeaker cone moves forward *i.e.* in the direction of propagation of wave, it pushes the layer of air closer. This air layer pushes the next air layer and the process goes on to form compressions. Production of regions of lower pressure: When the cone moves backwards, away from the direction of propagation of wave, it leaves a region of low pressure and the air layers move apart to from a rarefaction.

Note The regions of higher and lower pressure produced by a sound wave are called compression (high pressure) and rarefaction (lower pressure).

Q.2 (i) What is meant by the reflection of sound waves?

(ii) Describe an activity to study the reflection of sound.

Sol. (i) Reflection is the phenomena of reversion of wave going from one medium to the same medium after striking the second medium.

(ii) **Reflection of Sound** Take two identical pipes. Arrange them on a table near a wall. Keep a clock near the open end of one of the pipes and try to hear the sound of the clock through the other pipe. Adjust the position of the pipes so that you can best hear the sound of the clock. Measure the angle of incidence and angle of reflection, you will find that both the angles would be same which is the law of reflection of sound.

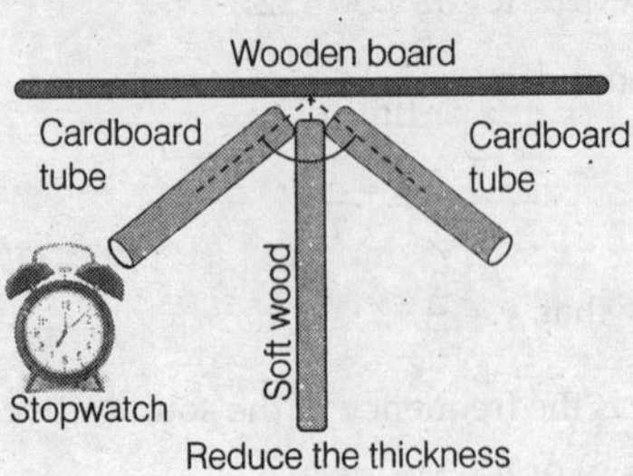

Improvement in Food Resources

CHAPTER 12

Important Points

01 Living organisms need food which supplies nutrients like carbohydrates, proteins, fats, vitamins and minerals. These are required for body development, growth and health.

02 The food is obtained from both agriculture and animal husbandry. This involves the cultivation of crops and rearing of animals, which provide a diverse range of nutrients essential of human consumption.

03 Different crops require different climatic conditions, temperature and photoperiod for their growth and completion of their life cycle.

04 The successful crop production depends on following factors:

(i) Understanding how crops grow and develop.

(ii) Effect of various nutrients, climate and water on the growth of the plant.

(iii) Modification and management of each factor for increasing the crop yield.

05 The crops which are grown in rainy season (June- October) are called **Kharif** crops. The Kharif crops include paddy, soyabean, pigeon pea, maize, cotton, green gram, black gram, etc.

06 The crops which are grown in winter season (November-April) are called **Rabi crops.** Examples, of Rabi crop are wheat, peas, mustard and linseed, etc.

07 The major activities which are involved in crop improvement can be classified as:

(i) Crop variety improvement

(ii) Crop production improvement

(iii) Crop protection management

08 Crop variety improvement depends on finding a crop variety that can give a good yield. It can be done by following methods:

(i) By hybridisation. (ii) By introducing a gene.

These methods aim to enhance the genetic make up of crops to achieve desired traits such as higher yield and disease resistance crops.

09 Hybridisation refers to crossing between genetically dissimilar plants. This crossing may be intervarietal (between different varieties), interspecific (between two different species of the same genus) or intergeneric (between different genera).

10 Introduction of gene provides the desired characteristics and results in genetically modified crops.

11 Some of the factors for which variety improvement is done are:

(i) **Higher yield** To increase the productivity of the crop per acre.

(ii) **Improved quality** Quality considerations of crop products vary from crop to crop. For example, baking quality in wheat, protein quality in pulses, oil quality in oil seeds, etc.

(iii) **Biotic and abiotic resistance** The biotic factors are diseases, insects and nematodes while abiotic factors are the drought, salinity, water logging, heat, cold and frost. Varieties resistant to these stresses can improve crop production.

(iv) **Change in maturity duration** The shorter the duration of maturity of crop, the more economical is the variety.

(v) **Wider adaptibility** This feature helps in stabilising the crop production under different environmental conditions.

(vi) **Desirable agronomic characteristics** It helps in developing desired agronomic characters for higher productivity. For example, tallness and profuse branching is required for fodder crops.

12 Crop production management can be done through various methods including nutrient management, irrigation and croppping patterns.

13 Plant require nutrients for growth which are supplied by air, water and soil. Essential nutrients are divided into macro-nutrients (needed in large amounts) and micro-nutrients (needed in small amounts) both of which are crucial for plant health and productivity.

Nutrients Supplied by Air, Water and Soil

Source	Nutrients
Air	Carbon and oxygen
Water	Hydrogen and oxygen
Soil	(i) **Macronutrients** Nitrogen, phosphorus, potassium, calcium magnesium and sulphur. (ii) **Micronutrients** Iron, Manganese, boron, zinc, copper, molybdenum and chlorine.

14 To increase the yield, the soil can be enriched with the nutrients in the form of manures and fertilizers.

15 Manure contains large quantities of organic matter and also supplies small quantities of nutrients to the soil. It is prepared by the decomposition of animal excreta and plant waste.

16 Based on the kind of biological material used manure can be classified as :

(i) **Compost** contains farm waste material such as livestock excreta (cow dung etc.), vegetable waste, sewage waste, straw, eradicated weeds, etc. These waste materials are decomposed in pits and this process of decomposition is called **composting.** The compost is rich in organic matter and nutrients.

(ii) **Vermicompost** is made by the decomposition of plant and animal refuse with the help of earthworms.

(iii) **Green manure** some plants like sunnhemp or guar are grown and then ploughed into the soil before sowing . These green plants thus turn into green manure. Which enrich the soil with nitrogen and phosphorus.

17 Fertilizers are commercially produced plant nutrients that supply nitrogen, phosphorus and potassium.

18 Fertilizers should be applied carefully in terms of proper dose, time and observing pre and post application precautions for their complete utilisation.

19 The continuous use of fertilizers in an area can lead to soil degradation, reduce soil structure and decrease biological activity over time.

20 In order to minimize the use of chemicals, organic farming is practiced. It relies on organic manures, recycled farm waste, and bio-agents for fertilization and pest control. It also incorporates healthy cropping systems like mixed cropping, inter-cropping and crop rotation.

21 Irrigation is very important for the success of crops. Various irrigation system include wells, canals, rivers and tanks.

(i) **Wells** are of two types, *i.e.,* dug wells and tube wells. In a dug well, water is collected from water bearing strata. Tube wells can tap water from the deeper strata.

(ii) **Canals** are an extensive irrigation system that receive water from reservoirs or from rivers. These are further branched into distributaries to irrigate fields.

(iii) **River lift systems** are useful in areas having irregular canal flow. Water is directly drawn from rivers for irrigation in areas close to rivers.

(iv) Tanks are small storage reservoirs that intercept and store the run-off of smaller catchment areas.

22 Cropping patterns are different ways of growing crops to get maximum production. The different cropping patterns are mixed-cropping, inter-cropping and crop rotation. These patterns optimises the use of available resources, enhance soil fertility and reduce pest and disease incidence.

23 **Mixed cropping** is growing two or more crops simultaneously on the same piece of land. For example, wheat and gram or wheat and mustard or groundnut and sunflower.

24 **Inter-cropping** involves growing two or more crops simultaneously on a same field in a definite pattern. A few rows of one crop alternate with a few rows of another crop.

For example, soyabean and maize or finger millet (bajara) and cowpea (lobia).

25 **Crop rotation** is growing of different crops on a piece of land in a pre-planned succession. The availability of moisture and irrigation facilities decide the choice of the crop to be cultivated after one harvest. If crop rotation is done properly then two or three crops can be grown in a year with good harvests.

Crop protection management involves practices that protect crops from weeds, insect pests, and diseases.

26 Weeds are unwanted plants in the cultivated field. *Xanthium* (gokhroo), *Parthenium* (gajar ghas), *Cyperinus rotundus* (motha) etc. These weeds compete for food, space and light and reduce the growth of the crop.

27 Weed control can be done by mechanical removal (most effective method). Some other preventive methods are proper seed bed preparation, timely sowing of crops, inter-cropping and crop rotation.

28 Insects pests generally attack the plants in three ways:

(i) They cut the root, stem and leaves.

(ii) They suck the cell sap from various parts of the plant.

(iii) They bore into stem and fruits.

These attacks can significantly reduce crop yield and quality if not controlled effectively.

29 Control of pests can be done by

(i) The use of disease resistant varieties.

(ii) The use of pesticides.

(iii) Summer ploughing, the fields are ploughed deep in summers.

30 Storage losses in agriculture are caused by biotic (insects, rodents, fungi, mites and bacteria) and abiotic factors (inappropriate moisture and temperatures) in the place of storage. These factors cause degradation in quality, loss in weight, poor germinability, discolouration of produce, all leading to poor market sale.

31 Control measures to prevent storage losses :

(i) Cleaning of produce before storage.

(ii) Proper drying of produce first in sunlight and then in shade.

(iii) Fumigation using chemicals that kill pests.

(iv) Proper treatment of the storage structures and systematic management of ware houses.

32 **Animal husbandry** is the scientific management of animal livestock. It includes feeding, breeding and disease control of the livestock. Animal based farming includes cattle, goat, sheep, poultry and fish farming.

33 Cattle husbandry is done for two purposes, milk and draught labour for agricultural work such as tilling, irrigation and carting.

34 Dairy animals require food for two purposes:

(i) **Maintenance requirement**, which is the food required to support the animal to live a healthy life.

(ii) **Milk-producing requirement,** which is the type of food required during the lactation period.

35 Animal feed includes roughage (fibre) and concentrates (low in fibre and contain relatively high levels of proteins and other nutrients).

36 Cattle suffer from a number of diseases. Vaccinations are given to farm animals, against many major viral and bacterial diseases. Regular vaccination programs help in preventing out break and maintaining cattle health.

37 **Poultry farming** is undertaken to raise domestic fowls for egg production and chicken meat. The cross-breeding programmes between Indian and foreign breeds of fowls for variety improvement are focused on to develop new varieties having desirable traits which are as follows

(i) Number and quality of chicks.

(ii) Dwarf broiler parent for commercial chick production.

(iii) Summer adaptation capacity/tolerance to high temperature.

(iv) Low maintenance requirements.

(v) Reduction in the size of the egg-laying bird with the ability to utilise more fibrous cheaper diets formulated using agricultural by products.

38 For good production of poultry birds, good management practices are important. It include mainting hygiene, monitoring health and providing adequate space and ventilation to ensure optimal growth and productivity.

39 Fish is a cheap source of animal protein for our food. Fish production includes finned true fish as well as shell fish such as prawns and molluscs.

40 Some marine fish are of high economic value, *e.g.*, finned fishes like mullets, bhetki and pearl spots, shell fish such as, prawns, mussels and oysters as well as seaweed. These fishes species are not only nutritionally valuable but also have significant market demand, contributing to the economy.

41 As marine fish stock gets further depleted, the demand for more fisheries can only be met by culture fisheries, a practice called **mariculture**.

42 Inland fisheries include fish capture from resources like canals, ponds, reservoirs, rivers and brackish water resources, such as estuaries and lagoons.

43 **Composite fish culture** system include a combination of five or six fish species in a single fishpond. These species are selected so that they do not compete for food among them having different types of food habits. For example, catlas are surface feeders, rohus feed in the middle zone at pond, mrigals and common carps are bottom feeders and grass carps feed on the weeds.

44 **Apiculture** is the rearing and breeding of honey bees for the production of honey and wax. The local varieties of bees used for commercial honey production are *Apis cerana indica* (Indian bee), *A. dorsata* (rock bee) and *A. florae* (little bee).

45 The Italian bees (*e.g.* A. *Mellifera*) are also used commercially. They have high honey collection capacity. They sting somewhat less. They stay in a given beehive for long periods and breed very well.

46 The quality and taste of honey depends upon the pasturage or the flowers available to the bees for nectar and pollen collection.

Intext Questions

On Page 141

Question 1 What do we get from cereals, pulses, fruits and vegetables?

Sol. Cereals (wheat, rice, maize, etc.) are the sources of carbohydrates which provide energy. They are staple foods that supply a major portion of the daily caloric need and are vital for sustaining physical activities. Pulses (pea, gram and soyabean, etc.) are the source of proteins. They are essential for muscle repair and growth. Vegetables and fruits provide us vitamins, minerals, and small amount of carbohydrates, proteins and fats. They are crucial for maintaining overall health thus boosting immune system and reducing the risk of chronic disease.

On Page 142

Question 1 How do biotic and abiotic factors affect crop production?

Sol. Biotic factors includes rodents, pests, insects, etc, and abiotic factors, includes temperature, humidity, moisture, etc. They affect crop production in following ways:

1. A pest feeds on crops, causing damage to agriculture by cutting various parts of plants or sucking cell sap, or boring.
2. Weeds also lower agriculture output by competing for nutrients, light and space with the primary crop.
3. Abiotic factors such as salinity, temperature etc. affect the net crop production.

Question 2 What are the desirable agronomic characteristics for crop improvement?

Sol. Desirable agronomic characteristics are:

(i) Tallness and profuse branching are desirable characters for fodder crops. These traits ensure a higher biomass yield, which is beneficial for feeding livestock, providing more food per plant.

(ii) Dwarfness is desired in cereals, so that less nutrients are consumed by these crops. This trait helps in reducing the risk of lodging (falling over), making the plants more stable and easier to harvest.

On Page 143

Question 1 What are macro-nutrients and why are they called macronutrients?

Sol. Macronutrients are essential elements that are required by plants in large quantities for their growth and development. They are called macro nutrients because they are needed in significant amounts compared to micro nutrients.

Some of the main macronutrients are nitrogen, phosphorus sulphur, calcium and magnesium.

Question 2 How do plants get nutrients?

Sol. Plants get nutrients from the air, water and soil. Air supplies carbon and oxygen, hydrogen comes from water and soil supplies the other nutrients to plants. Nutrients dissolved in soil are absorbed by the roots of plants. Which is then transported through out the plant body via the xylem tissue.

On Page 144

Question 1 Compare the use of manure and fertilisers in maintaining soil fertility.

Sol.

S.No.	Manure	Fertiliser
1.	It is obtained by the decomposition of cattle dung and plant residue.	It is man made inorganic salt.
2.	It makes the soil fertile.	It makes the soil fertile for a short time.
3.	It enriches the soil with nutrients.	High amount of fertiliser makes the soil dry and powdery.
4.	It is slowly absorbed by plants.	It is easily absorbed by plants.

On Page 145

Question 1 Which of the following conditions will give the most benefits? Why?

(i) Farmers use high-quality seeds, do not adopt irrigation or use fertilizers.

(ii) Farmers use ordinary seeds, adopt irrigation, use fertilizers.

(iii) Farmers use quality seeds, adopt irrigation use fertiliser and use crop protection measures.

Sol. Condition (iii) will give the most benefits because farmers using good quality seeds, adopting irrigation, using fertilizers and using crop protection measures will derive the maximum yield.

(i) The use of good quality seeds increases the total crop production. If a farmer is using good quality seeds, then a majority of the seeds will germinate properly and will grow into a healthy plant.

(ii) Proper irrigation methods improve the water availability to crops.

(iii) Fertilizers ensure healthy growth and development in plants by providing the essential nutrients such as nitrogen, phosphorus, potassium, etc.

(iv) Crop protection measures include various methods to control weeds, pests and infectious agents. If all these necessary measures are taken by a farmer, then the overall production of crops will increase.

On Page 146

Question 1 Why should preventive measures and biological control methods be preferred for protecting crops?

Sol. Preventive measures and biological control methods should be perferred for protecting crops because they are :

(i) **Simple** These methods are easy to implement and do not require complex procedures.

(ii) **Economical** They are cost-effective compared to chemical pesticides.

(iii) **Minimise pollution** They reduce the environment impact by avoiding harmful chemicals, thus preserving soil and water quality.

(iv) **Sustainable** These methods promotes sustainable agriculture by maintaining ecological balance.

Question 2 What factors may be responsible for the losses of grains during storage?

Sol. The following factors are responsible for loss of grains during storage:

(i) Abiotic factors such as excessive moisture and fluctuating temperature can lead to poor growth and spoilage.

(ii) Biotic factors like insects, rodents, birds, mites and bacteria can contaminate and damage the stored grains, leading to significant losses.

On Page 147

Question 1 Which method is commonly used for improving cattle breeds and why?

Sol. Cross breeding is a method commonly used for improving cattle breeds. It is a process in which indigenous varieties of cattle are crossed with with exotic breeds to get a cross breed which is high-yielding. Cross breeding aims to combine the best traits of both parents breeds to enhance productivity and over all performance of the cattle.

On Page 148

Question 1 Discuss the implications of the following statement. "It is interesting to note that poultry is India's most efficient converter of low fibre food stuff (which is unfit for human consumption) into highly nutritious animal protein food".

Sol. In poultry farming, domestic fowls are raised to produce eggs and chicken for this, the fowls are given animal feeds in the form of roughage, which mainly consists of fibres. Thus, by feeding animals a fibre rich diet, the poultry gives highly nutritious food in the form of eggs and chicken.

Question 2 What management practices are common in dairy and poultry farming?

Sol. Common management practice in dairy and poultry farming include.

(i) Provision of well designed and hygenic shelter.

(ii) Supply of proper food to get good yield.

(iii) Regular health check-ups and monitoring of animals and birds to detect and prevent diseases early.

(iv) Ensuring a constant supply of clean and fresh water to maintain health and productivity.

Question 3 What are the differences between broilers and layers and in their management?

Sol. Differences between Broilers and Layers in Poultry Management, are given in table below

	Broilers	Layers
(i) Definition	Broilers are chickens specifically bred and raised for meat production.	Layers are a special species of hens raised for egg production.
(ii) Growth and Nutrition	Broilers have a rapid growth rate and therefore require a protein-rich diet supplemented with fats. They do not need much space and lighting, as they are kept for a shorter duration until they reach market weight.	Layers require a balanced diet with lower protein and fat content. They require adequate space and lighting to ensure proper growth and egg production.
(iii) Raising Period	Broilers are typically raised for 6-7 weeks in poultry farms, after which they are processed for meat.	Layers begin laying eggs after approximately 18-20 weeks (around 5 months) and continue for several months, with peak production occurring around 25-30 weeks of age.
(iv) Diet and Care	Broiler chickens are fed a vitamin-rich supplementary feed to ensure good growth rates, feed efficiency, and carcass quality. Special care is taken to minimize mortality and maintain feathering.	Layers have simpler dietary needs compared to broilers. Their diet is focused on maintaining their health and optimizing egg production, with less emphasis on rapid growth.

On Page 150

Question 1. How are fish obtained?

Sol. Fish are obtained by two ways:

(a) Capture fishing-process of obtaining fish from natural resources.

(b) Culture fishery-practice of farming fishes.

Question 2. What are the advantages of composite fish culture?

Sol. Composite fish culture is done by a combination of five or six fish species in a single fish pond. The species are selected on the basis of food habits so that they do not compete for food among themselves. As a result, the food available in all parts of the pond is utilised without competing with each other. This increases the fish yield from the pond.

On Page 150

Question 1 What are the desirable characters of bee varieties suitable for honey production?

Sol. Desirable characters in varieties for honey production are:

(i) They should be able to collect a large amount of honey.

(ii) They should stay in beehive for a longer time.

(iii) They should have good breeding capacity.

Question 2 What is pasturage and how is it related to honey production?

Sol. Pasturage for bees is the flowers available for nectar and pollen collection. The quality and taste of honey depends on adequate quantity of pasturage and flowers available.

Exercises

Question 1 Explain any one method of crop production which ensures high yield.

Sol. Intercropping is one of the methods of crop production that ensures high yield. In this method, two or more crops are grown simultaneously on the same field in definite pattern. A few rows of one crop alternate with a few rows of second crop. For example, soyabean and maize or finger millet (bajara) and cow pea (lobia).

The crops are selected such that their nutrient requirements are different. This ensures maximum utilisation of the nutrients supplied. It also prevents pests and diseases from spreading to all the plants belonging to one crop in a field. This way, both crops can give better yields.

Question 2 Why are manure and fertilisers used in fields?

Sol. Manures and fertilisers are used in fields to enrich the soil with the required nutrients. Manure helps in enriching the soil with organic matter and nutrients. This improves the fertility and structure of the soil. On the other hand. fertilisers ensure a healthy growth and developement in plants.

They are good source of nitrogen, phoshorus and potassium. To get an optimum yield it is instructed to use a balanced combination of manures and fertilisers in the soil. Therefore, they help in good vegetative growth, giving rise to healthy plants that increares the crop production.

Question 3 What are the advantages of inter-cropping and crop rotation?

Sol. **Advantages of inter-cropping**

(i) Maintain soil fertility.

(ii) Increases productivity per unit area. Prevent pests and diseases to spread throughout the field.

(iii) Save time and labour.

(iv) Both crops can be easily harvested separately.

Advantages of crop rotation

(i) Improves soil fertilitiy.

(ii) Reduces pest infestation and diseases.

(iii) Helps in weed control.

(iv) Avoids depletion of a particular nutrient from soil.

Question 4 What is genetic manipulation? How is it useful in agricultural practices?

Sol. Genetic manipulation is the process of transferring desirable genes from one organisms to another to create plant varieties with specific beneficial traits. This technique is used to develop crops with characteristics like increased branching in fodder crops or higher yields in maize and wheat.

Uses in agricultural practices:

(i) Helps in increasing yield and quality.

(ii) Maturation period is shorter.

(iii) Better adaptability to adverse environmental conditions.

Question 5 How do storage grain losses occur?

Sol. Storage grain losses due to both abiotic and biotic factors.
Abiotic factor include moisture and temperatures which cause spoilage and deterioration of grains. Biotic factor include pests such as insects, rodents, birds mites and bacteria which can damage or contaminate the grains.

Question 6 How do good animal husbandry practices benefit farmers?

Sol. Benefits of good farming practices:

(i) Improved breeds of domestic animals.

(ii) Increased production of products like milk, egg and meat.

(iii) Proper shelter, feeding, care and protection against disease help the farmers to improve their economic conditions.

Question 7 What are the benefits of cattle farming?

Sol. Benefits of cattle farming are :

(i) Good quality and quantity of milk can be obtained.
(ii) Good quality meat, fibre and skin is obtained.
(iii) Good breed of draught animals can be obtained.

Question 8 For increasing production, what is common in poultry, fisheries and bee keeping?

Sol. The common factors for increasing production in poultry, fisheries, and bee-keeping include:

1. **Following Proper Management Techniques** Effective management practices are essential for optimising production, ensuring the health of the animals or organisms, and maximising yield.
2. **Regular Cleaning** Keeping the environment clean helps prevent the spread of diseases and maintains a healthy living condition for the animals.
3. **Temperature** Many species are sensitive to temperature changes, so maintaining an appropriate temperature is crucial for their optimal growth and production.
4. **Prevention and Cure of Diseases** Regular monitoring and prompt treatment of diseases prevent outbreaks and ensure that the animals or organisms remain healthy and productive.

Question 9 How do you differentiate between capture fishing, mariculture and aquaculture?

Sol. Differences between capture fishing, mariculture and aquaculture

S.No.	Capture Fishing	Mariculture	Aquaculture
1.	Method of obtaining fish from natural resources, like ponds, canals, rivers, etc.	Culture of marine fish in the open sea.	Production of fish from freshwater and brackish water resources.
2.	Locating fish is easy and can be captured by using fishing nets.	Fish can be located with the help of satellites and echosounders. These can be caught by many kinds of fishing nets using fishing boats.	Can be located easily and caught using fishing nets.

DIKSHA APP Questions

☐ Multiple Choice Questions

Q.1 Which of the following is called the surface feeder?

(a) Catla (b) Rohu

(c) Mrigal d) Grass carp

Sol. (a) Catla and Silver carp are surface feeders. Rohu feeds in the middle zone of the water body, while Mrigal is the bottom feeders. Grass carps feed on the weeds

Q.2 What is the process of growing two or more crops in a definite pattern?

(a) Crop rotation (b) Inter-cropping

(c) Mixed cropping (d) Organic cropping

Sol. (b) Inter-cropping refers to the practice of growing two or more crops together in a specific pattern to maximise the use of available resources and space.

Q.3 *Cyperinus* and *Parthenium* are types of

(a) diseases (b) pesticides

(c) weeds (d) pathogens

Sol. (c) *Cyperinus* and *Parthenium* are types of weeds. They are unwanted plants that can interfere with crop growth and reduce agricultural productivity.

Q.4 Preventive and control measures adopted for storage of grains include

(a) strict cleaning (b) fumigation

(c) proper drying (d) All of them

Sol. (d) Effective grain storage involves several measures including strict cleaning to prevent contamination, fumigation to control pests, and proper drying of grains to avoid spoilage.

Q.3 What is the relationship between pasturage and honey production?

Sol. The quality and quantity of honey produced are directly related to pasturage, which refers to the availability of flowering plants that bees visit for nectar and pollen. The type of flowers determines the flavor and color of the honey. Adequate and diverse pasturage ensures a steady supply of nectar, leading to higher honey production and better quality.

Q.4 (a) Why should preventive methods and biological control methods be preferred for protecting crops?

(b) Name the farming system in which only such above mentioned methods are followed?

(c) How does manure improve the soil structure of sandy and clayey soil?

Sol. (a) Preventive and biological control methods are preferred because they are environmentally friendly and reduce reliance on chemical pesticides. They help avoid pesticide resistance and reduce harm to non-target species, making them safer for both the environment and human health.

(b) Organic farming use only preventive and biological control methods avoiding synthetic chemicals and promoting ecological balance.

(c) **Manure improves** soil structure by adding organic matter:

- **In sandy soils** Manure increases water and nutrient retention, enhancing soil fertility and reducing erosion.
- **In clayey soils** Manure improves drainage and reduces waterlogging by breaking up the compacted soil, facilitating better root growth and aeration.

Q.5 (a) What are pesticides?

(b) Why is excessive use of pesticides not advisable?

(c) Name two preventive measures against pests.

Sol. (a) Pesticides are chemicals used to control or eliminate pests that damage crops, including insects, weeds, fungi, and bacteria. They can be applied to crops, soil, or seeds.

(b) Excessive pesticide use can lead to pesticide resistance, harm beneficial organisms, contaminate soil and water, and pose health risks to humans and animals. It can also result in environmental pollution and long-term ecological imbalances.

(c) Two preventive measures against pests are:

1. Proper seed bed preparation: Ensuring a clean and well-prepared seed bed reduces the initial pest load.
2. Timely sowing of crops: Sowing at optimal times can reduce the risk of pest infestations and improve crop resilience.

☐ Long Answer Type

Q.1 Describe composite fish culture system. What is the major problem in fish farming? How is it overcome?

Sol. The composite fish culture system involves stocking a pond with several fish species that occupy different feeding zones. For example, Catla feeds at the surface, Rohu in the middle Zone, Mrigal and Common Carp at the bottom, and Grass Carp consumes aquatic weeds. This method maximises resource use and increases overall fish yield.

Major Problem A significant issue is that many species breed only during specific seasons, leading to a shortage of quality fish seed. Additionally, wild-caught seeds may be mixed with unwanted species.

Solution To overcome this problem, hormonal stimulation techniques have been developed to breed fish is controlled environments, ensuring a consistent supply of pure, high-quality seeds.

Q.2 Enlist the criteria for the selection of crops for mixed cropping.

Sol. Criteria for selecting crops for mixed cropping include:

1. **Duration of Crops** Mix a long-duration crop with a short-duration one to optimize resource use.
2. **Growth Habit** Choose crops with different growth habits (e.g., tall and short) to utilise vertical space efficiently.
3. **Nutrient Demand** Select crops with varying nutrient requirements to prevent competition and optimize soil use.
4. **Root Pattern** Include crops with different root depths (deep and shallow) to improve soil utilisation.
5. **Water Requirement** Combine crops with different water needs to enhance water use efficiency and reduce competition.

Q.3 Describe the main irrigation systems that are adopted in India.

Sol. The main irrigation systems in India include:

1. Wells
    - **Dug Wells** Water is drawn from shallow water-bearing strata.
    - **Tube Wells** Water is extracted from deeper strata using pumps.
2. **Canals** An extensive system that channels water from reservoirs or rivers to fields through main, branch, and distributary canals.
3. **River Lift Systems** Water is lifted directly from rivers to irrigate fields in areas close to the river where canal flow is insufficient.

4. **Tanks** Small reservoirs that capture and store runoff from small catchment areas.

   New Initiatives Rainwater Harvesting and Watershed Management include constructing check-dams to increase groundwater levels, capture rainwater, and reduce soil erosion.

Q.4 (a) List four facilities that must be provided to cattle to ensure their good health and production of clean milk.

(b) State two ways of incorporating desired characters into crop varieties.

(c) How do good animal husbandry practices benefit farmers?

(d) What are the two purposes for which cattle husbandry is followed?

Sol. (a) Facilities that must be provided to cattle to ensure their good health and production of clean milk are :

1. **Well-ventilated shelter** To ensure proper airflow and prevent respiratory issues.
2. **Vaccination** To protect against various diseases.
3. **Proper diet** Balanced nutrition to maintain health and milk production.
4. **Regular health check-ups** To monitor and address any health issues promptly.

(b) Two ways of incorporating desired charcters into crop varieties are :

1. **Genetic Manipulation** Using techniques like genetic engineering to introduce or modify traits in crops.
2. **Hybridisation** Cross-breeding different crop varieties to combine desirable traits.

(c) Good animal husbandry practices improve animal health and productivity, leading to higher quality and quantity of milk, meat, or other products. This increases farmers' income by meeting the demand for animal products and reducing losses due to diseases.

(d) The two purposes for which cattle husbandry is used are as follows.

1. **Milk Production** To provide a source of dairy products.
2. **Draught Labour** To assist in agricultural work such as tilling, irrigation, and carting.

Q.5 Why is crop variety improvement important in cultivation? Describe the important factors for which crop improvement is done.

Sol. Crop variety improvement is essential to enhance productivity, quality, and resilience. It addresses the following factors:

1. **Higher Yield** To increase crop productivity and meet food demand.
2. **Quality** To improve characteristics like taste, texture, and nutritional value.
3. **Resistance** To develop varieties resistant to biotic (pests, diseases) and abiotic (drought, salinity) stress.
4. **Maturity Period** The shorter the duration of maturity of crop, the more economical is the variety. Uniform maturity makes the harvesting process easy and reduces losses during harvesting.
5. **Adaptation** To make crops suitable for diverse environmental conditions.
6. **Desirable Agronomic Characteristics** To enhance traits like dwarfness or branching, which can improve yield and reduce input costs.